THE

GEOGRAPHY

OF

THE BRITISH ISLES,

INTERSPERSED WITH

MANY HISTORICAL FACTS AND BIOGRAPHICAL SKETCHES;

SELECTED FROM THE BEST AUTHORS,

AND ILLUSTRATED WITH

SEPARATE BLANK MAPS AND EXPLANATORY KEYS;

SHOWING

THE RELATIVE SITUATIONS, BOUNDARIES, PRINCIPAL TOWNS,
RIVERS, &c., OF EACH COUNTY.

FOR THE USE OF YOUNG PERSONS AND SCHOOLS.

BY

MARY MARTHA RODWELL.

IN TWO VOLUMES.

VOL. II.

LONDON:

PRINTED FOR

LONGMAN, REES, ORME, BROWN, GREEN, AND LONGMAN,
PATERNOSTER-ROW.

1834.

29 6.

CONTENTS OF VOL. II.

DIRECTIONS FOR PLACING THE MAPS.

VOL. II.

GEOGRAPHY AND HISTORY

OF

THE BRITISH ISLES.

———◆———

SCOTLAND.

Mrs. Rowe.—THE remaining portion of the Island of Great Britain is the northern part, called SCOTLAND. Can you tell me what was its ancient appellation?

George.—*Caledonia*; the Caledonians being a tribe of the Celtæ, or Gauls.

Mrs. Rowe.—The first ages of the Scottish history are dark and fabulous; and the earliest account on which we can depend is derived from the Roman authors. When the Romans, under Agricola, first carried their arms into the northern part of Britain, A.D. 81, they found it possessed by the Caledonians, a fierce and warlike people; and having repulsed, rather than conquered them, they erected a strong wall between the Firths of Forth and Clyde, and thus fixed the boundaries of their empire. Adrian, on account of the difficulty of defending such a distant frontier, contracted the limits of the Roman province in Britain by building a second wall, A.D. 123, which extended from Newcastle to Carlisle; and in the year 421, when the Romans were obliged to abandon all their conquests in Britain, and recall their legions, in order to defend the centre of their empire, North Britain was, by their retreat, left under the

dominion of the Scots and Picts. If tradition may be re-
lied on, the former were a Scythian tribe, who first settled
in Ireland, and extending themselves by degrees, landed
on the opposite coast of Scotland about the beginning of
the fourth century, and fixed their habitations there : fierce
and bloody wars were for a long time carried on between
them and the Picts. Kenneth II. (the sixty-ninth king of
the Scots, according to their own fabulous authors,) obtained a complete victory over the Picts about the year
842, and united under one monarchy all the country from
the Wall of Adrian to the Atlantic Ocean. The kingdom
henceforward was called Scotland. The word Scot is no
other than a corruption of *Scuyth*, or Scythian, being originally from that immense country called Scythia by the
ancients.

GEORGE.—When was the independence of Scotland first
invaded?

MRS. ROWE.—Some of the northern counties of England
were early in the hands of the Scottish kings, who, as far
back as the feudal customs can be traced, held these possessions of the kings of England, and did homage to them
on that account. Henry II., having taken their king William the Lion prisoner, A.D. 1175, not only demanded an
exorbitant ransom for him, but compelled him to do homage for his whole kingdom; which claim his successor
Richard generously relinquished. Upon the death of Alexander III., the right of succession appeared, from the number of claimants, to be no less intricate than it was important; and in order to avoid the miseries of a civil war,
Edward I., King of England, was chosen umpire, by which
means he acquired an influence in Scotland which no English monarch had before possessed. Edward, imitating
the interested policy of Henry, pretended that the kingdom
was held as a fief of the Crown of England, and subjected
to all the conditions of a feudal tenure. In order to establish
his claim to the sovereignty, he seized the public archives,

ransacked the churches and monasteries, and getting possession, either by force or fraud, of many historical documents which tended to prove the antiquity or freedom of the kingdom, he carried some of them into England, and commanded the rest to be burned. From that time the national animosities of the two kingdoms were excited by the circumstances of frequent hostilities and national injuries; until, upon the death of Queen Elizabeth (nearly three hundred years afterwards), James VI. of Scotland was declared the legal heir to the Crown of England, thereby destroying the independence of Scotland. Upon the accession of Queen Anne, the Scots were offered their own terms, if they would agree to the incorporated union as it now stands; to which the Scotch parliament at length consented; thus firmly uniting two kingdoms, divided from the earliest records, but destined by their situation to form one great monarchy: and by this junction of its whole native force, Great Britain has risen to an eminence and authority in Europe which England and Scotland, while separate, could never have attained.—Describe the boundaries and extent of Scotland.

ANNA.—It is bounded on the north and west by the Atlantic Ocean, on the east by the North Sea, and on the south by England: it extends from north to south about 300 miles, and from east to west 150, and lies between 54 and 59 degrees north latitude, and between 1 and 6 west longitude.

MRS. ROWE.—This whole territory is divided into two distinct regions, which, on account of their strong dissimilarity, are respectively designated the Highlands and the Lowlands. The latter bear a near resemblance to England, to which they join; and it is only in the more remote part of the Highlands, where the country assumes the wildest irregularity, that their great difference is perceptible. With the exception of a few plains near the sea, the whole surface of Scotland is more or less hilly, and level tracts are

only to be found along the banks of its rivers.   The river
Tay forms a natural boundary to these divisions, which are
subdivided into thirty-three counties, thirteen of which
are in the Highlands and twenty in the Lowlands.—Can
you give me the names of the first-mentioned?

GEORGE.—The thirteen counties north of the Tay, called
the Highlands, are the Orkney and Shetland Islands (which
form one county), and the counties of Caithness, Sutherland,
Ross, Cromarty, Inverness, Nairn, Elgin or Murray, Banff,
Aberdeen, Kincardine or Mearns, Forfar or Angus, and
Perth.

THE ORKNEY AND SHETLAND ISLANDS.

ORKNEY ISLANDS.

Boundary.—Surrounded by the North Sea.
Town.—1, Kirkwall, in Pomona or Mainland.
Islands.—2, Pomona or Mainland; 3, Hoy Island; 4, South Ro-
    naldshay; 5, Burray; 6, Stronsa; 7, Sanday; 8, North Ro-
    naldshay; 9, Papay Westray; 10, Westray; 11, Rowsay.
Firths.—A, Pentland Firth; B, Stronsa Firth; C, Westra Firth.

SHETLAND ISLANDS.

Boundary.—Surrounded by the North Sea.
Town.—1, Lerwick, in Mainland.
Islands.—2, Mainland; 3, Yell; 4, Bulta; 5, Phedersray; 6,
    Skerries; 7, Whalsey; 8, Noss; 9, Foula; 10, West Burray;
    11, Fair Island.

MRS. ROWE.—THE Orkney and Shetland Islands comprise the most northerly county or stewartry of Scotland.
The Orkneys are also known by the name of *Orcades*,
which appellation they are supposed to have derived from
their situation near Cape Orchus, the ancient name of Dunnet Head in Caithness.—Have you any knowledge of the
number of them?

GEORGE.—This division of the county is said to consist of thirty islands, a part of which only are inhabited; the remainder are called Holms, and are appropriated to the pasturing of cattle, sheep, and rabbits. The principal of the inhabited islands are Pomona or Mainland, Hoy, South Ronaldshay, North Ronaldshay, Stronsa, Burray, Sanday, Papay Westray, Westray, and Rowsay.

MRS. ROWE.—Pomona, or Mainland, is the most extensive island, and is situated in the centre of the group:—tell me its extent and principal towns.

GEORGE.—It is computed to measure, from north-west to south-east, about 30 English miles; the breadth of it varies from 6 to 16 miles; and near the middle it is so narrow as to form an isthmus, which is little more than a mile across, thus dividing the island into two peninsulas. Its chief parishes are Kirkwall, Stromness, and Deerness.

MRS. ROWE.—Kirkwall, the capital, is the only royal borough in the county or stewartry: it is supposed to have been of considerable importance at an early period, but of the nature of its constitution, and the extent of its immunities at that time, little is now known. The chief object of curiosity in the town is the cathedral church of St. Magnus, the seat of the Bishop of Orkney, and remarkable as the only cathedral in Scotland, besides that of Glasgow, which survived the Reformation. This is altogether an imposing and magnificent structure, and is supposed to have been built by Reginald count of Orkney, in 1138, in honour of his uncle St. Magnus, to whom it was dedicated: a portion of it is used as the parish church. Opposite the cathedral are the ruins of the King's Castle, a building of considerable size and antiquity: it is said to have received its royal name from having been the customary residence of the royal governors, chamberlains, or farmers of the islands. The ruins of the ancient bishop's palace are also worthy of note: this building must have been of great consequence as early as the thirteenth century, being noted for having then afforded accommodation to the celebrated Haco king of Norway, with his retinue, on his return from his last expedition against the Scots. Several gentlemen of property reside in this town, as well as a number of merchants and tradesmen: the harbour is safe and capacious, having a sufficient depth of water, and so firm a clay bottom, as to afford secure anchorage for vessels of considerable burden.

The village of Stromness is situated on the south-western corner of Pomona, and has an excellent harbour, by means of which it enjoys a considerable coasting trade: its inhabitants are mostly sailors, shipmasters, pilots, and small proprietors of land, and are an industrious and enterprising people.

The parish or rather territory of Deerness is at the eastern extremity of the island, peninsulated by the encroachment of two bays, both well calculated to afford a retreat for shipping. The soil of this district is generally poor, and the cultivated land lies in a declivity towards the south. —Are there any lakes in this island?

ANNA.—In the western part is the great Loch of Stenness, which extends about five miles in a northerly direction: trout, flounders, and other kinds of fish are found in it. This lake is so situated at the head of Kerston Bay, that the tide at its flux and reflux alternately fills and almost empties it.

MRS. ROWE.—A ridge of hills, of moderate height, rises in the eastern extremity of this island, and on the western boundary is another chain, called the Mountains of Stromness and Sandwick: these hills are generally green on their sides, and the soil of them is in many parts productive, when cultivated.

Hoy lies to the south-west of Pomona, and is noted for containing the highest land in the county, almost the whole of it being occupied by three large hills, which are beautifully covered with alpine plants. It is chiefly appropriated to the pasturage of sheep. Besides the hills, there is a stupendous rock, called the Beary, which is noted for producing a bird called the Layer, supposed to be a species of the penguin.

South Ronaldshay is a populous island, measuring about 18 square miles. The arable and grass lands here form a larger proportion to the rude ordinary pastures than elsewhere : much kelp is manufactured on the shores.

North Ronaldshay contains about 4 square miles, and is almost a level tract: it is chiefly noted for the great quantity of kelp manufactured on its shores.

Stronsay is a considerable island, being about 7 miles long and 4 broad ; its soil is very various, and while it equals several of the islands in its production of the fruits of the earth, it enjoys an advantage over them, in its eligible situation for an extensive and lucrative fishery : here are two harbours or rather places of retreat for ships, Linga Sound on the west, and that of Papay on the north-east.

Burray is parted from South Ronaldshay by a ferry about a mile broad, and is nearly 4 miles long and 1 mile in breadth. Potatoes, carrots, peas, onions, cabbages, and turnips, are raised here in greater perfection than in the other islands, and white and red clover abound in the natural pastures.

Sanday derives its name from the nature of its soil: it lies to the north-east of Stronsa, from which it is separated by a channel from two to three miles broad, and is about 12 miles in length, and from 1 to 3 in breadth. The making of kelp is the chief employment of the people in summer.

Papay Westray is a beautiful little island, about 4 miles long and 1 mile broad : it is pleasant and fertile, abounding with fine natural clover, and its south-eastern corner is adorned with a lake of fresh water.

Westray is a larger island, to the south of the last-named, and contains a great quantity of peat : much corn is also raised on it ; and in the boisterous seas around, abundance of fish is caught.

Rowsay lies to the north of Pomona, and is about 9

miles long and 4 broad: the greatest part of it is hilly ground, but it has some arable land on the coast, and is accounted one of the most pleasant of the Orkney Isles.

Few countries exhibit such variety of scenery in a narrow compass as the Orkneys. Hills and valleys, lakes, streams, and bays, interspersed with small green islets, are grouped together within the space of a few miles. But their prominent features are to be found in their rock and sea scenery; these indeed are magnificent. The ocean is here diversified by numerous islands, which divest it of its usual monotony, while it exhibits aspects of more terrific grandeur than elsewhere. Pressed by a collection or flood of waters through the narrow channels which separate the islands, the currents, setting in from opposite directions, rush through the straits, and meeting in full force, boil up into vast billows, even in the calmest day.—Name the principal islands of the Shetland group.

GEORGE.—They are said to consist of about 17 inhabited ones, and a number of rocks called, as in the Orkneys, Holms, which are principally appropriated to the feeding of sheep, cattle, and rabbits. The largest of the inhabited islands are, Mainland, Unst, Noss, Foula, West Burray, and Fair Island.

MRS. ROWE.—Mainland is not less than 60 miles from north to south, and in some places it is upwards of 12 in breadth: it is on all sides so deeply indented with bays and harbours, that a very small portion of it lies above three miles from the sea, consequently the territory may be considered as wholly maritime: the principal parishes in it are Lerwick and Scalloway. Lerwick, the capital of these isles, stands near a spacious harbour of the same name, from which it derives its consequence, being the rendezvous of the vessels employed in the whale fishery; and what renders it particularly commodious, is its having two entries, one from the north and the other from the south.

ANNA.—It was to this remote region that the infamous

Bothwell resorted after his expulsion from Scotland; and it is well known that for some time he and his followers subsisted by piratical practices. It is said, that after the dispersion of his small squadron by Kirkaldy of Grange and Tulliebardine, Bothwell escaped by the north passage of Bressa Sound, as Kirkaldy, in a ship called the Unicorn, closely pursuing him, came in at the south; for when his enemies were gaining fast upon him, and his capture appeared inevitable, Bothwell's pilot, who was well acquainted with the course, passed close by a sunken rock in safety, while Kirkaldy, unconscious of the hidden danger, struck his vessel against it, and was wrecked. The rock, which can be seen at low water, is called the Unicorn to this day.

Mrs. Rowe.—Scalloway is a small place, supposed to be more ancient than Lerwick: it lies on the south coast, and has an excellent harbour, but the only building in it worthy of remark is its Castle, which was erected by Patrick earl of Orkney.

Unst is deserving of note as being the most northerly of the British Isles: its surface is diversified by several extensive and moderately high hills. It is not intersected by rivers, but contains many small fresh-water lakes, around which the scenery is very pleasant.

Noss is situated on the east of Mainland, and is one of the finest and most fertile of the Shetland Isles.

Foula, or Fule, lies to the west of Mainland, and was known to the ancients by the name of *Ultima Thule*: it is about three miles long and one and a half broad, and is very bold and steep: the only landing-place, called Hain, lies on the east side. This island is much resorted to as a fishing station.

West Burray is a small island, situated also on the west of Mainland, from which it is parted by a narrow sound.

Fair Island lies nearly midway between the Shetland and Orkney Isles, from both of which its towering rocks are plainly to be seen.

GEORGE.—It was on the east side of this small island that the Duke of Medina Sidonia, Admiral of the Spanish Armada, was wrecked in 1588; and after eating up all the provisions of the island, the crew had to get themselves transported to Mainland, and from thence to France, in a small pinnace belonging to the island.

MRS. ROWE.—It is said that the Admiral lodged at the house of Malcolm Sinclair, an old gentleman who had seen the world; and imagining the natives regarded him with profound admiration, the vain Spaniard one day desired his interpreter to ask his host if he had ever seen such a man: "Farcie on that face!" exclaimed Sinclair, "I have seen many a prettier man hanging in the Burrow-moor." The dark winter nights of these islands are often illumined by that splendid and beautiful phænomenon of nature the northern lights, or aurora borealis, commonly called the Merry Dancers. The grandeur and magnificence of its appearance is beyond conception: it begins with faint streaks of light, which suddenly burst forth into the most brilliant and heterogeneous mixture of moveable bodies of fire.—Travelling is usually performed here on the small horses called shelties, and a person proposing to sojourn in Shetland cannot be equipped with any articles that will serve him better than a saddle and bridle. Formerly these islands belonged to Denmark, and it was only by the marriage of James VI. with Anne of Denmark that they fell irrecoverably under the dominion of a British monarch. Perhaps the most remarkable thing to be mentioned about the Orkney and Shetland Islands is the total absence of trees.

CAITHNESS-SHIRE.

Boundaries.—Sutherlandshire, Pentland Firth, and the North Sea.
Towns, &c.—1, Wick; 2, John o' Groat's House; 3, Thurso;
    4, Durlet; 5, Clyth; 6, Knockglass; 7, Berrydale.
Rivers.—a, the Wick; b, Thurso.
Islands.—A, Pentland; B, Skerries; C, Strona.
Capes and Bays.—D, Dunnet Head; E, Clyth Ness; F, Ord of
    Caithness; G, Wick Bay.

Mrs. Rowe.—DESCRIBE the situation, extent, and chief
towns of Caithness-shire.

Anna.—Caithness is bounded on the north by the Pentland Firth, which separates it from the Orkney Islands, on
the west by Sutherlandshire, and on the south-east by the
North Sea: it is of triangular shape, ending at the south
with the promontory called the Ord of Caithness; its greatest length is 35 miles from north to south, and its breadth
20 from east to west. Its chief towns are Wick, Thurso,
John o' Groat's House, and Durlet.

Mrs. Rowe.—Wick, the county town, is a royal burgh,
on a small river of the same name, the mouth of which
forms the harbour. It is a bustling, thriving town, and
contains several good buildings. Within the last few years
a new pier has been erected, by which the harbour was
both extended and improved; and on the south side of the
river, under the auspices of the British Herring Fishing
Company, many buildings have been raised. Its chief
branch of commerce is fishing, which is prosecuted with
great industry: the coast consists principally of high rocks,
underneath which are many creeks and coves, with hideous
caverns, where boats can harbour.

Thurso stands on the northern side of the county, at the
extremity of a beautiful and spacious bay, where the river

Thurso falls into the sea. The principal manufactures of this town are coarse linen and woollen cloth; besides which it has a share of the fishing trade, though it is not so populous as Wick. The coast to the west is said to increase in wildness and grandeur, till it terminates at Cape Wrath. A highly ornamental structure has been built in this neighbourhood, by Sir John Sinclair, to the memory of Harold earl of Caithness, who was slain on the spot upwards of six centuries ago. John o' Groat's House is reckoned the most northerly dwelling in Scotland;—can you remember any tradition relating to it?

GEORGE.—It is said that in the reign of James IV., two brothers of the name of John o' Groat came from the Lowlands to Caithness, bearing a letter from the king recommending them to the gentry of the county. They procured land in this remote spot, where they settled, and became the founders of families; and when the race had increased to eight branches, a quarrel arose amongst them regarding precedency, at one of the anniversaries to celebrate their arrival at that place, each affirming that he was chief: this dissension became at last of so serious a nature, that one of them, named John, who was the proprietor of a ferry-boat over to Orkney, rose and declared he would project a building for them to meet in upon equal terms; and to fulfil the engagement, he erected one of an octagonal shape, having a door and window at every side, and furnished with a table of the same form; so that at their next carousal they entered at their respective doors, and took their places at the table, and as they were all upon an equal footing, their former harmony and good humour was restored.

MRS. ROWE.—Durlet is a district noted only for its Castle, which stands in a beautifully romantic spot, on a round, high, and nearly perpendicular rock, overhanging the river Thurso: this place is said to have been of great strength in the days of rapine and plunder.—Can you tell me the names of the rivers of this county?

ANNA.—The Wick and the Thurso are the most considerable.

MRS. ROWE.—The Wick issues from a small loch, and runs easterly into the sea a little below the town of the same name.

The Thurso rises in the centre of the county, and after passing by the Castle of Durlet, runs northerly through the western point of Dunnet Bay to the sea.

GEORGE.—I see in the map three small islands near this coast.

MRS. ROWE.—They are the Pentland Skerries: the largest of those two situated at the north-eastern extremity is inhabited by one family, who take care of the light-houses erected here in 1794; the other is named Strand, and is very inconsiderable. On this coast are several capes or promontories, of which Dunnet Head on the north, Clyth Ness on the east, and the Ord of Caithness on the south, are the principal: along the side of the latter mountain a capital post road has been cut, which is the only entrance into this county from the south.

The men of Caithness appeared in great strength at Flodden Field, where they suffered so severe a loss, that it has since been superstitiously regarded as unlucky to cross the Ord on a Friday, that being the day on which this unfortunate band left their native country.

Caithness is in general a fertile and level district, though but ill cultivated, and almost destitute of everything in the shape of trees: it being, however, excellently situated for the herring fishery, its coast is occupied by fishing towns. On the south-western side are some mountains, which are the abode of wild roes and other animals, and its lakes are the resort of swans and various water-fowl.

SUTHERLANDSHIRE.

Boundaries.—Caithness-shire, Ross-shire, the Atlantic Ocean, and Dornoch Firth.

Towns.—1, Dornoch; 2, Skelbo; 3, Creich; 4, Invershin; 5, Brora; 6, Mowadale; 7, Strathy; 8, Shanwell; 9, Tongue; 10, Strathbeg; 11, Carkaig.

Rivers and Lochs.—a, Helmsdale River; b, Strathy River; c, Loch Brora; d, Loch Buy; e, Loch Navern; f, Loch Loyal; g, Loch Eriboll; h, Loch Tongue; i, Loch Laxford; k, Loch Shin.

Capes, Firths, and Bays.—A, Faro Head or Cape Wrath; B, Farout Head; C, Dornoch Firth; D, Calvo Bay; E, Farr Bay; F, Strathy Bay.

Mrs. Rowe.—WHAT are the boundaries, extent, and chief towns of Sutherlandshire?

George.—It is bounded on the north and west by the Atlantic Ocean, on the east by Caithness-shire and the North Sea, and on the south and south-west by the Firth of Dornoch and Ross-shire; it measures from east to west about 46 miles, and from north to south, somewhat more: its chief towns are Dornoch, Skelbo, Brora, Tongue, and Invershin.

Mrs. Rowe.—Dornoch, the county town, is situated at the entrance of a fine firth of the same name: it was formerly of much importance, and the residence of the bishops of Caithness. A part of the ancient Cathedral still serves as the parish church. This edifice is said to have been erected by Gilbert Murray, who was bishop in 1222.

Anna.—I have read that for a long time the Archbishop of York claimed a jurisdiction over the Scottish Church, and that this claim was patronized by the King of England, and favoured by the Pope's legate; in consequence of which a convention was held at Northampton, in presence of the

Kings of England and Scotland. The Scotch bishops were
at first greatly intimidated by the arguments of the legate,
until Gilbert Murray (then one of the inferior clergy), who
had attended his bishop to England, rose, and with a vehe-
ment and intrepid eloquence defended the independence of
the Scottish Church: his abilities gained the applause of
the assembly and roused the spirits of his associates; and his
adversaries, judging that he spoke the sentiments of his
country, prudently broke up the convention.

MRS. ROWE.—On his return home, Murray was re-
warded for his intrepidity by being promoted to the See
of Caithness: he died in 1245, and was afterwards canonized. Here are also some remains of the ancient bishop's
Castle, which appears to have been a stately edifice.

GEORGE.—In 1567 this town was nearly destroyed by
fire, owing to some dissensions between the Earls of Caithness and Sutherland, when a tribe of the Murrays (friends
of the latter,) were obliged to take shelter in the Castle,
where they for some time defended themselves with great
valour, but were at length compelled to capitulate, and deliver up three hostages, who were soon after murdered.

Skelbo is an extensive parish, situated in a bare and
dreary district; but it has of late years undergone considerable improvement, and the gardens here plainly demonstrate what labour and attention can effect, as apples, pears,
and cherries are successfully cultivated, and some peaches
and apricots are grown, even in this northern latitude.

Brora is an inconsiderable village in the eastern part of
the county, seated on a river of the same name, which descends from a vale of the most romantic and savage character, usually called Strathbrora.

Tongue, a parish in the northern part of the county,
contains the ruins of a very ancient building, which is so
covered with earth that its original form cannot be ascertained: it is called by the natives Dun Bhuidh, 'The Yellow
Heap,' and is said to have been erected by Dornadilla,

King of the Scots, at a very early æra. Rocks, crystals, pebbles, and beautiful garnets are found on the coast of this parish, and here are also several veins of coals, but their quality is not considered good.

Invershin is situated at the northern extremity of the Firth of Dornoch, and is remarkable for a waterfall and salmon leap, where the fish that fail in the leap are caught in baskets, which are placed for that purpose.—Which are the largest rivers in this county?

ANNA.—The Helmsdale, Strathy, and Brora.

MRS. ROWE.—The river Helmsdale is the most northerly along the eastern coast : it descends from lofty mountains, through a considerable territory of arable land, and by its inundations serious injury is often sustained.

The Strathy issues from Loch Buy, and flowing north-ward, falls into the sea, through a bay of the same name.

The Brora flows from an inland loch of the same name, and taking a south-easterly course, falls into the sea at the village of Brora.—Which are the principal lochs and bays?

GEORGE.—Brora, Navern, Loyal, Shin, and the Bays of Tongue and Eriboll, to which may be added the Firth of Dornoch.

MRS. ROWE.—Loch Brora is a beautiful sheet of water, in the eastern part of the county, about four miles long and nearly one broad : in its centre is a small island, which has some appearance of being artificial ; and among the mountains near it are some beautiful plantations and villages.

Loch Navern is situated considerably to the north-west of the last-mentioned.

Loch Loyal, or Laoghall, lies in the parish of Tongue.

Loch Shin is near the south-western boundary of the county, and is about twenty miles long, and from one to two broad : its banks (especially on the southern side,) are beautifully covered with natural wood. These lochs are generally well stored with fish, particularly trout of various sizes.

Tongue Bay, or Loch Tongue, is a long arm of the sea, which stretches five miles into the land : it is skirted on each side by corn-fields, inclosed pastures, and farm-houses.

Loch Eriboll is a spacious bay, in which even the smallest sloops may lie in perfect safety.

The Firth of Dornoch, sometimes called the Firth of Tain, is that arm of the sea which divides the southern part of Sutherlandshire from Ross-shire : its entrance is nearly fifteen miles wide, which gradually becomes narrower, till at about three miles west of the town of Dornoch it is not more than two miles across, where it is called the Mickle Ferry of Dornoch, from its possessing a boat for the conveyance of passengers, &c.

ANNA.—Cape Wrath is situated at the most northwesterly point of the Island of Great Britain, and is justly the dread of mariners, as the rapid tide bursts with incredible fury against its rugged and lofty cliffs.

The south-western portion of this county is termed Assyut, in which are large strata of white marble equal to the Parian.

The hills of Sutherland, viewed externally, are so dismal and wild, that in crossing the firth towards them the traveller can scarcely abstain from shuddering at the prospect of entering such a land. This alpine region is, however, intersected by vales of great fertility, and sometimes by lakes, which soften the harshness of the landscape. Freestone, limestone, and slates abound here; besides which, iron stone, and veins of iron ore rich in silver, have been found in some parts of the county. Stags are numerous on the hills, as well as roes, grouse, ptarmigans, and black game. The county of Sutherland is much indebted to the munificence and exertions of some of its noble owners for having risen from a state of romance and indolence to one of activity and industry.

ROSS-SHIRE.

Boundaries.—Sutherlandshire, Inverness-shire, Atlantic Ocean, Firths of Murray and Dornoch.

Towns.—1, Tain; 2, Dingwall; 3, Invergordon; 4, Fortrose; 5, Lovat; 6, Beaulieu; 7, Pool Ewe; 8, Udrigall; 9, Kylscow; 10, Tarbat; 11, Sandwick.

Rivers and Lochs.—a, the Fairry; b, Conan; c, Grady; d, Loch Ennard; e, Loch Mealy; f, Loch Broom; g, Loch Ewe; h, Loch Mari; i, Loch Gare; k, Loch Torridon; l, Loch Kisserne; m, Loch Carran; n, Loch Luag.

A, Firth of Cromarty.

Islands and Capes.—J, Lewis; K, Harris, containing towns,— 1, Stornaway; 2, Barvie; B, Schant Islands; C, Housaness; D, Romarnish; E, Bible Head; F, Hempen Head; G, Salts Head; H, Oreby Point, or Butt of Lewis.

Lochs in Lewis.—4, Loch Tarbet; 5, Loch Stornaway; 6, Loch Shell; 7, Loch Birkins; 8, Bernera; 9, Hamaway Loch; 10, Skarpa.

MRS. ROWE.—DESCRIBE the boundaries, extent, and chief places of Ross-shire.

GEORGE.—It has the county of Sutherland on the north, Inverness-shire on the south, the Atlantic Ocean on the west, and on the east the Firths of Murray and Dornoch. From north to south it extends near 60 miles, and from east to west 70. Its chief towns are, Tain, Dingwall, Fortrose, Tarbat, Invergordon, Pool Ewe, and Beaulieu.

MRS. ROWE.—Tain, the county town, is irregularly built on the south side of the Firth of Dornoch, in the neighbourhood of a well cultivated country. It contains many handsome houses, and is a prosperous and pleasant little town. Its church was formerly collegiate, and is supposed to have been built in the fifth century. At a short distance are to be seen the remains of a small chapel: both these edifices were dedicated to St. Duthus.

ANNA.—It is said that King James IV. once made a pilgrimage on foot from Falkland to the shrine of St. Duthus, for the expiation of some offence : he travelled with unusual expedition, resting only a short time at the monastery of Pluscardine, near Elgin.

MRS. ROWE.—There is also a tradition, that soon after the royal visit this edifice was burnt by a party of the Mackrays, who were in pursuit of some person offensive to them, that had fled to it for shelter.

Dingwall was made a royal burgh by Alexander II., in 1226. It is pleasantly situated at the western termination of the Firth of Cromarty, which is navigable for small vessels as far as this town. It is an ancient place, built in the fashion of a Dutch town, consisting of one main street and a few smaller ones branching off from it. A few ruins of its strong and impregnable Castle, formerly one of the residences of the Earls of Ross, are now standing : it was surrounded by a deep ditch, and a regular glacis still remains. The church is a fine building, near which is an obelisk, erected on an artificial mount by George first earl of Cromarty, Secretary of State to Queen Anne, and intended as an ornament to the spot he designed as the cemetery of his family, and where he was buried. Some linen is manufactured in this town, and there is a lint-mill in the neighbourhood.

Fortrose, called also Rosemarkie, is an ancient town, seated on the Murray Firth, and consists of the towns or villages of Rosemarkie and Canonry, joined together by a charter confirmed by King James II. in the year 1444, which was ratified by James VI. in 1592, and made in a still more complete form by that monarch in 1612. Here the Bishop of Ross formerly resided, and the episcopal See was founded by David I.; but the period at which the Cathedral was erected is unknown, and of this ancient building there are only a few remains. Fortrose is spoken of as having once been a flourishing town, and the princi-

pal seat of divinity, law, and physic in this part of the
kingdom. It is now principally inhabited by weavers, who
find constant employment in manufacturing linen from flax
grown and prepared by themselves.

Beaulieu, ' Fine Plàce', is a pretty little town, worthy o
its name, situated at the head of the river Fairry, or Beaulieu, which here becomes a sort of inland firth, in continuation of that of Murray. Near this place stand the ruins of
a priory, founded in 1230, and peopled at first by monks
from France, who gave the town its name : it is a plain
structure, in the form of a cross, remarkably entire, the in-
ternal area being used as a burying-ground. The Kilmo-
rack Waterfalls are another object worthy of notice in this
neighbourhood.

Tarbat, once the pride of Ross, both for situation and
picturesque grounds, was the most favoured seat of the
Earls of Ross; but during the attainder of that family, i
was not only neglected, but dismantled of its greatest or
naments : the largest forest-trees ever seen in this countr
were then cut down, and sold to a company at Leith ; muc
of the ground within the Park was parcelled out to dis
banded soldiers and sailors; and this most elegant and best
finished house of three counties was then allowed to fa
to ruins.

Invergordon, seated on the north side of the Firth c
Cromarty, is noted for its Castle, which, having recentl
undergone many improvements, is a beautiful residence.

Pool Ewe, or Ulla Pool, on the western coast, is one c
the most advantageously situated fishing stations belongin
to the British Herring Fishery Company, having a good an
commodious harbour in one of the best fishing lochs c
that coast. It was begun to be built in 1788, and has eve
since been gradually increasing.—Name the principal rive
in Ross-shire. .

George.—The Fairry, or Beaulieu; the Conan; an
the Grady, or Orrin.

Mrs. Rowe.—The Fairry, or Beaulieu, rises near the western side, and for some distance forms a boundary between this county and Inverness-shire.

The Conan also finds its source in the west, and flows eastward into the Firth of Cromarty. It abounds with salmon, and pearls were formerly found near its mouth.

The Grady, or Orrin, rises in the west, and flows eastward into the Conan.—Which are the principal lochs and firths?

Anna.—The lochs are those of Broom, Mari, Carran, and Luag; and the Firth of Murray or Beaulieu.

Mrs. Rowe.—The western part of this county is very deeply indented with bays or arms of the sea, here called lochs: one of the largest is Loch Broom, extending inland to a great distance. It is one of the noted retreats of the shoals of herrings in their passage southward; and on its banks many fishing stations have been established.

Loch Mari is to the south of the former, and is of considerable extent, containing many islands: on the largest, called Island Mari, there are the remains of an ancient Druidical edifice, and around it a burial-place, where the inhabitants on the north side of the loch inter their dead.

Lochs Carran, and Luag, like the other arms of the sea on this coast, are excellent fishing stations, and safe retreats for ships.

It would be impossible to specify the most remarkable hills in a county so wholly mountainous as Ross-shire; that of Tulloch Ard, in the south-west corner, claims particular attention, on account of its importance in ancient times. Like the Roman temple of Janus, it indicated peace or war; for when the latter was begun, a barrel of burning tar on the highest point was the signal, and in twenty-four hours all the tenants and vassals of Seaforth appeared armed at the Castle of Donan. This mountain is the crest of the arms of Seaforth.

Ben Wyvis, in the eastern part of the county, is also

worthy of note for towering above the rest, and having its summit almost perpetually covered with snow.

GEORGE.—The proprietor of Ben Wyvis holds his estate in Ross-shire by the following singular tenure of one of the early Scottish kings : That he must bring three wainloads of snow from the top of that hill whenever His Majesty should desire it; and if the fulfilment of the tenure had been insisted upon in September 1826, he must have forfeited the manor, as this mountain was then known for the first time to be destitute of snow. It is said it was claimed by the Duke of Cumberland to cool his wine with when he was residing at Inverness in the summer of 1746.

ANNA.—Do not the islands of Lewis, and the Schant, or Holy Islands, belong to Ross-shire?

MRS. ROWE.—They are a part of a cluster called the Hebrides, or Western Isles; and tradition affirms them to have been under their own princes till the destruction of the Pictish kingdom by Kenneth II. in the ninth century, when they formed a part of his dominions, since which they have been claimed at different periods by the kings of Norway, England, and Scotland, who have pretended to dispose of them at their pleasure, although the descendants of their ancient chiefs still kept possession, exercised the power, and often assumed the title of kings over them; but at length these haughty Lords of the Isles were reduced into British subjects; and if we except those few which constitute the county of Bute, they do not now form separate provinces, but belong to the counties of Ross, Inverness, and Argyle.

GEORGE.—These nobles long retained that pride of spirit which results from independence : one of them, named M'Donald, when in Ireland was invited by the Governor to an entertainment, who asked him to sit beside him. Lord M'Donald, who did not understand English, asked, " What says the Carle?" " He bids you move to the head of the table," was the answer. "Tell the Carle," said M'Donald, "that wherever M'Donald sits, that is the head of the table."

Mrs. Rowe.—The opinion conceived by these Lords in their own country is emphatically expressed in a short epitaph discovered on one of their tombs, which has been thus translated : " Fate alone could lay M'Donald there."

The island of Lewis is the most northerly and one of the largest of the Western Isles : it is said to be about 35 miles long, and in its mean breadth 13. Its principal parishes are Stornaway and Barvie ; the former is a place of considerable size, and has an excellent harbour, which will admit vessels of great burden. The principal employment of the inhabitants is in the herring fishery. It is a port of the Custom House, and has a port officer, and a regular packet, which sails every week with the mail and passengers.

Barvie is situated in the western part, and is known as a fishing station. Numerous lochs and bays intersect both the eastern and western coasts of the island, and springs, lakes, and rivulets, furnish abundance of fresh water. The climate may be thus described : the spring is uncommonly cold and backward ; summer warm ; autumn accompanied with profuse rains ; and winter, though without long and severe frosts or very heavy falls of snow, is attended with constant stormy and cold winds. In this island are to be found deer ; and numbers of wild fowl frequent the shores, lakes, and cliffs of the mountains ; among which is the Eider goose, so noted for its valuable down. Immense shoals of fish, of a variety of species, haunt the coast.

The Schant, or Holy Islands, are well known to mariners : in one of them, named Moair, or Mary's Island, are the remains of a Popish chapel. Black cattle are pastured upon all of them, and they are famous for fattening sheep ; but particularly some small rocks in the neighbourhood, which have grass on their tops.

The county of Ross stretches across the island from sea to sea, and is divided into two districts, respectively called

Eastern and Western Ross. The latter is a frightful tract of hill, penetrated by a few lonely roads, and thinly inhabited. Eastern Ross is, on the contrary, a beautiful, well cultivated and wooded plain, bordering on the North Sea. In the woods is that beautiful bird called Capercailzie, or Cock of the Wood: it is of a bright azure colour, and almost as large as a common turkey. The ptarmigan, a simple bird, somewhat less than a partridge, is also found on the mountains: it is often indebted for its safety to its grey colour, which resembles the stones among which it lodges; in winter it becomes as white as snow, in which it often buries itself.

CROMARTY.

Boundaries.—The Firth of Cromarty, Ross-shire, and Firth of Murray.
Town.—1, Cromarty.
Firth.—1, Firth of Murray.

MRS. ROWE.—WHAT are the situation, extent, and chief towns of Cromarty?

ANNA.—It is bounded on the north by the Firth of Cromarty, east by Murray Firth, and south and west by Ross-shire. From east to west it measures 12 miles, and about 3 in its greatest breadth. Its chief town is Cromarty.

MRS. ROWE.—Cromarty, or Cromartie, is the capital of this small county, and is as flourishing and improving a place as any of its size in Scotland: it stands on a promontory jutting into the firth, and being slightly elevated, it has the advantage of a dry as well as a pleasant situation. This town has a manufacture of hempen cloth, and an extensive coasting trade in fish, which affords employment for the greater proportion of the common people. Chambers, in his Picture of Scotland, says, that "in September 1826 he saw two hundred women engaged in cleaning and salting the fish, which the innumerable boats were bringing ashore, while twenty-nine vessels lay in the firth waiting to convey the barrels, on being made up, to various ports." The truly excellent harbour of Cromarty, the *Portus Salutus* of the Romans, is of very considerable extent : the entrance is narrow and bold, being formed by two huge lofty rocks, which are called by the natives the Sutors of Cromarty. The state of the shore and anchorage ground on both sides, for several miles up this bay, is so favourable and smooth, that were a vessel driven from her anchors and cast ashore, there would be little or no damage incurred. In violent easterly winds ships flock into this harbour when they dare not venture into any other port on the eastern coast of Scotland, from the Firth of Forth northwards : and from Wick, in Caithness, to this firth, a distance of 60 miles, the shore is utterly inadmissible to sea vessels of any size, the waters of Dornoch excepted, which, however, are of no great utility to navigation, in consequence of shallows and quicksands. Crabs and lobsters are dragged from holes among the rocks ; and seals and otters are often found on this coast.

The county of Cromarty is tolerably fertile in corn and pasturage. The two rocks at the mouth of the firth are perfectly uniform, except in artificial adornment. They are called the North and South Sutors ; and the latter, which overhangs Cromarty, is most beautifully wooded, being a part of a park attached to a fine seat called Cromarty House. There is a deep chasm in the front of the hill, termed Macfarquhar's Bed, besides a petrifying spring, called the Dropping Well. Near the North Sutor are seven sunk rocks, which are never to be seen except at the neap tides ; they are named The Seven Kings' Sons, because, according to tradition, seven individuals who bore that re-

lation to Majesty were shipwrecked and drowned upon
them in coming home from France.

INVERNESS-SHIRE.

Boundaries.—Ross-shire, Murrayshire, Banffshire, Aberdeenshire,
Perthshire, Argyleshire, and the Atlantic Ocean.

Towns.—1, Inverness; 2, Culloden; 3, Gents. Hut; 4, Fort
Augustus; 5, Urquhart; 6, Bealada; 7, Bernea; 8, Pitmain; 9, Ruthven; 10, Dalwhinie; 11, Catleach; 12, Garry-
more; 13, Letter Findley; 14, Kepach; 15, Fort William.

Rivers and Lochs.—a, River Spey; b, Loch Ness; c, Loch Oich;
d, Loch Garry; e, Loch Quick; f, Loch Arkek; g, Loch
Lochy; h, Loch Laggan; k, Loch Linnhe; l, Loch Shiel;
m, Loch Halluort; n, Loch Ranach; o, Loch Nus; p, Loch
Morer; q, Loch Nevisk; r, Loch Urn.

Islands.—A, Skye; B, Raasay; C, Ronay; D, Sculpa; E, Egg;
F, Rum; G, Muck; H, Canay; I, Helscar; J, North Uist;
K, South Uist; L, Barra; M, Monach; N, Waterness;
O, Bishops; P, Benbecula.

Lochs in Skye.—s, Loch Eyford; t, Loch Brittil; u, Loch Eynord;
v, Loch Brakadale; w, Loch Fallart; x, Loch Snisort.

Mrs. Rowe.—DESCRIBE the boundaries, extent, and
chief towns in Inverness-shire.

George.—The county of Ross bounds it on the north;
those of Nairn, Murray, Banff, and Aberdeen, east; Perth
and Argyle south; and the Atlantic Ocean on the west. It
measures about 45 miles from north to south, and 75 from
east to west. Its chief towns are Inverness, Fort Augustus,
Fort William, Culloden, Pitmain, and Urquhart.

Mrs. Rowe.—Inverness, the capital, is an ancient royal
burgh: its first charter was the grant of Malcolm Canmore. It is situated chiefly on the south-east bank of the
river Ness, over which a handsome bridge, having seven

arches, was built in the reign of Charles II. and between
the first and second arches from the east end there is a
vault, only five or six feet square, accessible by a trap-
door at the top, and lighted by a little grated window on
the upper side of the bridge: this was formerly used as a
jail, and afterwards as a place for insane persons. Below
the town, where the Ness joins the Seal are to be seen the
remains of a fort built by Oliver Cromwell: its area is
now occupied by a tribe of weavers. The Castle of Inverness, which was really the scene of Duncan's murder,
is an object of much interest. This edifice stood on an
eminence to the east of the town, a spot well worthy the
description given of it by the poet:

"This Castle hath a pleasant seat; the air
 Nimbly and sweetly commends itself
 Unto our gentle senses," &c.

When Malcolm Canmore overthrew the murderer of his
father and the usurper of his Crown, he thought proper to
destroy this Castle; he, however, built another fortress, which
stood on a lofty hill overhanging the town. The latter edifice continued for seven centuries to be an occasional royal
residence. It is said that when Queen Mary visited this
place in 1562, the governor refused to admit her on account of her hostility to his superior, the Marquis of Huntly-
ley, and she was obliged to reside in an old house, which
is still shown near the bridge, till her attendants had taken
the Castle, and killed the governor. This fortress was, at
a great expense, converted into a fort for the subjugation
of the Highlands at the Revolution: it being, however,
taken by Prince Charles Stuart in 1746, he ordered it to
be destroyed by explosion; and of this once famed building there now only remains the wall of an exterior rampart. The church of Inverness is a plain structure; the
Tolbooth is a more modern building, with a handsome
spire, the top of which was twisted by the earthquake in

1816. Its academy has long been a distinguished seminary
for the Highland youth. The inhabitants of this place
have, till within a very few years, been averse to any de-
parture from their original habits; and when the magi-
stracy had resolved upon instituting the system of clearing
the streets, it was with difficulty that a scavenger could be
found, as none of the natives would accept so degrading an
office; and a person of very low estate, on being requested
to undertake it, asked, with tears in his eyes, what act of
meanness, or what crime, he or his father, or his grand-
father, or his great-grandfather, or any of his ancestors or
relatives had ever committed, that this shame should await
him. In testimony of the same fact, it may be stated that
there were no roads near Inverness till the military ways
were formed about a century ago; and the first coach ever
seen in Inverness was one belonging to the Earl of Seaforth, in 1715, when the country people looked upon the
driver as the most important person belonging to it, and
accordingly made suitable obeisances to him. A manufacture of ropes and canvass is carried on here; and the
salmon fishery is also considerable.

Fort Augustus is the central one of the chain along the
lochs extending from north-east to south-west: it stands
at the head of Loch Ness, having Loch Oich to the south-
west. It is a regular fortification, in good repair, but by no
means a place of strength, being commanded by the surrounding hills. This fort was taken by the Highlanders
in 1746, who, after demolishing what they could, deserted
it. The neatness of its appearance, and the surrounding
plantations, give it very much the resemblance of an English country seat.

Fort William is the last of the chain of forts erected for
the subjugation of the Highlanders, and is situated at the
western corner of this county; it was first built of earth,
under the direction of General Monk, during the usurpation
of Cromwell, when it occupied much more ground than at

present, as in the reign of William and Mary it was rebuilt with stone and lime on a smaller scale; but it is now in a state of decay, owing to a part of its walls having been undermined by the river Nevis.

GEORGE.—I have read that neither threats nor entreaties could induce the brave Sir Ewan Cameron, Laird of Lochiel, to abandon the cause of King Charles I., although all the neighbouring chiefs had yielded to General Monk, who commanded the forces of Oliver Cromwell. He stationed himself on an eminence, whence he could see the progress of the enemy, who were engaged in erecting this fort; and being informed of their design to cut down his wood, and carry away his cattle, he determined to make them pay dearly for every tree and bullock's hide: then calling a council of war, in a short but spirited speech he represented to his followers, that if they had any regard for their lawful sovereign, their chief, or their honour, they would attack the English; "for," said he, "if every one kills his man, which I hope you will, I will answer for the rest." Upon this they all consented, but requested that he and his younger brother would stand at a distance, and only view the danger. To this proposal, with regard to himself, he would not listen, but commanded his brother (who, with all the ardour of youth, was with pleasure anticipating the conflict,) to be bound to a tree, and left a little boy to attend him. The unwilling prisoner soon prevailed on the child to release him, and eagerly ran to take an active part in the engagement, which was long and obstinate; for though the English defended themselves with great bravery, they were compelled to give way, and retreated to their ships with their faces towards the enemy, fighting with astonishing resolution. In this way did the bold chief harass the new garrison in the neighbourhood, making them often pay dearly for their depredations; till at last, finding his country impoverished, and his people almost ruined, he listened to the solicitations which were made to him, and submitted to terms of his own dictating; on receiving which, Macleod immediately wrote him a letter of thanks.

Urquhart Castle, now only the picturesque ruin of a Highland fortress, stands on the western side of Loch Ness. Abercromble records that this fortress was reduced by Edward I. in 1309, when the governor, Alexander Boice, and the garrison who defended it, were basely put to death.

Anna.—The same author states, that in 1306 Robert Lauder, their governor, bravely defended it for Baliol against the English.

Mrs. Rowe.—In the year 1509 James IV. bestowed this fortress upon the Laird of Grant.

Culloden, on the Murray Firth, is rendered of importance in historical annals from the battle between the Highland army and the Duke of Cumberland being fought on its Moor, April 16, 1746, when the English gained a decisive victory, and the hopes of the House of Stuart were for ever extinguished.

George.—Prince Charles (the son of the Pretender), who had raised and conducted the Highland troops, was forced from the field of battle by one of his officers; for several days wandered about the country, and found refuge in caves and cottages, or concealed himself in forests: he was constantly pursued by the troops of the conqueror, who offered a reward of 30,000l. for taking him, either dead or alive. In the course of a very short period he had occasion to trust himself to fifty-nine different persons, whose sense of honour and veneration for his family outweighed their avarice. It is said that a person of the name of M'Ian (though no friend to his cause,) watched over him with inviolable fidelity for weeks, and even robbed, at the risk of his own life, for his support. At last, after innumerable hardships and adventures (in the course of which Prince Charles was once disguised as a laundry-maid), he

and the place where Montrose, in 1645, gained one of his celebrated victories.—What is the course of the river Nairn?

Ans.—[The Nairn rises] in the hills of Inverness-shire, and proceeding towards the north-east, falls into the Murray Firth at Nairn. It is called in the Gaelic *Kisg Nearn*, signifying ' the Waters of Alders,' from the number of those trees which grow on its banks.

Mas. Bowne.—The soil of this small county, though rocky, is fertile, and is in general well cultivated, for which it is more adapted than the hilly districts which encompass it: it is also remarkable for the salubrity of its climate : its lakes abound in fish, and it has some plantations of firs.

Though not peculiar to this district, but to the whole Scottish nation, I will here notice that celebrated musical instrument the Bagpipe, of which there are two varieties, one with short pipes, played on with the fingers, the other with long ones, and only sounded by the mouth : this last, which is the loudest and most ear-piercing of all music, is the genuine Highland pipe, and suited well the warlike spirit of the ancient Caledonians, amongst whom it was in such universal use, that when every chieftain was a prince, and had his officers of state, who had lands allotted them for their subsistence, the piper was a regular appendage to their dignity. His office was, by the sounding of his pipe, to rouse their courage in battle, to alarm them when in danger, to collect them when scattered, to solace them in their long and painful marches, and in times of peace to keep up the memory of the gallantry of their ancestors, by tunes composed after signal victories ; but they too often awakened the spirit of revenge, by airs expressing the defeats or massacres of rival clans.

The village of Auldearn is situated in the centre of the great roads between the towns of Elgin and Inverness, and is chiefly worthy of notice for being a borough brunty,

island from Fort George in the north-east to Fort William
in the south-west: it measures about three miles in length,
and the scenery along its banks is very grand.

Loch Lochy is the most western of the fresh-water lakes
in this chain: it measures about 14 miles in length, and
from 1 to 2 in breadth. The hills surrounding this lake
are very steep, and in some parts covered with wood.

Loch Laggan is situated in the south-eastern district,
and is about 15 miles long, and 1½ mile broad: on the
south side of it is the Coil More, the most considerable
remnant of the great Caledonian Forest.

Loch Shiel and Loch Eil are two arms of the sea, which
form a part of the boundary between this county and Argyleshire.

Inverness-shire is intersected by the Great Glen of Scotland, that wonderful natural hollow, which stretches in a
straight line from south-west to north-east, and is almost
entirely filled by lakes and arms of the sea, so as nearly
to isolate the northern half of the kingdom, thus seem-
ing to have been formed by nature to be fashioned into
a canal when the proper time should arrive: and it would
really appear, from the general tradition of the Highlands, that some native seer many centuries ago pre-
dicted what has actually taken place, "a passage for white-
sailed vessels along the lonely glen of the lakes"; foreseeing,
by a mere exertion of the understanding, that advantage
would ultimately be taken, in that way, of the natural con-
figuration of the territory. The Caledonian Canal was
commenced in 1803, and opened in 1822, after an expense
of upwards of 800,000l. It is 20 feet deep, 50 wide at the
bottom, and 110 at the top: its length is 60 miles, exclu-
sive of the important estuary of Loch Linnhe, through
Loch Eil, where it begins; and after extending through
numerous lochs in its course to Inverness, it forms through
the heart of Scotland a communication between the Atlantic Ocean and the North Sea. The western part of this

county is very mountainous, particularly where its lofty hills are in appearance piled one upon another in terrific magnificence. The celebrated Ben Nevis, the highest hill in Great Britain, stands to the south of Fort William; it affords pasturage for sheep, and from its summit one of the most extensive and beautiful prospects in Scotland. The northern district is mountainous and barren, the woody parts of which are the haunts of stags and roes; and the capercailzie is sometimes seen among the lofty pines. The heath is the resort of wild fowl and ptarmigans, and alpine hares are sometimes found here. The extensive plains which surround the lakes are in general fertile; and upon their high grounds many sheep and black cattle are fed, the rearing and selling of which is the chief employment of the inhabitants. Limestone and iron ore are the principal minerals, with some beautiful rock crystals of various tints; but no mines have hitherto been worked with much success.—Which are the most considerable of the Hebrides that belong to this county?

Gibson.—The islands of Harris, Skye, North and South Uist, Raasay, Sculpa, Ronay, Egg, Canay, Rum, and Muck.

Mrs. Rowe.—The island of Harris, though belonging to this county, is a continuance southward of that of Lewis, and is about 15 miles long, and at the southern extremity 6 broad. Like most of the Scottish isles, it is greatly intersected by arms of the sea, and is generally wild, bleak, barren of wood, and little fitted for cultivation.

Skye is the largest of the Hebrides, being nearly 50 miles long, and 20 broad: on the south-east it is parted from Inverness-shire by a very narrow channel. Its principal parishes are Portree and Slate, the inhabitants of which trade chiefly in black cattle, small horses, and kelp: the latter parish terminates in a rugged promontory on the south-eastern side of the island, called the Point of Slate. Notwithstanding some mountainous tracts, a great portion of this island is level ground, affording excellent pasturage, and great numbers of deer are found in it: it abounds with limestone and marble. It has been said that a cave in the east end afforded shelter to the disappointed Pretender and his faithful guide for two nights in 1746.

North Uist lies to the south of Harris, and is of a very irregular shape, about 20 miles long, and varies in breadth, from the coast being much intersected by numerous inlets of the sea, which afford excellent harbours. On the morasses in this island grows that long grass known through Scotland by the common name of Bent, which is unfit for pasture, but is manufactured by the inhabitants into ropes, and used also for thatching and other purposes. Innumerable species of land and water fowl frequent this isle, and fish of almost every variety swarm round the coast.

South Uist, so called from its situation with regard to the last-mentioned island, is about 30 miles long, and from 2 to 9 broad. A great number of cows are annually sold here, but the principal source of emolument is from the making of kelp. Druidical temples are here to be seen as well as Dúns or Pícts' houses.

Raasay is a small isle on the eastern side of Skye, about 12 miles long, and from 2 to 5 broad. Its chief produce are black cattle and sheep: goats and small horses are also fed here in great numbers.

Scalpa is a low heath-covered island. Its land dimensions are not easily ascertained, through a singular intervention of freshwater lakes and arms of the sea. Its extreme points, from east to west, may be computed 3 miles distant. In the eastern extremity is a light-house, which was erected in 1788; and near the western are two of the best natural harbours in the Hebrides. Mariners call Scalpa the Isle of Glass.

Ronay is north of Raasay, about 4 miles in length and nearly 2 in breadth: it is rocky and barren, but affords pasture for cattle, and has a good harbour, though sailors seldom put into it unless forced by the weather.

Egg, Canay, Rum, and Muck form a parish, called Small Islands; concerning which it may be remarked, that the inhabitants are all excellent fishermen, and mainly depend upon the productions of the ocean for their support. North Uist lies to the south of Harris, and is of an irregular shape, about 20 miles long, and varies in breadth from the coast ——————

NAIRNSHIRE.

Boundaries.—The Firth of Murray, Murrayshire, and Inverness-shire.

Towns.—1, Nairn; 2, Fort George; 3, Auldearn.

River.—a, the Nairn.

MRS. ROWE.—DESCRIBE the situation, extent, and chief places of Nairnshire.

ANNA.—It is bounded on the north by the Firth of Murray, on the west by Inverness-shire, and south and east by Murrayshire. Its length is 12 miles, and breadth 8. The chief places in it are Nairn, Fort George, and the village of Auldearn.

MRS. ROWE.—Nairn, the capital, and the only royal burgh in the county, is pleasantly seated on a small river of the same name, near the shore of the Firth: it is supposed to be of considerable antiquity, but the exact æra of its foundation is unknown; and although undistinguished as a port by trade or manufactures, it may be considered an agreeable and improving place. The boundary line of the Highlands passes so exactly through the centre of it, that it is a remarkable circumstance that the Gaelic language is spoken in one part, while English, or rather lowland Scotch, is the dialect of the other.

GEORGE.—I have read, that when James VI. ascended

ELGIN OR MURRAYSHIRE.

Boundaries.—Nairnshire, Inverness-shire, Banffshire, and Murray
or Moray Firth.

Towns.—1, Elgin; 2, Findhorne; 3, Forres; 4, Dulse; 5, Gran-
town; 6, Avemore; 7, Lossiemouth; 8, Gairmouth.

Rivers.—a, the Spey; b, Duinan; c, Findhorne; d, Lossie.

MRS. ROWE.—TELL me the situation, extent, and chief
towns of Elginshire.

GEORGE.—It is bounded on the north by the Firth of
Murray, east by Banffshire, south by Inverness-shire, and
west by the latter county and Nairnshire. Its length is
about 40 miles, and its breadth nearly as much. It contains
the towns of Elgin, Forres, Lossiemouth, and Gairmouth.

MRS. ROWE.—Elgin, the See of a bishop, and the capital of the county, is a fine old-fashioned city, pleasantly
situated on the little river Lossie. The county buildings,
episcopalian chapel, and many modern private edifices
are remarkable for the neatness of their architecture, and
the beauty and purity of the pale sandstone with which they
are built. This stone is superior to any other found in Scotland, and a considerable quantity of it was exported to
London, in 1826, for building the New London Bridge.
The greatest object of attraction in this city is its ancient
and venerable Cathedral, which was founded in the early
part of the 13th century. In 1390 Alexander Stuart, commonly called the 'Wolf of Badenoch,' owing to his resentment
against Bishop Bar, burnt the Cathedral and many other
buildings. It took years to repair this disaster of a day;
but by the exertions of the bishops, who successively devoted one third of their revenues to the pious undertaking,
it was restored to its former splendour, and remained in

its complete state till it was reduced to ruins in 1568, when, by an order of the Privy Council at Edinburgh, the Sheriff of Aberdeen with some others, was appointed to remove the lead from the cathedral churches of Aberdeen and Elgin, and sell the same for the maintenance of the Regent Murray's soldiers.

ANNA.—This unholy deed did not, however, answer the desired purpose; for it is recorded that the vessel employed to transport the metal to Holland for sale, had scarcely left the harbour of Aberdeen before it sunk with all its cargo.

MRS. ROWE.—The ruins of this Cathedral attest (what has been generally allowed,) that it was by far the most splendid specimen of ecclesiastical architecture in Scotland; and enough still remains to strike the beholder with admiration and astonishment. There are many monuments in it, including some which represent the deceased lying in complete armour: it is also noted for containing the remains of Duncan, who was murdered by order of Macbeth in 1040. Elgin has no manufactures, but possesses a distinguished brewery. At the west-end stands Guy's Hospital, which owes its origin, as well as the free school for poor children, to the bounty of a native.

Forres is situated on an eminence, and is renowned for its ancient Castle, which was the scene of the murder of Duffus, one of the early kings of Scotland, by Donwald, Governor of the Castle, under circumstances from which Shakspeare certainly formed his dramatic version of the murder of King Duncan by Macbeth. In consequence of this atrocious act the Castle was destroyed, but another was erected on its site, the ruins of which still exist. This town is also celebrated by the genius of our immortal bard as having been the scene of the greater part of his tragedy of Macbeth; and the waste called Hard Moor (not far from hence) is, according to all the old historians (whom Shak-

predictions.　　　　　　　　　　often frequented by wild swans.

... On the east of Forres is erected a pillar ... the memory of the immortal Nelson; and it is said that every individual, man and woman, in Forres ... instance of their patriotic feeling, by contributing either by money or labour, to the construction of this public work. In the vicinity of this place is an ancient column called King Swinol's Stone, or Danish Pillar: on it are carved figures of soldiers on horseback and on foot; and it is supposed to have been erected by Malcolm II. in commemoration of the final retreat of the Danes from Scotland after he had defeated them in 1008.

... mouth derives its name from its situation at the mouth of the river Lossie, and is only noted for being the harbour of Elgin, from which great quantities of corn are annually exported.

Gairmouth is a small village at the mouth of the river Spey, which here forms a good harbour: it has a considerable salmon fishery.—Which are the principal rivers of the county?

... The Findhorne, Spey, and Lossie.

... The Findhorne rises in Inverness-shire, and pursuing a north-easterly direction, falls into the Murray Firth.

The Spey, which has already been mentioned as rising in the hills of Inverness-shire, terminates its course at the village of Gairmouth, and is remarkable for its rapidity, as well as for producing excellent salmon and trout.

The Lossie has its source in this county, and pursuing a north-easterly direction, falls into the firth at the port of Lossiemouth.—Describe the lochs in this county.

GEORGE.—Loch Spynie is about three miles long, and one mile broad: it is supposed to have been formerly a

often frequented by wild swans.

every individual, man and woman, in Forres...

esteemed as having been the founder of a free school...

the mean condition of a private soldier to...

...dral of Elgin, where the mother of Anderson, an indigent and infirm widow lived for many years when he was a boy; and ... was perhaps the most abject ... permitted to make provision for ... such outcasts as he had himself been.

The Lossie has its source in this county, and pursuing a north-easterly direction, falls into the firth at the port of Lossiemouth.—Describe the lochs in this county.

GEORGE.—Loch Spynie is about three miles long, and one mile broad: it is supposed to have been formerly a

BANFFSHIRE.

Boundaries.—Murrayshire, Inverness-shire, Aberdeenshire, and Murray or Moray Firth.

Towns.—1, Banff; 2, Portsey; 3, Cullen; 4, Fochabers; 5, Abertour; 6, Macduff; 7, Keith.

Rivers.—*a*, the Devon, or Devoron; *b*, Spey; *c*, Avin.

MRS. ROWE.—THIS county forms the remainder of the province of Murray. Describe its boundaries, extent, and chief towns.

GEORGE.—It is bounded on the north by the North Sea, on the west by Inverness-shire and Elginshire, and on the east, south-east, and south, by Aberdeenshire. From north-east to south-west it measures upwards of 50 miles; and its breadth, in its widest part, is upwards of 30, which varies considerably, till its south-western extremity terminates in a point. It contains the towns of Banff, Cullen, Portsey, Macduff, Fochabers, and Keith.

MRS. ROWE.—Banff, the capital, is situated at the mouth of the river Devon, or Devoron, and, according to tradition, owes its origin to the 12th century, having been founded by Malcolm Canmore in 1163: it was erected into a royal burgh, and endowed with the same privileges as Aberdeen in virtue of a charter granted by Robert II. in 1372, but has several well-built streets, and is said to be the most fashionable town north of Aberdeen. It was here that the noted robber named M'Pherson was executed. About a century ago this marauder, who had long robbed with impunity, was at length taken by an intrepid ancestor of the Earl of Fife, and underwent the sentence of the law; and it is said that when led to the place of execution, he took his violin (on which instrument he was a great proficient,) and played his own funeral march, that he had previously composed, and then he resigned himself to his fate with the most indignant countenance.—The salmon fishery of the Devon is a source of great wealth, but the harbour is much injured by the continual shifting of the sands.

Cullen is the other royal burgh in this county, and was anciently called Invercullen, from its situation on the little river Cullen at its junction with the sea. It may be said to consist of three distinct towns; the New Town, a well built place near the sea, with a good harbour; the Auld Town, more inland, and adjoining to the Park of Cullen House; and the Fish Town, a low village exclusively inhabited by fishermen. In the centre of these is an eminence, named the Castle Hill, on which the ruins of a house are still shown, where it is said that Elizabeth, queen of Robert Bruce, died. Cullen House, the seat of the Earl of Seafield, is one of the most princely mansions north of the firth, and lies imbedded in an umbrageous forest in the vicinity of this town. In a small sandy bay are three lofty aspiring rocks, formed of flinty masses, known by the appellation of 'The Three Kings of Cullen.' Not far from thence is an assemblage of cairns, or monuments, supposed to have been raised to the memory of those slain in a victory obtained by Indulphus over the Danes in the year 986.

Portsoy is a thriving little port, situated at the head of one of those small bays with which this part of the coast is so frequently indented : it carries on some trade in linen, thread, &c., but is principally famous for beautiful marble, and other mineralogical productions found in its neighbourhood.

Macduff is a modern village and a sea-port situated on the opposite side of the river Devon, or Devoron, about a mile from Banff, to which it is accessible by a fine bridge thrown across the river; and having a better harbour, it may be said to possess more trade than that town. The church is a fine structure, erected on an eminence, and ornamented by a handsome cross.

Fochabers stands at the western extremity of the county, on the river Spey, and is chiefly remarkable for being an appendage to Gordon Castle, which is a magnificent structure, situated in a beautiful park, and surrounded by a delightfully picturesque country.

Keith is a thriving manufacturing town, with weekly markets, and well attended annual fairs. The parish school has long been famous as an initiating seminary for youths intended for the University, owing to the attention of the proprietors in procuring able teachers to fill that important office.—Which are the principal rivers in Banffshire?

George.—The Devon or Devoron, Avon, and Spey.

Mrs. Rowe.—The Devoron enters on the eastern side of the county from Aberdeenshire, and first proceeds in a north-easterly direction, then suddenly turning due north it flows through Banff, and mixes with the waters of the North Sea.

The Avon finds its source at the southern extremity of the county, on the confines of Aberdeenshire and Inverness, and flows northerly to unite its waters with the Spey, which has been described in "Murrayshire."

Banffshire contains many lofty mountains, of which the most noted are Belrinnes, rising 2690 feet, and Knockhill, which is 1500 feet above the level of the sea. It is remarkable for possessing many relics of the Caledonians, or Danes, among which have been found stone coffins, urns, ashes, and other sepulchral appendages.

The province of Murray comprehends the three small counties of Banff, Elgin, and Nairn, and may be described as forming the southern shore of the Murray Firth. On the east it is separated from Aberdeenshire by the Devoron, on the west it is bounded by Inverness-shire. Unlike all the districts which surround it, it is remarkable for equality f surface, fertility of soil, and salubrity of climate; and here is an old popular saying, that it enjoys forty days more of fair weather than any other part of the kingdom. t was anciently considered and designated the Granary of Scotland. The province of Murray suffered more perhaps than any other district of Scotland by the civil wars: the people were then generally attached to the Covenant, and as Montrose chose to make it one of his principal scenes of action, the peaceable farmers were not permitted to enjoy their opinions and their goods undisturbed. In his descent upon Murray in 1645, after his battle at Inverlochy, he destroyed all the houses of such as did not join his standard, and gave up the towns of Banff, Cullen, and Elgin to indiscriminate pillage; but the province has now an appearance of comfort and beauty more appropriate to its character for amenity and productiveness.

ABERDEENSHIRE.

Boundaries.—Murray Firth, North Sea, Mearnshire, Angusshire, Perthshire, Inverness-shire, and Banffshire.

Towns.—1, Aberdeen; 2, Old Aberdeen; 3, Kintore; 4, Inverury; 5, Ellon; 6, Peterhead; 7, Strichen; 8, Fraserburgh; 9, Tarriff; 10, Fyvie; 11, Segaat; 12, Old Meldrum; 13, Huntley; 14, Cabild Forbes; 15, Monemusk; 16, Kincardine; 17, Midmar; 18, Tullich; 19, Cargraff Castle; 20, Galdia; 21, Braemar.

Rivers.—a, the Dee; b, Don; c, Ythan; d, Ugge; e, Brogie; f, Ured.

Capes.—Kinsird's Head and Nairn's Head.

Districts.—B, Mar; C, Formarten; D, Buchan; E, Garrioch.

Mrs. Rowe.—WHAT are the boundaries, extent, and chief towns of Aberdeenshire?

shire.—It is bounded on the north and east by the
North Sea, on the south by Mearnshire, Angusshire, and
Perthshire; and by Inverness-shire and Banffshire on
the west: from Kynaird's Head in the north-east, to its
south-western extremity, it measures more than 80 miles,
and its breadth may be computed at 30, though in some
places it is considerably more. The most important places
in it are Old and New Aberdeen, Peterhead, Fraserburgh,
Inverury, Kintore, Old Meldrum, Huntley, Tarriff, and
Midmar.

Mar Rows.—Old Aberdeen is seated on the river Don,
about a mile north of the New city, with which it is connected by long streets, though it is quite distinct with respect to municipal government. It is noted for its remote
antiquity, and is the seat of a College and Cathedral; by
means of the former, and a few manufactures, it is said to
maintain its present importance. It is remarkable throughout history for the singular learning, piety, and public spirit
of its bishops; and the names of Cheyne and Elphinstone
are honourably associated with the public buildings of
Aberdeen. In 1494 Bishop Elphinstone procured a Bull
from Pope Nicholas V., granting him permission to found
its College, and the institution being afterwards taken under
the protection of royalty, it was denominated 'King's College.' Its buildings consist of a large quadrangle, and a
church of great antiquity, but in good repair. This College has a good library, which has the privilege of having
a copy of every new publication. The Medical school of
Aberdeen is one of those acknowledged by the College of
Surgeons in London. The only remains of the Cathedral,
and its precincts, is a church with two steeples, usually
called the Church of St. Machar, and it is said there is more
of the massive than the elegant in this relic of Gothic architecture; yet it possesses a noble western window, and is
decorated within in a style which cannot fail to command
admiration. The bridge over the Don, in the vicinity of this

city, may rank as another object of antiquity deserving of
notice: it consists of one spacious Gothic arch, stretching
from the rock on one side to that on the other, so that it
is raised to a prodigious height above the stream. It was
built by Bishop Cheyne in the reign of Robert Bruce, who,
having opposed the interests of that monarch, fled to England on his becoming successful; but, after a series of
years, he returned to his native country, and out of his ac-
cumulated revenues erected this stately fabric.

New Aberdeen is situated on a slight eminence between
the rivers Dee and Don, which, after traversing the mountainous district of Mar, here approach each other and fall
into the sea: it has all the bustle of trade and appearance
of opulence which usually distinguish a metropolis, and is
justly considered the third city in Scotland for trade, beauty,
and extent. Amongst its public buildings may be mentioned the bridge in Union-street, consisting of one arch,
the span of which, 132 feet, with a rise of only 32, is believed to have scarcely its equal in the world. The grey
granite with which Aberdeen is built is found in great profusion in the neighbourhood, and vast quantities, cut into
small blocks, are annually exported to London for paving
the streets. Castle-street, at its eastern extremity, derives its name from a fortification built by Oliver Cromwell, where there is now a barrack: it is considered the
pride and boast of Aberdeen. Its Cross, with its stone enta-
blature containing portraits of ten Scottish sovereigns, and
its graceful column pointing to the sky, is not less valuable
for its rarity than its beauty. The College of New Aberdeen was founded in 1593, by a member of the Noble family
of Marischal, whose name it bears, and is now attended by
nine professors, though its buildings at this time exhibit an
appearance of decay. The harbour has been much improved
by a series of expensive works, and a pier running out into
the sea to the amazing distance of 1206 feet: it is constructed
with immense blocks of granite, bound together by strong

bars of iron, which are found to be scarcely capable of sustaining the violence of the waves. A canal extends from the harbour along the north side of the town, and penetrates a considerable way into the interior of the country. The fishing of the Don and Dee contributes greatly to the commercial importance of this port. Its manufactures are those of woollen, cotton, and thread stockings, particularly the former, for which it has obtained great celebrity.

Peterhead, the second whale-fishing station in the United Kingdom, (being inferior only to Hull,) is situated at the mouth of the river Uggi, on the most easterly point of land in Scotland, and is particularly celebrated for its mineral waters, which render it a place of fashionable resort. It has a manufacture of sewing-thread; but it is in the harbour and shipping, and in the singular activity of the inhabitants, that the glory of Peterhead principally lies. Immense quantities of cod and ling are annually exported from hence. A little to the southward of this place is that natural wonder the Buller of Buchan; it is a bold rocky coast, at least 200 feet high, against which the waves never cease to dash. In one of the most prominent headlands there is a spacious pit, into which boats sail from the sea, under a natural arch resembling a large Gothic window, through which, in violent storms, the waves rush with great noise and impetuosity. This natural curiosity cannot be viewed without striking the beholder with a mixture of awe and admiration. In the neighbourhood of this stands Slaines Castle, the seat of the Earl of Errol, which is remarkable for the peculiarity of its situation, being on the edge of a crag, so close to the sea-side, that it may be said that his lordship's neighbour on the north-east is the King of Denmark: the desolating influence of the sea-breeze prevents its being adorned by so much as a single tree.

GEORGE.—It was near this seat that a celebrated battle was fought in the eleventh century, between Malcolm II.

and Canute the son of Sweyn, afterwards King of England,
it which the former was victorious.

Mr. Rows.—Fraserburgh, a town and burgh of regality,
is situated at the extreme north-east angle of this part of
Scotland; and owing to the construction of a large harbour
during the last war, to serve as a place of retreat for British
ships, it has risen from comparative obscurity to be a port
of considerable importance; but from its remote situation
it can scarcely be expected ever to attain to great distinction
in point of ordinary trade.

Inverury stands on a point of land formed by the Don
and Urie. Its oldest existing charter is from Queen Mary,
though it is traditionally asserted that it was made a
royal burgh by Robert Bruce, in consequence of his having
here obtained a signal victory over Cummin of Badenoch,
general of the English forces. Its situation on a peninsula
long retarded its prosperity, it being inaccessible on all
sides but one (except by boats); but from the erection of
a bridge over the Don, it has become of more importance
in a commercial point of view.

Kintore is a pleasant little town on the river Don, and
has some claim to antiquity, as it is said to have been made
a borough by Kenneth MacAlpine, in the ninth century;
but none of its records are extant of an earlier date than a
charter of confirmation by James V. This town is well
built, and has a neat town-house.

Old Meldrum is a small town, which has risen out of a
village, and is still in a state of advancement, though the
inhabitants have had no other inducement for their exertions
than each having the secure possession of a sufficient
portion of fen land for a house and garden. It has a good
weekly market and a well-attended annual fair.

Huntley is a neatly built and thriving village, seated on
a point of land formed by the confluence of the rivers Bogie and Devoron, and has a considerable manufacture of
linen cloth.

Turreff, or Tarriff, is seated on the banks of the Devoron and was made a free burgh or barony in 1511 by King James IV. It has considerable manufactures of linen-yarn thread, and brown linens; besides which there is a large bleaching-field.

Midmar is principally noted in historical annals for being the scene of a battle between the Earl of Murray (general of the forces of the unfortunate Queen Mary) and the Marquis of Huntley, who fell in the engagement.—Which are the principal rivers of this county?

Anna.—The Dee, Don, Bogie, Uggi, and Urie.

Mrs. Rowe.—The Dee springs from the Grampian Hills proceeds in an easterly course between the defiles of those mountains, and after dividing this county from Kincardineshire, falls into the sea at New Aberdeen.

The Don rises in the south-western part of the county and after receiving many tributary streams in its curvilinear passage, unites its waters with the ocean at Old Aberdeen

The Bogie rises in the west, and flows northerly through the town of Huntley, to join the Devon, or Devoron.

The Uggi rises in the centre of the northern part of the county, and proceeds in an easterly course till it reaches the sea, a little to the north of Peterhead.

The Urie rises in the west, and runs south-easterly to join the Don at Inverury.

The catching and curing of salmon, with which all these rivers abound, is the staple branch of business in this county, and the fishing for haddocks, cod, ling, and tusk is carried on with greater spirit in the north-eastern corner of Aberdeenshire (where many pleasant little fishing villages are situated,) than in any other part along the coast of Scotland. The numerous and active inhabitants of these places are enabled by their industry to live in easy circumstances, and contribute not a little to the prosperity as well as to the national security of the country, by furnishing number of hands for the navy whenever circumstances require der it necessary. The small fish they catch are generally disposed of in the surrounding towns; but the larger ones are salted, dried, and usually sent to Leith. A great many lobsters are also caught here for the London market.

Aberdeenshire was formerly divided into four districts, of which only the names and boundaries are now known: they are, Mar, which comprehended all the country between the rivers Dee and Don; Formarten, which extended along the coast from the Don to the Ythan, and was bounded on the west by a ridge of hills near Old Meldrum; Buchan was the most northerly division, and included all that country between the rivers Ythan and Devoron; and the district of Garrioch comprehended the remainder of the county, which chiefly consisted of one extensive inland vale, intersected by little knolls rising one above another, and affording a beautiful and picturesque appearance. The southern or south-western part of the county is very mountainous, forming a portion of the Grampians; but towards the north-east the general appearance of the surface may be described as being agreeably diversified by irregular depressions and gently swelling slopes; thus exhibiting scenery which is tolerably uniform, though the particular feature of it is varied at every step. The agriculture, in the immediate vicinity of Aberdeen, is uncommonly excellent, approaching nearly to the art of gardening. The chief mineral production of this county is granite, of which it has inexhaustible stores.—Can you mention any distinguished character to whom Aberdeenshire has given birth?

GEORGE.—John Barbour, chaplain to King David Bruce, the most memorable events of whose reign he recorded in verse: he was one of the earliest Scottish poets.

KINCARDINE- or MEARNS-SHIRE.

Boundaries.—Aberdeenshire, Angus-shire, and the North Sea.
Towns.—1, Inverbervie; 2, Dunnotter Castle; 3, Fordun; 4, Chance
    Inn; 5, Stonehaven; 6, John's Haven; 7, Fettercairn.
Rivers.—a, the Dee; b, North Esk; c, Carron; d, Bervie.
Bay and Hills.—A, Stonehaven Bay; B, Grampian Hills.

Mrs. Rowe.—Describe the situation, extent, and chief places in Kincardineshire.

Anna.—It is bounded on the north and west by Aberdeenshire, on the south by Angus-shire, and on the east by the North Sea: from north-east to south-west it measures 40 miles, and its width is somewhat less than 20. Its chief towns are Inverbervie, Stonehaven, John's Haven, Fettercairn, and Fordun.

Mrs. Rowe.—Inverbervie, or Bervie, is situated at the mouth of a small river of the same name, and is the only royal burgh in the county; it acquired that privilege from David II., as a testimony of gratitude for the humane and hospitable treatment he received from the inhabitants when he was driven ashore off the coast of this town on his return from France. It formerly possessed a small harbour for fishing boats, but from the inconvenience of it, the fishermen have almost all removed to a place called Gordon, about two miles to the south.

Stonehaven, or Stonehive, is a large town, situated at the mouth of the little river Carron, in the bottom of a bay, and flanked on both sides by lofty hills. The oldest part of the town is irregularly built, but on the north bank of the river there is a new town, consisting of neat and regular streets. The harbour is excellent, and has lately been much improved by the erection of a handsome pier. Not far from hence is that magnificent curiosity Dunnotter Castle, the

ruined seat of the ancient family of Keith, earls of Marischal, erected by an ancestor of that family about the time
of the contests between Bruce and Baliol for the Scottish
Crown.

GEORGE.—In 1298 history records that this fortress was
taken from the English by that celebrated hero Sir William
Wallace, who consigned it to the flames, with 4000 persons
constituting its garrison.

MRS. ROWE.—It was again fortified by Edward III.,
King of England, when he was endeavouring to place Edward Baliol on the Scottish throne, A.D. 1336; but Sir
Andrew Murray, regent for David II., soon after captured
it. In March 1745, Dunnotter Castle underwent a severe
siege, and did not surrender until the garrison was compelled by famine. In the year 1650 it was selected as the
strongest place in the kingdom for the preservation of the
regalia: fortunately, these time-honoured relics were secretly removed, before the Parliamentarians besieged and
took the Castle, and were buried, for greater security, under
the pulpit of the parish church of Kinneff (in the neighbourhood), where they remained till the Restoration. In the
reign of Charles II. Dunnotter was used as a state prison.
It was dismantled soon after the civil war of 1715, when its
proprietor, James earl Marischal, was attainted for high
treason: but though dismantled, the buildings are nearly
entire, excepting the roofs and floors. The battlements, with
their narrow embrasures, the strong towers and airy turrets, the hall for the banquet, and the cell for the captive,
are all alike whole and distinct, and remain to attest the
different state of things which once prevailed here.

John's Haven, at the mouth of the North Esk, was anciently noted as a fishing station, but owing to several boats
being lost, and the severe exactions demanded from hence
for the navy (besides the impress service), it has much declined, and may now be considered a manufacturing town,
being a sort of colony for the manufacturers of Dundee.

Fettercairn is a small village, chiefly worthy of notice for its romantic bridge over the North Esk, which stands on two stupendous rocks, elevated to a great height above the river.

ANNA.—It was at Fenella Castle, in this parish, that King Kenneth III. was assassinated, in revenge for having put to death Crathilinthus, the son of a powerful lady of the name of Fenella, and grandson of the Earl of Angus.

MRS. ROWE.—The manner in which this murderous design was perpetrated is singular, and displays both the ingenuity and base cunning of the Lady Fenella, who invited the monarch to her castle, and under pretence of amusing him with a sight of the architectural elegance of her mansion, conducted him to the upper room of a lofty tower, where, in the midst of splendid drapery and curious sculptures, she had placed a brass figure holding a golden apple, which she said was intended as a present for her royal guest, and courteously invited him to take it : no sooner had the king complied with her request, than some concealed machinery was set in motion, which acting upon some crossbows behind the arras, caused a number of arrows to traverse the rooms, from one of which he received a fatal stroke : and as soon as Fenella perceived her design had succeeded, she fled from the just vengeance of the king's attendants.

Fordun is worthy of notice, as having been for some time the residence (and is the supposed burying-place) of St. Palladius, who was sent, in the fifth century, by Pope Celestine to oppose the Pelagian heresy ; and it was thought that by him bishops were first placed at the head of the Scottish clergy, as before that time the prelates were always members of the monasteries, and subject to their government.—Which are the principal rivers of this county?

GEORGE.—The North Esk, Bervie, and Carron.

MRS. ROWE.—The North Esk may perhaps be more properly considered as a river of Angus-shire, as it rises in that county, and after an easterly course, by which it forms the southern boundary of Kincardineshire, it falls into the sea near John's Haven.

The Bervie rises in the centre of the county, and after a circuitous route, runs into the ocean near the town of the same name.

The Carron is a smaller stream, rising also in the middle of the county, and flowing eastward to the sea at Stone-haven.

Kincardineshire derives its appellation of Mearns from having been at an early period the property of Mernia, brother of King Kenneth II. The northern part of the county is chiefly formed by a chain of the Grampian Hills, those mighty barriers of ancient independence, which terminate at the north-eastern corner of this county. The southern side is pleasantly diversified with hill and dale, particularly along the banks of the North Esk, from whence to Stonehaven, along the coast, the soil is good : but agricultural improvements have not been carried on here with so much spirit as in the more southern districts. The mineral production of this county consists chiefly of limestone of the best quality.—Can you name any distinguished characters who were natives of this county?

ANNA.—John de Fordun, author of the *Scotichronicon*, one of the most ancient and authentic histories which has been published in Scotland. By some biographers he is supposed to have been a man possessed of great property in this country : by others it is conjectured he was a monk, who resided in it.

Lord Monboddo, who is well known in the literary world by his writings on ancient metaphysics, and the origin and progress of language.

Dr. Arbuthnot, the celebrated physician to Queen Anne, and one of a distinguished triumvirate with Pope and Dr. Swift.

FORFAR- or ANGUS-SHIRE.

Boundaries.—Aberdeenshire, Mearns-shire, Perthshire, the North
    Sea, and the Firth of Tay.
Towns.—1, Forfar; 2, Montrose; 3, Brechin; 4, Aberbrothick, or
    Arbroath; 5, Inverpefer; 6, Dundee; 7, Glamis.
Rivers and Lochs.—a, the South Esk; b, Isla; c, Lunan; d, Dighty;
    e, Forfar Loch.
Capes, Firths, &c.—A, Red House Head; B, Firth of Tay; C,
    Bell Rock Light House.

Mrs. Rowe.—WHAT are the boundaries, extent, and
chief places of Angus-shire?

George.—It is bounded on the north by Kincardineshire
and a part of Aberdeenshire, on the east by the North Sea,
on the south by the Firth of Tay, and on the west by Perthshire: from north to south it measures about 30 miles, and
from east to west somewhat less. It contains the towns of
Forfar, Dundee, Montrose, Arbroath or Aberbrothick,
Brechin, and Glamis.

Mrs. Rowe.—Forfar, the capital of the county, is an
ancient inland burgh, and was a royal residence in the time
of Malcolm Canmore: it is now a town of pleasant appearance, though situated in the lowest part of a country
declining towards it on all sides; and in its environs is a
considerable lake. Forfar possesses a handsome suite of
county buildings, and a new church and steeple have been
recently built. King Malcolm resided in a Castle to the
north of the town, and it is said that he held the parliament
here, in which titles and surnames were first conferred on
the Scottish nobility. His illustrious consort had a separate establishment, consisting of a nunnery, situated on a
small artificial island on the north side of the loch, which is
still called the Inch, from a tradition of its having been

connected with the land by a passage capable of giving access to only one person. The inhabitants of Forfar celebrate an annual fête here in honour of Queen Margaret.
It possesses a small manufacture in weaving.

Dundee is situated on the north bank of the Tay, where
that river has all the appearance of an arm of the sea. The
harbour is safe, commodious, and easy of access to ships of
great burden. The ground on which the city is built rises
gradually from the shore, and its external appearance quite
justifies the appellation of "bonny Dundee": its massive
steeple, innumerable suburban villas, crowded harbour,
the majestic river in front, and the beautiful country behind,
form the materials of a splendid landscape, and denote the
importance and prosperity of the place. It was anciently
denominated *Alectum*, and is said to have received its present appellation at the time of the foundation of St. Mary's
church, by Henry earl of Huntingdon, brother of William
the Lion, on his return from the third crusade. It is noted
for its sugar-house and glass manufactory, besides manufactures of coarse linen, sail-cloth, cordage, leather, and
hats.

ANNA.—History relates that King William, being very
much attached to his brother Henry, vowed, in the spirit of
the times, that he would bestow upon him the spot of
ground on which he should first land; and the earl being
driven to Dundee by stress of weather, the king accordingly
performed his promise, and Henry chose to mark his gratitude to Heaven for his signal deliverance from the perils
of the sea, by erecting the present church and steeple.

MRS. ROWE.—This ecclesiastical structure is a large and
curious, though somewhat irregular pile, and contains four
distinct places of worship: the steeple, or rather tower, is
a massive square fabric, the glory of Dundee, and unques-
tionably the finest thing of the kind in Scotland.

GEORGE.—I have read that when the town was captured
by Monk, Lumsden the governor, with a small party, held

out for a long time in the steeple; but being at last compelled to surrender, he suffered for his unavailing bravery
by being immediately beheaded.

MRS. ROWE.—Montrose is a beautiful little town, situated on the north side of the South Esk, near its junction
with the sea. Its harbour is very commodious, and in it
are docks for building and repairing ships. A considerable
number of vessels belonging to this port are employed in
the coasting and Baltic trade. Its principal manufactures
are of linen-yarn and thread, sheeting, and sail-cloth; besides which it has several extensive tan and rope works.
It is a gay town, distinguished as the residence of people
of opulence and fashion, and may be justly styled the seat
of wealth and amusement, as well as that of industry and
commerce. There was in it very lately a house of peculiar
interest in history, for having been the residence of the
Noble family of Montrose, and where the marquis was born.

ANNA.—It was also famous for being the last abode of
the Pretender in Scotland, who slept in it on the 13th of
February 1716, the night before he escaped to the Continent.

MRS. ROWE.—Arbroath, or Aberbrothick, is a royal
burgh of great (though unknown) antiquity, situated at
the mouth of the little river Brothick, from which it is supposed to derive the latter appellation. The harbour is neither safe nor spacious; but, nevertheless, it possesses considerable trade with Russia, and manufactures a great
quantity of sail-cloth. The town is regularly built, and
exhibits a state of exemplary neatness. Its abbey, now in
ruins, was founded in 1178 by William the Lion, and is
noted for having been one of the most dignified and wealthy
establishments of the sort in Scotland. John king of England was a patron of this abbey, and by charter under the
great seal, granted it an exemption in every part of his
kingdom, except London.

GEORGE.—This venerable edifice is noted in history for

having been the place where, in 1320, Robert Bruce assembled the nobility, and composed a letter of remonstrance to Pope John, who had favoured the claims of Edward to the Scottish throne; in which he traced to the remotest period the antiquity and independency of Scotland. This representation had great weight with the Pope, who immediately sent a Bull to Edward king of England to exhort him to make peace with the Scots, at the same time stating, that any operations against the infidels might be pursued without interruption.

MRS. ROWE.—A cave on the coast near this town is said to have been, so recently as the polished æra of the fifteenth century, the retreat of a family of cannibal banditti, who pursued their execrable means of procuring subsistence by quietly stealing, or taking by violence, young men and children, for the purpose of devouring them, for which they were all apprehended and burnt.

ANNA.—Is not the Bell Rock Light-house situated near this town?

MRS. ROWE.—It stands about eleven miles south-east of it, where formerly stood a wooden beacon; but the dangerous reef surrounding this rock rendered it important to have a more substantial erection of the kind, and in the year 1807 Mr. Stephenson undertook to build a stone light-house here upon principles similar to those upon which the Eddystone is erected in the English Channel, which, in a nautical point of view, adds to the safety and comfort of the mariners, at the same time that it affords protection to property along the whole line of coast of the eastern shores of Great Britain.

Brechin is an ancient royal burgh, the seat of a bishopric, which was established and liberally endowed by David I. in 1150: it is romantically seated on the South Esk, and was formerly the county town. Its Cathedral was a magnificent Gothic pile; the beauty of which has been within the last few years almost destroyed in repairing the western extremity, which now serves for the parish church. The tower, a square edifice, at one of the corners of this building, still remains entire. It has a spire at the top, of modern erection, and there is a door at the bottom, the sideways of which are adorned with figures carved in an antique style; and at the top are four windows corresponding with the cardinal points. This edifice is conjectured to have been a watch-tower. Brechin was one of the seats of the Culdees long before it became a bishopric, and it is supposed that the site of their establishment was adopted as that of the Cathedral. Its Castle, in the immediate neighbourhood of the town, is an object of admiration. It possesses a small manufacture of sail-cloth.

ANNA.—I have read, that in 1303 this fortress stood a siege of twenty days, and only surrendered in consequence of its brave governor, Sir Thomas Maule, being killed by a stone thrown from an engine.

MRS. ROWE.—Glamis is a pleasant little village, in the vicinity of Forfar, famous for its Castle, situated in the midst of an extensive park, exhibiting a princely and antique appearance, consisting of irregular congregations of tall towers, erected at different æras; which, while history, poetry, and the works of Shakspeare remain, will always excite interest and attention. The spot where Malcolm II. fell, by the hands of assassins, and the more pleasing scene where the bards took their places and sung the heroism of their patrons and ancestors, are objects of great curiosity. In the churchyard is a stone, called the gravestone of Malcolm, as the sculpture on it alludes to his murder.

GEORGE.—The punishment due to these murderers soon overtook them; for, as they fled from the spot where they had perpetrated the cruel deed, they lost their way, and coming unwarily on the Lake of Forfar (owing to the country being covered with snow), the ice gave way, and they sunk to rise no more.

MRS. ROWE.—It is related, that when the head of the

exiled family of Stuart visited this mansion in 1715 (on which occasion eighty-eight beds were provided for him and his retinue), he declared "he had never seen a finer chateau anywhere in Europe."—What are the names of the principal rivers that water this county?

ANNA.—The South Esk, Isla, Lunan, and Dighty.

MRS. ROWE.—The South Esk springs from the Grampian Hills, in the north-west part of the county, and after pursuing a south-easterly course, turns easterly, and passes through a fertile country to the sea at Montrose.

The Isla rises also in the Grampian Hills, and flows southerly into Perthshire, which it separates for some distance from this county.

The Lunan finds its source in the vicinity of Forfar, and passing through a chain of lakes, runs along a fertile vale into a bay of the same name.

The Dighty rises from the Lake of Lundie, and flows east of Dundee into the sea.

The principal loch in this county is that of Forfar.

The hills are the Grampian and Sidlaw: the former extended into the northern district, and contain many fine valleys. One of the highest of this range is the Catlaw, rising 2264 feet above the level of the sea, from the summit of which a fine prospect is obtained. The Sidlaw extends westward into Perthshire, two chains of which run parallel in that direction; and a third (the highest range,) stretches to the north-east. Freestone abounds in many parts of this county, as well as slate, and there are some quarries of limestone; but all the districts north of the Tay are destitute of coal. Great numbers of cattle are reared and fed here. The three counties of Forfar, Kincardine, and Aberdeen are included in the popular term of the 'East Coast,' and comprehend a fertile and important part of Scotland. The inhabitants of this district may be said generally to display more constitutional activity and lively ingenuity in the pursuits of commerce and agricul-

ture, and the desire of the substantial comforts of life, than
the rest of their countrymen.   This district formed a great
part of the Pictish kingdom, and its inhabitants still retain
marked features of the characteristics of that peculiar people; and from their having been more intruded upon by
the adventurers of the North of Europe than the Southern
Lowlanders, they differ in many respects from the latter.

PERTHSHIRE.

Boundaries.—Inverness-shire, Aberdeenshire, Angus-shire, Fifeshire, Kinross-shire, Stirlingshire, Argyleshire, the Firth of
  Tay, and the Firth of Forth.
Towns.—1, Perth; 2, Dunkeld; 3, Scone; 4, Kinnoul; 5, Errol;
  6, Couper; 7, Blair Gowrie; 8, East Haugh; 9, Urrard;
  10, Blair Athol; 11, Kinloch; 12, Dull; 13, Kenmore;
  14, Killin; 15, Clifton; 16, Comrie; 17, Crieff; 18, Callandar;
  19, Dumblane; 20, Abernethy; 21, Culross; 22, Doune.
Rivers and Lochs.—a, the Tay; b, Garry; c, Blackwater; d, Lyon;
  e, Bran; f, Erne; g, Forth; h, Isla; i, Loch Erach; k, Loch
  Kennach; l, Tamel, or Tummel; m, Lyon; n, Tay; o, Erne;
  p, Veal; q, Ketterin; r, Arde; s, Menteith.
Firths.—A, Firth of Tay; B, Firth of Forth.

Mrs. Rowe.—WHAT are the boundaries, extent, and
chief towns of Perthshire?

George.—It is bounded on the north by the counties of
Inverness and Aberdeen; on the east by Angus-shire, the
Firth of Tay, and part of Fifeshire; on the south by Kinross, Clackmannon, and Stirlingshire; and on the west by
Argyle and Dumbartonshire: from its most northerly point
to the Firth of Forth in the south, it measures more than
60 miles, and from east to west it is upwards of 50.   It

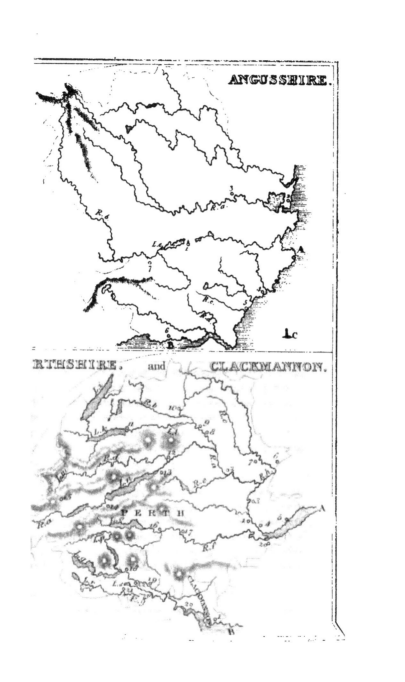

RTHSHIRE. and CLACKMANNON.

thriving manufactures, all conspire to render it a desirable place of residence to a great number of affluent people, who have a beneficial influence over the minds of the population.

Culross, situated on the Firth of Forth, has a very picturesque appearance. It formerly possessed extensive salt-works, and a manufacture of girdles, the round iron plates on which the Scottish people bake their unleavened bread. It was also the site of an abbey, of which scarcely a vestige remains except the chapel, which has been converted into the parish church.

Luncarty, in this neighbourhood, is noted for an engagement which took place between the Danes and the Scots, in the reign of Kenneth III., who must inevitably have been vanquished had it not been for the valour of a peasant and his two sons, who were ploughing in sight of the engagement, and seeing their countrymen fly, they, with no other weapon than the yoke which they snatched from their oxen, opposed the invaders, and by their example reanimated the courage of the Scots, led them back to the battle, and ultimately drove the Danes into the river. When the conflict was over, the old man is said to have expressed his sensation of fatigue by the common exclamation of "Hech hay!" The king coming up at the instant to thank him for his timely assistance, said, "Then Hay shall your name be;" at the same time conferring upon him peculiar honours. He is also said to have given the venerable champion the choice of the hound's chase or the falcon's flight, as a possession suitable to his honours: he chose the latter. The bird took its flight from the spot where the Danish camp had been, and alighted upon a stone near the river Tay, a mile to the south of the House of Errol, which is still called the Falcon's or Hawk's Stone. The yoke and motto (*Serva jugum*) adorn the arms of the noble family that bears that name.

Scone is famous for its ancient palace, built by the Earl

of Gowrie, after whose death James VI. presented it to his
favourite Sir David Murray, in whose possession it remained
till the destruction of the abbey by a mob rendered furious
by the preaching of Knox : an old aisle is the only remaining portion of this ancient building. The House of Scone,
the seat of the Earl of Mansfield, occupies the site of the
old palace, where the kings of Scotland at an early period
used to be crowned. Charles II. of England was crowned
here previous to the battle of Worcester. It has been believed, from time immemorial, that invisible hands brought
Jacob's pillow from Bethel and dropped it on the site of
this palace; and this famed stone became, in some mysterious
way, so connected with the sovereignty of Scotland, that
the kings always sat upon it when they were crowned: an
inscription upon it testified that wherever it should be, there
the Scots should enjoy sovereignty, which was so fully believed, that Edward I., in order to break the hope of the
Scottish people that their kingdom should ever be restored,
transferred it from Scone to London, and it is now preserved
in Westminster Abbey, forming part of the coronation chair
of the British monarch.

Dumblane is a village of great antiquity, seated on the
banks of Allan Water, supposed to have been originally a
cell of the earliest Christian clergy of Scotland, called the
Culdees. It was erected into a bishopric by David I.,
who in 1142 founded the Cathedral, which is now one of
the most entire edifices of that sacred character in North
Britain. The east end (or nave) is fitted up in a peculiarly
handsome fashion as the parish church, and great care is
taken to preserve the rest from further decay. Some of
the prebendaries' chairs (or stalls) are still to be seen in
the church : this is the only known remains of popish fur-
niture existing in any ecclesiastical structure north of the
Tweed.

GEORGE.—The celebrated battle of Sheriffmuir was

fought in the vicinity of this place in 1715, and was by the king's party termed the Battle of Dumblane.

MRS. ROWE.—Crieff is, in point of situation, one of the most delightful towns in Scotland, occupying the face of a gentle declivity on the north bank of the river Erne. It formerly possessed a large annual fair, at which the Highlanders attended with numerous herds of black cattle; but this traffic has since been transferred to Falkirk; and Crieff is still a thriving town, and may be said to derive considerable importance from being a favourite summer retreat for invalids and others, who are attracted by its beauty and salubrity.

Comrie is of fearful interest in the eyes of a stranger, in consequence of its being occasionally visited by earthquakes, which are happily more frequent than mischievous. It underwent, however, a shock of a serious nature on the 5th of November 1789.

ANNA.—Some historians assert that the last and most distinguished battle fought between the Britons (under a leader named Galgacus,) and Agricola took place near this town.

MRS. ROWE.—This assertion is supposed to have some foundation, from the discovery of an entire Roman camp in its immediate vicinity; and the plain on which it is situated is of sufficient extent for a battle of such magnitude.

Blair Athol is so called from its Castle, which stands on an eminence above the plain, watered by the impetuous river Garry. This place was once fortified. It is now an occasional residence of the Duke of Athol.

Blair Gowrie is a small village, seated on the river Blackwater: it was erected into a burgh barony in 1634.

Dunkeld is now a small place on the river Tay: it was called by the ancients *Castrum Caledoniæ*. It has a manufacture of linen, and is much frequented by invalids for the purpose of drinking goats' milk and whey. This place became the seat of religion at a very early period. Constantine III., King of the Picts, is said to have founded a monastery here in honour of St. Columba in 927, the monks of which were not enjoined celibacy, but interdicted from living with their families during their turn for officiating. David I., who was famed for his piety, made the town an episcopal See, and converted the abbey into a Cathedral, in the year 1127: some remains of this building are still to be seen. In the present church, which was erected in 1436, are the effigy and tomb of Alexander Stuart earl of Buchan, third son of Robert II., who, for his cruelty and impiety, was styled the 'Wolf of Badenoch.' The cascade, which is formed by a fall of the little river Bran, is considered the greatest curiosity of Dunkeld: it precipitates itself with incredible fury through a chasm of granite, and agitates by its violence the prodigious masses which form the surrounding rocks. It is hardly possible to conceive a more striking spectacle, and few objects will more amply repay the traveller for the trouble of visiting them.

Abernethy, though now only a small village, was once the capital of the Pictish dominions, and possessed a monastery, which was one of the most extensive establishments of the Culdees. It is said to have been founded about the year 460; but of this extensive fabric there now remains only one tower.

Doune is seated on the river Teith, at its confluence with the Ardoch, and formerly had an extensive manufacture of Highland pistols, which has declined. The general appearance of this place was greatly improved by the erection of a new parish church, in the Gothic style, in 1826. For this useful public work the parishioners were indebted to the munificence of the Earl of Moray, the patron and chief heritor of the parish. The ruins of Doune Castle are very striking: this great baronial fortress stood on an elevated peninsula, formed by the junction of the two rivers on which the town is built; and there still remains a huge square building, with a lofty tower rising to a great height above the trees which encompass it. It is uncertain when or by whom it was built, but it has long been the property of the Noble family of Moray, who derive from it the secondary title of Baron Doune.

GEORGE.—History records that this Castle was the favourite residence of the two successive Dukes of Albany, who usurped the government of Scotland during the captivity of James I. in England, in the early part of the fifteenth century; and that in the sixteenth century it was often inhabited by Margaret, widow of James IV. and daughter of the English king Henry VII.

MRS. ROWE.—Which are the principal rivers in this county?

ANNA.—The Forth, Tay, Tummel or Tamel, Garry, Tilt, Bran, Isla, Ericht, and Erne.

MRS. ROWE.—The Forth enters this county in the south-west, and after forming a boundary between it and Stirlingshire, discharges itself into the sea, through a broad estuary called the Firth of Forth.

The Tay, the noblest of all the Scottish rivers, and which pours into the ocean a greater quantity of fresh water than any other of Great Britain, rises in the western extremity of this county, under the name of Fillan, which it retains till it reaches Loch Dochart, when it assumes that name to Loch Tay, through which it passes, and from thence, under its own name, (receiving in its passage many tributary streams,) flows on to Perth, a little below which it forms a broad estuary called the Firth of Tay, through which it discharges itself into the sea.

The Tummel, or Tamel, rises on the confines of Argyleshire, under the name of Gawer, and flows to Loch Rannoch, or Kennach, through which it runs, and from thence assuming its own name, passes through Loch Tummel, forming, in its rapid descent to join the Tay above Dunkeld, the most romantic and picturesque cascades.

The Garry, Tilt, and Brura unite their waters at Blair

lthol, and proceed, under the name of Garry, in a south-rly direction to the Tummel.

The Isla flows from Angus-shire, in a south-westerly ourse, to join the Tay.

The Ericht is a rapid stream, which flows in a southerly irection, under the name of Blackwater, to join the Isla ear Cupar.

The Erne springs from a loch of the same name, and lows easterly through Grieff, or Crieff, and Abernethy, till t falls into the Firth of Tay.—Which are the most consilerable lochs in Perthshire?

GEORGE.—Those of Tay, Erne, Rannoch or Kennach, ind Ketterin.

MRS. ROWE.—Loch Tay is an extensive piece of water, iituated near the centre of the county, in a tract unparalleled or the variety of its beautiful and magnificent scenery. In 1784 a singular phænomenon occurred in it: the water bbed and flowed several times in a quarter of an hour, vhen suddenly it rushed from east to west in opposite cur-ents, so as to form a ridge, leaving the channel dry to the listance of one hundred yards from its usual boundary. At ength the waves burst with a clashing noise and much oam: the waters then flowed out five yards beyond the isual limits. This wonderful flux and reflux lasted two iours, after which it gradually decreased. A similar mo-ion was observed for several days, but not so violent as he first. The banks of this lake are finely wooded, and n it is a small tufted island, on which are the ruins of a ıriory, erected in the reign of Alexander I.

Loch Erne lies to the south of Loch Tay, and is about 3 miles long, and 1½ mile broad. Near each end of it is a small artificial island, on one of which are the remains of ın ancient Castle. The banks of this loch are covered with ıeautiful woods, and present a great variety of scenery.

Loch Rannoch, or Kennach, is situated in the western ıart of the county, and is about 12 miles long and from 1

to 2 broad: in it is a small island, partly artificial, on which
are the remains of an old Castle or fortress, which was once
the residence of the chief of the clan of Robertsons.

Loch Catherine, or Ketterin, is one of a chain of lakes
lying to the north-west of the river Forth, and which are
apparently only expansions of the beautiful little river
Teith: the rugged tract along this chain is called the Tros-
sacks. The surrounding rocks are stupendous, and present
such an assemblage of wildness and rude grandeur as
must fill the mind of the beholder with the most sublime
conceptions. Besides these lochs there are many others,
which, though of less magnitude, are equally famed for
their beautiful scenery and for the production of fish, particularly salmon, trout, pike, and char.

The mountains of this county may be said to consist of
three chains, the Grampians, Ochil, and Sidlaw. The first
chain runs along the northern and north-western sides of
the county, and consists of enormous piles, from the exposed summits of which the soil has been washed by the
beating of wintry storms. The Ochil range lies to the
south, from which the country descends to the Firth of
Forth. The Sidlaw may be considered a continuation of
the Ochil, running from Perth towards the north-east, in a
parallel direction to the Grampians.

The general aspect of this county, both from its extent
of surface, and from its including some of the wildest parts
of the Highlands, as well as some of the most fertile of the
Lowlands, is greatly diversified, comprehending scenery of
every description of excellence, from the savage and romantic to the beautiful and champaign.

The extensive tracts of Strathmore extend from the foot
of the Grampians, and comprehend those parts of the
county where the tributary streams pursue their courses to
the Erne and Forth. Strathearn may be considered as a
continuation westward of Strathmore.

The celebrated pass of Killicrankie is in the north of

the county, and is simply that particular part of the Vale
of Garry where the hills on both sides approach very near,
and descend in precipitous rugged steeps to the rough
channel of the river Garry. It is clothed in natural woods,
and abounds in dense shades and horrid depths, which have
lost much of their former dreadful appearance by a broad
new road having been led securely through them.

GEORGE.—The upper extremity of this pass is famed in
history for having been, in 1689, the scene of the engagement between the Highland clans, under Viscount Dundee,
and the troops of William III., headed by General Mackey:
the former were victorious, though with the loss of their
gallant leader, who fell by a random shot ; and his fate so
paralyzed his army, as to prevent all further pursuit.

MRS. ROWE.—The districts of the Carse of Gowrie, and
that on the Forth, of similar fertility, must not be omitted.
The level territories of these tracts are considerable, and
consist of an extremely rich and fertile soil of the finest
sort of alluvial land, similar to that which forms the celebrated Delta of Egypt, or plain at the mouth of the Nile :
the higher grounds comprise pasturage, and no district in
Scotland enjoys a climate more mild and favourable to vegetation. Lime and marl are the principal mineral productions of the county. At Culross, on the Forth, coal has
been wrought for ages, but is of little importance to Perthshire.—Can you mention any celebrated character who was
born here ?

ANNA.—James Crichton, who, from the singular endow-
ments of his mind and body, obtained the appellation of
the 'Admirable Crichton'. Nature, fortune, and education,
combined to form this extraordinary character, and his attainments almost exceed credibility : in his disputes in the
foreign Universities with the most learned professors, he was
generally victorious. Sir Thomas Urquhart observes, that
he obtained the esteem of kings and princes by his magna-
nimity and knowledge ; of noblemen and gentlemen, by his

courtliness; and of knights and ladies, by his honourable
deportment. The circumstances of his death are doubtful;
though it has been asserted that it happened at an early
period through the treachery of his pupil, who hired some
ruffians to assassinate him, but himself gave the mortal
stab.

MRS. ROWE.—We have now concluded the descriptions
of the Highlands : can you name the twenty counties lying
south of the Tay, which are called the Lowlands?

GEORGE.—They are Clackmannon, Fife, Kinross, Stirl-
ing, Dumbarton, Argyle, Bute, Ayr, Renfrew, Lanerk,
Linlithgow or West Lothian, Edinburgh or Mid Lothian,
Haddington or East Lothian, Berwick, Roxburgh, Selkirk,
Peebles, Dumfries, Kirkcudbright, and Wigton counties.

CLACKMANNONSHIRE.

Boundaries.—Perthshire, and Firth of Forth.
Towns.—1, Clackmannon; 2, Alloa.

MRS. ROWE.—DESCRIBE the situation, extent, and places
of most note in Clackmannonshire.

GEORGE.—This small county is surrounded on all sides
by Perthshire, except on the south, where it is parted from
Stirlingshire by the Firth of Forth. It measures from east
to west 8 miles, and from north to south about 5. Its chief
towns are Clackmannon and Alloa.

MRS. ROWE.—Clackmannon, the capital, is an inferior
place, but was once of note as the residence of King Robert
Bruce. The palace was demolished, because the materials
were required to erect some other edifice, and nothing re-

mains to demonstrate the former grandeur of the town but a tower on the top of a hill, which is a tall and impressive structure. The church is a handsome modern edifice in the Gothic taste, with an elegant tower. The privileges of this town are supposed, in some mysterious way, to depend upon the existence of a huge shapeless blue stone, which having been broken in pieces, is bound together with iron, and is regarded by the inhabitants with great veneration.

ANNA.—Its legendary history is important, as it records that when Robert Bruce was residing in the Castle, before there was a town attached to it, he happened one day to leave his glove on this stone, and upon missing it desired his attendant to return to the *clack* (the Gaelic word for ' stone',—for King Robert usually spoke his native tongue), and bring his *mannan* (or glove): the servant said, " If ye 'll just look about ye here, I 'll be back with it directly." From this trifling circumstance arose the name of the town which was subsequently reared round the stone; and a farm at the place where the glove was missed still bears the name of ' Look about Ye.'

MRS. ROWE.—Alloa is a thriving sea-port and manufacturing town, containing many good buildings, among which a modern church, in the Gothic style, is preeminent. But its greatest pride is the seat of the Earl of Mar, a building of the 13th century, which has so frequently undergone repairs, as to render but little of the ancient edifice discernible. In it James VI. and his eldest son were successively nurtured and educated, under the care of the Mar family. The cradle and nursery chair of the former, and Prince Henry's golfs, were in the tower till a recent period, and are still kept, with the care and veneration due to such valuable heir-looms, by some member of the family of Mar. The country around this place is very beautifully interspersed with numerous fine seats and pleasant little villages.

The only stream of any consequence is the Devon, which

enters the county in the north-east, and proceeds in a due
westerly course till it falls into the Firth of Forth on the
borders of Perthshire.

This county has extensive coal-fields, and numerous collieries are in constant work. The mountains contain some
precious minerals, as veins of copper and lead have been
found; and some years ago an attempt was made to work
a silver mine; but the mass, which consisted of the finest
quality, was speedily exhausted, as was also one of cobalt:
they also produce granite or whinstone. Though Clackmannon possesses great advantages from its mineral productions, and its vicinity to a navigable river, yet having
this on one side, and the Ochil mountains on the other, it
is rendered a sequestered spot.

FIFESHIRE.

Boundaries.—Perthshire, Kinross-shire, Firth of Tay, Firth of
    Forth, and the North Sea.
Towns.—1, St. Andrews; 2, Dairsie; 3, Coupar; 4, Falkland;
    5, Morton; 6, Crail; 7, Kilrenny; 8, Kirkaldy; 9, Inver-
    keithing; 10, Dunfermline; 11, Kinghorn.
Rivers and Lochs.—a, the Leven; b, Eden; c, Loch Lindores;
    d, Kinghorn; e, Killcongahar.
Firths, Capes, Bays, and Islands.—A, Firth of Forth; B, Firth of
    Tay; C, Largo Bay; D, Fife Ness, or East-Neuk o' Fife;
    E, Inch Keith; F, Inch Colm Islands.

MRS. ROWE.—WHAT are the boundaries, extent, and
chief towns of Fifeshire?

GEORGE.—It is bounded on the north by the Firth of
Tay, on the east by the North Sea, on the south by the
Firth of Forth, and on the west by the counties of Perth

and Kinross. It measures from north-east to south-west near 40 miles, and varies in breadth from 7 to 16. Its most important places are St. Andrews, Kirkaldy, Coupar, Falkland, Dunfermline, Inverkeithing, Kinghorn, Kilrenny, and Crail.

Mrs. Rowe.—St. Andrews is situated on the eastern coast of Fifeshire, and was formerly the seat of the Primate of Scotland, but is now only celebrated for its University, founded by Bishop Wardlaw in 1411: it is justly supposed to be one of the earliest settlements in Scotland, not only of religion, but of population. According to the common legend it became the residence of St. Regulus in the sixth century, and was for some time denominated Kilrule. The name of the city was changed to St. Andrews on the union of the Scottish and Pictish kingdoms by Kenneth II.

George.—I have read that St. Regulus, or St. Rule, a Greek, was warned by a vision to visit Albion, and to take with him some of the remains of St. Andrew. He accordingly set out with some companions in the year 570, and after being tossed by tempests, was shipwrecked on the coast of Otholima, now the Firth of Tay, in the territory of Hergustus king of the Picts, who no sooner heard of the arrival of the pious strangers with their precious relics, than he gave them the most hospitable reception; and having accommodated St. Regulus with his own palace, built a church near it, which still bears the name of that devotee.

Mrs. Rowe.—Here Regulus established the first Christian priests in this country, called Culdees, or dwellers in cells. These long professed a pure religion, and withstood the power of the Pope; but David I. agreeing with His Holiness, they lost the authority of choosing their own bishops, and the superstitious rites of popery were introduced. The ruins of St. Regulus's Chapel, with an entire tower, are still to be seen near the Cathedral, being without

E 2

exception or doubt the oldest relics of ecclesiastical architecture in Scotland. The Cathedral was founded by Bishop Arnold in 1162, and finished by Bishop Lamberton in 1318. This magnificent fabric, which took 156 years in building, was in 1559 destroyed by the zealous followers of John Knox, who by his declamations first inflamed, and then permitted his furious disciples to overthrow edifices dedicated to that Being he pretended to honour. Its demolition was the work of a single day: only a few remains of this prodigious fabric are now to be seen. The Priory was founded by King Alexander I. in the year 1122, the immense extent of which may be seen by the walls, which are all that remain of it. The ruins of the Castle, erected by Bishop Trail in 1401, and afterwards rebuilt in the reign of Queen Mary by Archbishop Hamilton, are worthy the attention of the curious. Of the former edifice, in which James III. was born and Cardinal Beaton assassinated, scarcely a vestige remains: the pile now shown to strangers is part of the comparatively recent structure erected by Archbishop Hamilton. Besides the support which St. Andrews derives from its literary establishment, this town possesses some advantages as a sea-port; but as its harbour partakes of the dangerous character common to all the ports on this coast, it has but little trade.

Kirkaldy is a sea-port on the Firth of Forth, possessing a dock-yard for building small vessels, and a considerable silk manufactory. Its trade in salt and coals is also extensive. The precise time of its erection is unknown, but it was a haven of considerable note as early as the 14th century, when David II. made it a burgh; and it was afterwards erected into a free royal burgh, with considerable privileges and immunities.

Coupar is a small neat town on the river Eden, and from being the principal of an extensive and productive country, is very properly styled a prosperous one. It formerly possessed a Castle, which was long the residence of the Earls of Fife, but afterwards became a national fortress. Wallace recovered it from the English in 1297, and Wishart bishop of Glasgow afterwards held it for Bruce; but being besieged and taken in arms, he was conducted in that uncanonical character to the Castle of Nottingham in 1306. This Castle was again recovered by the Scots; and during the minority of David II. it was repossessed by the English under Edward III., after which it was entirely demolished.

Falkland, situated on the south of the river Eden, was, in consequence of its frequently being the residence of royalty, made a borough by James II. in 1458. The palace was originally a strong-hold belonging to Macduff earl of Fife, but was appropriated as a hunting-seat by one of the Scottish monarchs. The present fabric, which is but one out of three sides that formerly existed, was erected by order of James V., who died in it of grief, occasioned by an affront he had received from his barons in 1542. The last royal inhabitant was Charles II., who during his captivity among the Presbyterians made it his abode for ten days.

Anna.—Robert duke of Rothsay, brother to James I., was starved to death in a dungeon of the original fortress by his inhuman uncle the Duke of Albany, to whose ambitious views he was offensive; and history relates that this unhappy prince was for a long time supported by two tradesmen's wives in the town; but being at length discovered, his supplies were cut off, and he perished from hunger in 1402.

George.—Falkland has a more recent claim upon history for importance, as in 1715, after the battle of Sheriff-Muir, it was garrisoned by the famous Rob Roy with a party of Macgregors, who laid the country under contribution for miles round; and after continuing their violent practices with impunity for a considerable time, they retired with a large booty.

Mrs. Rowe.—Falkland has been noticed for its simplicity; and the principal employment of its humble inhabitants is that of weaving.

Dunfermline is populous, and has large manufactures of diapers, damasks, checks, and ticking: ironstone also abounds in its neighbourhood, and there are numerous collieries. At different periods this place has been the residence of Scottish monarchs, and some remains of a Palace and Castle are still to be seen. A magnificent Abbey was begun by Malcolm Canmore, and completed by Alexander I., a great portion of which, in 1303, Edward I. burnt down, alleging as an excuse that it afforded a shelter for his enemies; and extensive as the ruins of this edifice still are, it is supposed they were originally of much greater size and magnificence.

Anna.—The palace of Dunfermline, which is a massive fabric in the vicinity of the Abbey, derives a melancholy interest from having been the birthplace of Charles 1. and his sister the Princess Elizabeth; and as long as virtue is admired and misfortune pitied, the memory of that unfortunate sovereign must be cherished with respect and affection.

George.—Amongst the antiquities of this town is a stone called St. Margaret's Stone, from its having been the resting-place of Margaret, who with Edgar Atheling fled from England at the time of the Conquest, and landing in Scotland, soon after became the queen of Malcolm III. She was the grand niece to Edward the Confessor; and in addition to her many noble virtues, her memory is entitled to the respect of all Britons, as through her the House of Brunswick may be said to add their descent from the Saxon dynasty to their other claims upon the British Crown. By her piety and learning she softened the ferocious disposition of her husband; and such was the estimation in which she was held, that her body was eventually transported to France, and invested with the honours of canonization.

Inverkeithing is situated on a bay of the same name,

which is large and safe, and affords excellent shelter for ships in all winds. It is a burgh of very high antiquity: its first existing charter is from William the Lion, confirming one of earlier date. It is said to have been in those early times the residence of many noble families, and even of royalty itself. In 1651 its neighbourhood was the scene of a battle between the English Parliamentarian army and the Scottish loyalists, in which the latter were defeated.

Kinghorn is a place of some antiquity, though it was not made a royal burgh till the time of Charles I. It has a harbour formed by a ridge of rocks, with the assistance of a pier, and possesses a small share of trade, with some manufactures.

ANNA.—In the vicinity of this town King Alexander III. was killed, March 19, 1285, when, as he was returning from hunting, the evening being dark, he was precipitated down a precipice, called the Black Rock, and died on the spot.

Kilrenny is a small parish, formerly connected with Eastern and Western Anstruther, and has some manufactures. When united, these three villages, or rather fishing towns, were of considerable importance. Eastern Anstruther is now the most extensive, and by means of its port, trades to the Baltic and Holland.

Crail is situated in the south-eastern corner of the county, and was formerly written Carle, Caryle, or Caraille. It possesses great capabilities for the construction of a harbour, but at present has but little trade. A little east of it is the East Neuk o' Fife, a spot which gives name to a popular Scottish air, and where is shown a cave in which King Constantine II. was beheaded by the Danes, who were in the frequent habit of invading this coast, A.D. 863.

GEORGE.—Mary of Lorraine, consort of James V., landed in this neighbourhood from stress of weather, and took shelter in a house near the cave, which has since been demolished.

Mrs. Rowe.—Which are the principal rivers in this county?

Anna.—The Leven and Eden.

Mrs. Rowe.—The Leven issues from a loch of the same name in Kinross-shire, and after an easterly course of some miles in this county, it falls into the Firth of Forth.

The Eden rises near Falkland, and runs easterly through Coupar to the village of Dairsie, when taking a more northerly course, it mixes its waters with the sea north of St. Andrews.

Fifeshire contains several lochs, though none of them are very extensive:—can you tell me the largest?

George.—Those of Lindores, Killcongahar, and Kinghorn.

Mrs. Rowe.—Loch Lindores is situated in the northern part of the county, and is a beautiful sheet of water, nearly a mile long, and of equal breadth, frequented by wild ducks and other water fowl, and abounding with pike and perch.

Loch Killcongahar lies in the south-eastern corner of the county: it is nearly of an oval form, and about two miles in circumference; and from its being situated in a fertile country between large plantations and inclosures, it becomes an interesting object, and adds beauty, variety, and richness to the scene.

Loch Kinghorn lies on the north side of the town of the same name, and forms a natural reservoir, from which the cotton and flax machinery at Kinghorn is supplied with water. Besides these inland waters, the county has along the greater part of its boundary the sea coast, which renders almost every part of it accessible to commerce.

The principal islands belonging to this county are Inch Keith and Inch Colm. The former lies in the centre of the Firth of Forth, opposite to Kinghorn, and is about a mile long. It is said to have derived its name from the gallant Keith, who signalized himself in 1010.

George.—This hero was a young commander in Mal-

colm's army, and is said to have been a native of Germany,
and prince of a colony of Celti that had settled in the
county of Caithness. He, when in pursuit, having overtaken and killed the Danish General Canrus, a Scottish
officer disputed the glory of the action with him : the king
coming up in the midst of their contention, ordered them
to decide it by single combat. Again Keith proved victorious, and killed his antagonist, who with his dying breath
confessed the justice of his opponent's claim; upon which
Malcolm dipped his finger in the blood, and marked the
shield of Keith with three strokes, saying, "Truth over-
comes," which has ever since been the armorial bearing and
motto of the family of Keith.

MRS. ROWE.—The ruins of a chapel, dedicated to St.
Marnock, are to be seen on this island. On the west side
of it are vast strata of coral; and the shore is bold and
rugged, exhibiting several deep caverns, shelving cliffs, and
towering rocks. About six miles west of this is the Isle of
St. Colomba, commonly called Inch Colm, famous for the
ruins of its monastery, founded by Alexander I., in the
year 1123, as a grateful memorial of the hospitable reception he met with from a hermit, who fed him with the milk
of his cow and a few shell-fish for three days, when he was
driven upon the island by a violent tempest. During the
reign of Edward III. of England, this place did not escape
a sacrilegious violation; but the plunderers being afterwards overtaken by a storm, many of them perished in the
deep.

Fifeshire exhibits much variety of soil, which, where it
has no great elevation above the sea, is for the most part
of excellent quality: in many places it is remarkably fertile,
producing luxuriant crops of all kinds: on the other hand
large tracts of land are yet either covered with heath, or
soured with a superabundance of moisture. This county
has long been famed for its breed of horned cattle, the
prevailing colour of which is black. Flax is cultivated to

a very considerable extent in Fifeshire. Its minerals con—
sist of coal in vast quantities, limestone, freestone, ironstone, and marl.—What eminent character can you mention
as having been a native of this county?

ANNA.—Alexander Selkirk, so well known as the renowned hero Robinson Crusoe, was born at Nether Largo
in the year 1676; and being a youth of high spirit and
uncontrollable temper, he was for some offence obliged to
submit to the mortifying censures of the Church in their
severest forms. When the term of his punishment expired, he left his native town in disgust, and enlisted himself in a ship bound to the South Seas. In consequence of
a disagreement with his captain, he was left on the desolate
island of Juan Fernandez, where he remained four years
and four months in complete solitude, from which he was
relieved and brought to England by Captain Wood Rogers;
but from his long seclusion from intercourse with man he
had so far forgotten the use of speech as to be almost un-
intelligible.

KINROSS-SHIRE.

Boundaries.—Perthshire and Fifeshire.
Town.—1, Kinross.
Loch.—G, Loch Leven.

MRS. ROWE.—DESCRIBE the boundaries, extent, and
chief towns of Kinross-shire.

ANNA.—This small county is bounded on the east and
south by Fifeshire, and on the north and west by Perthshire: it measures from east to west nearly 12 miles, and
from north to south about 9. The general figure of the

county is somewhat oval, although the boundary line is irregular. The only important place is Kinross.

Mrs. Rowe.—Kinross, from which this little territory takes its name, is situated on the west shore of Loch Leven. The general appearance of the town is rather mean, but it is delightfully placed on a promontory, which advances into the water: it has no independent manufactures, but is inhabited by weavers, who procure employment from Glasgow. The church, situated in the centre of the town, and unconnected with the churchyard, is a pleasing and picturesque object. But the great ornament of the county is that beautiful and magnificent piece of water called Loch Leven, which possesses, according to tradition, the following remarkable peculiarities: it is eleven miles round, is encompassed by eleven hills, is fed by eleven streams, contains eleven kinds of fish, and is studded with eleven islands. But it is principally of note for its island fortress, which was the prison of the unfortunate Mary queen of Scots in 1567. This Castle stands on an island of about two acres, near the north-west extremity of the lake, and directly opposite the promontory before mentioned. It belonged originally to Dougart king of the Picts, was inhabited by Alexander III., besieged by Edward I. of England, and latterly possessed by the Douglases. When the queen escaped from the Castle, her deliverers are said to have landed at a place called Babbinny, on the south side of the lake, from whence she was conducted across the moors to the ferry: she stopped a few hours during the night at Niddry Castle in West Lothian, and arrived next morning at Hamilton palace, forty miles from the place of her confinement. Some trees, perhaps coeval with this unfortunate princess, still grace the sequestered spot.

The surface of this county is varied: the middle portion, which comprehends nearly half of it, is low, and may be considered as a flat plain varied with gentle rising grounds: the boundaries are formed of higher land. The air is gene-

rally clear, which is conducive to the health of the inhabitants.   Flax is here grown in considerable quantities ; but
wheat is seldom sown.   Black cattle and sheep are to be
found upon most of the farms.

The mineralogy of this county is not important, whinstone and freestone composing the chief.—Can you name
any distinguished characters who were natives of this
county?

GEORGE.—Sir William Bruce, one of the most eminent
Scottish architects.

Andrew Winton, prior of Lochleven in the reign of
James I.   He was author of a work in Scottish metre, entitled "The Lochleven Chronicle, or a History of the World
from its Creation to the Captivity of James I.," a copy of
which is in the Advocates' Library, and has been frequently
appealed to by later historians.

John Douglas, of the family of Pittendriech, celebrated
for being the first Protestant Archbishop of St. Andrews :
he was appointed to that dignity in 1571.

Michael Bruce, who, though he died at the early age of
twenty-one years, displayed uncommon poetical talents :
he was the son of a weaver, but had received a liberal education at the University of St. Andrews.   His poetical description of Lochleven Castle is well known, and has been
frequently quoted by tourists.

STIRLINGSHIRE.

Boundaries.—Perthshire, Dunbartonshire, Lanarkshire, Linlith-
gowshire, and the Firth of Forth.
Towns.—1, Stirling; 2, Carron; 3, Falkirk; 4, Kilsyth; 5, St.
Ninian's; 6, Grangemouth; 7, Bannockburn; 8, Camelon;
9, Milltown.
Rivers.—a, the Forth; b, Carron; c, Bannock; d, Avon.
A, Firth of Forth.

Mrs. Rowe.—WHAT are the boundaries, extent, and
chief towns of Stirlingshire?

Anna.—This county has on the north Perthshire, on
the north-east and east the Firth of Forth and Linlithgowshire, on the south Lanarkshire, and on the west Dunbartonshire. It is nearly 40 miles in length and from 8 to 15
in breadth; and its chief towns are Stirling, Falkirk, Carron, Camelon, Grangemouth, Bannockburn, St. Ninian's
and Milltown.

Mrs. Rowe.—Stirling, the capital, from which it derives its name, is a fine ancient town, and possesses a Castle
of great strength and beauty, which has undergone many
revolutions: it has frequently been the residence of royalty,
and from the lofty battlements the monarch could with pride
behold the bold outline of an unconquered kingdom. The
Grampian, Ochil, and Pentland Hills, with the majestic
course of the river Forth and its tributary streams, present
a romantic and pleasing prospect. Stirling is so much
connected with the memorable occurrences in Scotch and
English histories, that to give an account of the vicissitudes
it has undergone, would be to relate a portion of the annals
of both nations; nor is it more remarkable for being the
scene of bloodshed in national conflicts, than for that which
has flowed under the hand of the executioner; as an emi-

nence called Hurlie Haw, in the vicinity, was the ordinary place of execution, and is addressed as such in Douglas's apostrophe to those scenes by the author of the Lady of the Lake.

GEORGE.—I well remember the lines to which you allude. They are—

> " Ye towers! within whose circuit dread
> A Douglas by his sovereign bled ;
> And thou, O sad and fatal mound !
> That oft hast heard the death axe sound,
> As on the noblest of the land
> Fell the stern headsman's bloody hand...."

MRS. ROWE.—The last execution of any note that took place here was that of Hamilton archbishop of St. Andrews, Primate of Scotland, and a partisan of Queen Mary's. He was hanged in 1571 for being an alleged accessory in the murder of the Regent Murray. This town has a manufacture of carpets and cotton goods, contains a great number of prosperous and opulent merchants, and is celebrated for the number of its hospitals.

Falkirk is an old town, famous for its large cattle fairs, called Falkirk Trysts, at some of which as many as 15,000 head of cattle have been reported to have been sold.—Can you relate any historical event that occurred in this town?

GEORGE.—In the year 1298 a battle was fought between the English commanded by Edward I. and the Scots by Sir William Wallace, in which the latter were totally routed.

MRS. ROWE.—It appears to have been the precipitancy of the Scots which caused their ruin, as, had they protracted the campaign, their enemies, from want of provisions, must have made an inglorious retreat. The slaughter of the Scots was dreadful, and among the slain were Macduff, and Sir John Graham, styled the right hand of Wallace : he lies buried in the churchyard under a plain stone. This town possesses a great deal of trade, and is a busy and prosperous place.

Carron, on a river of the same name, is justly celebrated for its extensive iron-works, the largest manufactory of the kind in the world: it was founded in 1761, on a spot where there was not a single house, and is said to afford constant employment to at least 1600 men. All kinds of cast-iron goods are made here, from the most trifling article for domestic use to cannon of the largest calibre: the machinery constructed by Mr. Smeaton deserves admiration for its elegance and correctness. In the vicinity of the foundries (on an elevation above the river) stood the celebrated antiquity called Arthur's Oven, supposed to have been a *sacellum* (or repository) for the Roman standard. This matchless edifice was destroyed by a Gothic knight, who made a mill-dam of the materials; but in less than a year (as if to punish him for his sacrilege) the whole was destroyed by a flood.

Camelon is a village a little north-west of Falkirk, situated near what is now styled Old Camelon, a Roman city, built by Vespasian, and which, when afterwards possessed by the Picts, is said to have had twelve brazen gates. Of this magnificent place no other vestige exists than a fragment of an upright wall and a few straggling trees, which are said to mark the extent of its site.

Grangemouth stands at the place where the Forth and Clyde canal joins the Firth of Forth, and is a sea-port of considerable importance: besides having a commodious harbour, it possesses a dry dock, rope-walk, custom-house, and large warehouse for goods. Vast quantities of timber, deals, hemp, flax, and iron are here imported from the Baltic, Norway, and Sweden, besides grain from the coasts of England and Scotland.

Bannockburn, on the river Bannock, is sufficiently famed in history for a battle fought near it in the year 1314, between 30,000 Scots, headed by Robert Bruce, and an immense army of English, under their sovereign Edward II., who was totally defeated, and Scotland was for some time completely emancipated from the English yoke.

St. Ninian's, a small village a little to the south of Stirling, is noted for its manufactories for nails and leather. The steeple of this place is a distinguished curiosity, as the church which was attached to it was used by the Highlanders in 1746 as a powder magazine, and was accidentally blown up immediately before their retreat to the north, and though scarcely a stone of it was left, the steeple remained uninjured.

Milltown is chiefly remarkable for an extensive manufacture of nails.

ANNA.—I have read that the barons of Scotland, being dissatisfied with the administration of James III., rose in rebellion against him, and prevailed on the king's eldest son to be of their party. In 1488 a battle was fought near this town, in which the king's party was defeated: but before the fate of the day was decided, His Majesty fled, alone, from the field, and in attempting to cross the Bannockburn, his horse started at sight of a pitcher with which a woman was lifting up water, and which she threw away upon seeing an armed man riding towards her; upon which the king was thrown from his charger, and fell upon the ground in a state of insensibility. As the disaster happened within a few yards of a mill, His Majesty was carried thither: the miller and his wife, though unconscious of the rank of their guest, humanely administered to him such cordials as their house afforded. On recovering his recollection, James asked for a priest, and to the repeated inquiries of who he was, replied, "I was your king this morning": on hearing which the miller's wife ran out, wringing her hands, and calling for a confessor for the king. "I am a priest," (said one of his enemies, who was then in pursuit of him,) "lead me to him." He found the unfortunate monarch in a corner of the mill, covered with a coarse cloth; and ap-

proaching on his knees, (under pretence of reverence,) inquired if His Grace thought surgical aid would recover him;
to which the king no sooner replied " Yes!" than the ruf-
fian pulled out a dagger and stabbed him several times to
the heart.

Mrs. Rowe.—The spot where this happened is called
Little Coglan, but the engagement is usually styled by
historians 'the battle of Sanghieburn'.—Name the principal rivers of Stirlingshire.

George.—The Forth and the Carron.

Mrs. Rowe.—The Forth bounds this county a long way
on the north and north-east, and though (perhaps) not the
largest, is the most distinguished river in all Scotland: it
enters it from Perthshire, and a little above Stirling its importance is greatly increased by the receipt of some tributary streams.   It is navigable for vessels of a large size
throughout its whole course, and is a peculiarly serpen-
tine river.   At Alloa it expands into the estuary or firth
which bears its name.

The Carron rises in the south, and flows in a north-
easterly direction into the Firth of Forth.

George.—The banks of this river are famed for having
been the scene of warfare during the earliest period of history : many battles described in Ossian's Poems took place
here ; and the decisive one between the Scotch and English
in 1298 also happened on its banks.   The course of that
great Roman antiquity, St. Antoninus's Wall, is from this
river to the Clyde: it was first marked out by Agricola, and
completed by Antoninus Pius, and was defended at proper
distances by forts and watch-towers.   It is called by the
common people Graham's Dike, from a tradition that a
Scottish warrior of that name first scaled it.

Mrs. Rowe.—Stirlingshire is not only one of the most
beautiful counties in Scotland, but one of the most celebrated, having once formed the boundary of four kingdoms,
the Cumbrian and Northumbrian on the south, and the

Scots and Picts on the north; and in consequence it became the battle-ground of all these conflicting nations: and
there is scarcely a foot of accessible ground which has not
felt the tread of marching armies; and the eye may view
in all directions the field of some memorable contest.   Although the appearance of the county is generally mountainous, yet it is not without the interruption of various morasses and vales. The plains (styled the Carses) of Falkirk
and Stirling are extensive and fertile, and abundance of coal
and lime are found in the south part of the county.—Can
you name any great character to whom this county has
given birth?

GEORGE.—Sir Ralph Abercrombie, a brave British general, who entered the army in 1750 as a cornet, and rose
through the several gradations of rank to that of major-
general, to which he was promoted in 1787. He had been
upwards of forty years in the army, and served with distinction in the wars, when he was employed upon the Continent, under the late lamented Frederick duke of York:
he then succeeded Sir Charles Grey as commander-in-chief
of the British forces in the West Indies. By his active exertions the forts of Demerara and Essequibo, with the islands of St. Lucia, St. Vincent, and Trinidad, were added
to the British conquests.   On his return to Europe he was
made Knight of the Bath, sent as commander-in-chief to
Ireland, afterwards to Scotland, and at length was chosen
by his sovereign to dispossess the French in Egypt; and
on the 21st of March 1801 he received a mortal wound
at the battle of Alexandria, and died eight days after, universally beloved and lamented.

DUNBARTONSHIRE.

Boundaries.—Argyleshire, Perthshire, Stirlingshire, Lanarkshire, Renfrewshire, and Loch Loung.
Towns.—1, Dunbarton; 2, Kilmarnock; 3, Buchanan; 4, Tarbet; 5, Luss; 6, Renton.
Rivers.—a, the Clyde; b, the great Canal uniting the Forth and the Clyde; c, Leven; d, Fruin.
Lochs.—A, Loch Lomond; B, Loch Loung.

Mrs. Rowe.—WHAT are the boundaries, extent, and chief towns of Dunbartonshire?

Anna.—This singularly formed county terminates in a point between the counties of Argyle and Perth: the latter and Stirlingshire bound it on the east, Lanarkshire and Renfrewshire on the south and south-west, and Argyleshire and Loch Loung on the west: its length from north-west to south-east is about 40 miles, and its extreme width nearly 30, though it varies to about 6. Its chief town is Dunbarton, besides which it contains the villages of Luss, Tarbet, and Renton.

Mrs. Rowe.—Dunbarton, the capital of the county, is seated at the confluence of the rivers Leven and Clyde, and was erected into a royal burgh by Alexander II. in 1221. Its Castle stands on a two-headed rock of stupendous height, near which are the ruins of a light-house, supposed to have been a Roman pharos. From the natural strength and immense height of the rocks, this fortification was considered impregnable. It resisted all the efforts of Agricola; but in the year 1571, by a desperate and successful scalade, it was taken.

George.—In the time of the Bruce and Baliol wars this fortress was governed by Sir John Monteith, so celebrated in history as the betrayer of Wallace into the hands of the

English; and it is asserted that that unfortunate hero was imprisoned here for some time prior to his removal to England to take his trial.

MRS. ROWE.—This town is of small extent, though possessed of considerable commerce and manufactures, particularly that of glass.

Luss is a small village at the north-east point of Loch Lomond, on a promontory which juts into it, principally inhabited by fishermen. It is also much resorted to in summer by tourists, in search of the picturesque.

Tarbet is a small and remote place on the north-west side of Loch Lomond, and derives its name from the district of Tarbet, which is so called from its situation between two lochs, that being the term always given to narrow pieces of land which intervene between two pieces of water.

Renton is a village situated on the Leven, midway between the southern end of Loch Lomond and Dunbarton, chiefly occupied by persons engaged in bleaching, which branch of manufacture flourishes to a greater extent in this district than in any other part of Scotland on account of the limpid purity of the stream.—Which are the principal rivers of this county?

ANNA.—The Leven and the Fruin.

MRS. ROWE.—The course of the Leven, though not more than six miles, is most exquisitely beautiful: it issues from Loch Lomond, and proceeds due southward through Renton and Dunbarton into the Firth of Clyde.

The Fruin rises in the eastern part of the county, and flows westerly into the south-eastern corner of Loch Lomond. The great glory of this county are its lochs, of which those of Lomond and Loung are preeminent. The first-mentioned extends about 24 miles in length and 8 in breadth at the widest part, and contains twenty-four small islands, some of which are inhabited, and others afford a shelter for eagles and ospreys. The surrounding scenery of

towering mountains, deep and gloomy glens, with the view
of the rivers Leven and Clyde, altogether form a prospect
beyond conception majestic and sublime, and render it the
most celebrated of the Caledonian lakes. At the north-east
stands the lofty Ben Lomond, towering above his alpine
brethren : this mountain is a great resort for wild fowl,
particularly ptarmigans. At the foot of this hill is Rob
Roy's Prison, so called from a rock at the bottom of this
tremendous precipice, on which the Macgregors used to
drop their culprits who were guilty of capital offences,
where they perished, either for want of food or in the lake,
into which, from despair, they frequently plunged themselves.

GEORGE.—A tract in this county called Glen Fruin was
the principal seat of the Macgregors, a murderous clan,
infamous for excesses of all kinds, who were finally pro-
scribed and hunted down like wild animals, and it was considered penal to bear their name.

MRS. ROWE.—Loch Loung is an arm of the sea nearly
parallel with Loch Lomond, and is a beautiful sheet of water,
the head of which is distinguished by a grotesquely grand
peak called Ben Artur, (or The Cobbler, in consequence of
its resembling in shape the attitude of that artizan when at
work).

ANNA.—It is recorded that the Norwegians, who invaded
Scotland in 1263, (but who were eventually defeated by
Alexander III.,) sent a part of their army up this loch to
ravage the country. On reaching the head they transported their boats over the beautiful little vale into Loch
Lomond, on which they again embarked, and sailing in all
directions, laid waste the whole of the surrounding country
within their reach, particularly the western part of Stirlingshire.

MRS. ROWE.—Dunbartonshire, often denominated the
Lennox, and under that name giving title to that ancient
Scottish dukedom, may be described simply as the basin

of the extensive loch it contains, which comprehends its whole surface, except a narrow tract which surrounds it, and a broader one in the south-eastern part. It is a county of subordinate importance in a political point of view, as well as in its territorial wealth and population; but as it contains scenery of an unparalleled description, it may excite a more lively interest with strangers than many others of North Britain. In all the rivers of this county salmon is caught in great abundance, and the fisheries of Loch Lomond and Loch Leven are of great value : these fish are cured in a peculiar kind of way, called 'kippering'; and throughout Scotland kippered salmon is a favourite dish. This county consists of a mixture of natural pasture, wood, and arable lands. Its mineral productions are coal, limestone of various qualities, and slate : large quantities of the latter are annually sent to Greenock, Glasgow, and Paisley, and some across Loch Lomond to Stirlingshire.—Can you name any distinguished person who was born in this county ?

GEORGE.—Dr. Tobias Smollett was an eminent physician, who possessed considerable abilities and an independent mind. He is better known as an author of history, novels, and political tracts. When he died he had in hand a new edition of the Ancient and Modern Universal History.

George Buchanan, tutor to James VI., was a Scottish historian and Latin poet.

ARGYLESHIRE.

Boundaries.—Inverness-shire, Perthshire, Dunbartonshire, and the Atlantic Ocean.

Towns.—1, Inverary; 2, Cladich; 3, Bunan; 4, King's House; 5, Appen; 6, New York; 7, Kindra; 8, Rahoy; 9, Oban; 10, Kilmore; 11, Melford; 12, Ormick; 13, Killener; 14, Cairndow; 15, St. Catherines; 16, Batnaca; 17, Otter; 18, Aird; 19, Tarbet; 20, Skipnith; 21, Cambelton.

Lochs.—a, Loch Fyne; b, Loch Cambelton; c, Loch Tarbet; d, Loch Etive; e, Loch Linnhe; f, Loch Awe; g, Loch Sunart; h, Loch Shiel.

Islands and Districts.—A, Mull Island; B, Staffa; C, Icolnkill; D, Isla; E, Jura; F, Col; G, Tirey; H, Colonsa; I, Ormsay; J, Cowall District; K, Cantyre; L, Lorn; M, Appen; N, Glenorchy; O, Morven; P, Sunart.

Mrs. Rowe.—ARGYLESHIRE is a very extensive and irregular county, divided by its lochs into the districts of Cowall, bordering upon Dunbartonshire, and separated from thence by Loch Loung. Kintire, or Cantyre, and Argyle Proper project southwards, and are divided from Cowall by Loch Fyne; to the north of these are situated the inland districts of Lorn, Appen, and Glenorchy; and on the west of them, and parted from them by Loch Linnhe (the mouth of the Caledonian Canal), lie those of Morven and Sunart.—Can you describe its situation, extent, and chief places?

Anna.—It is bounded on the north by Inverness-shire, on the east by Perthshire and Dunbartonshire, and on the south and west by the Atlantic Ocean, by which it is broken into islands and peninsulas, with bays and inlets, which afford good harbours for shipping. It is upwards of 100 miles from the Mull of Cantyre to its north-eastern extremity: its breadth is very unequal, measuring in its northern extremity 40 miles, in the centre of the county about 30, whilst across the Cantyre it does not exceed 5. Its chief towns are Inverary, Cambelton, Oban, and Cairndow.

MRS. ROWE.—Inverary is pleasantly situated on Loch Fyne (an arm of the sea), within sixty miles of the Western Ocean. Its Castle was for many ages the residence of the Campbells, whose power, and the difficulty of its approach, preserved it (except in two instances) from hostile insult. In December 1644, during a severe snow-storm, the enterprising Montrose poured down his troops on this town, through ways apparently impassable; when the Marquis of Argyle with difficulty escaped in a fishing-boat, and left his people to the fury of the merciless invaders. The second calamity was in 1685, when another clan, armed with the dreadful writ of fire and sword, carried destruction among the Campbells, seventeen of whom were instantly executed.

GEORGE.—This place was saved from falling into the hands of the rebels in 1715, by the resolution of Archibald duke of Argyle and earl of Hay, who collected a body of troops here, and preserved this important pass for King George I.

MRS. ROWE.—Till within the last few years this town was rarely visited by strangers, owing to its inaccessibility; but from the numerous vehicles, terrestrial and marine, which ply to it daily from Glasgow, it is now much more frequently resorted to. It was made a royal burgh by Charles I. when he was a prisoner in Carisbrooke Castle. The principal support of this town is its herring fishery, those caught in Loch Fyne being particularly excellent; besides which it has some woollen manufactures.

ANNA.—I have read of a singular instance of pride in one of the Campbell family: his name was Colin, better known by that of 'Jongallach, or the Wonderful,' on account of his adventures. He set fire to his own house at Inverary, that he might be compelled to entertain the

O'Neills (illustrious guests from Ireland) in his magnificent field equipage.

Cambelton is pleasantly seated near the southern part of the district of Cantyre, on the banks of a beautiful semicircular bay of the same name, and is remarkable as having been (under the name of Dalruadhain) the first capital of the Scottish kingdom. It is a clean and well-built town, and possesses an excellent harbour, by means of which it exports great quantities of fish, potatoes, and excellent whiskey: the distilleries for manufacturing the last-mentioned article are here very numerous.

Oban, a flourishing modern village, was founded in 1713 by a trading company belonging to Renfrew: it is the place of general rendezvous for the herring-boats on the west coast, and is admirably situated for trade.

GEORGE.—It was near the spot where this village stands that King Alexander II. died, while he was lying with a small fleet in this bay, and meditating the conquest of the Hebrides, then possessed by the Norwegians.

MRS. ROWE.—Cairndow is a small place, situated at the northern extremity of Loch Fyne, noted only for being the place where travellers procure boats to convey them down the loch to Inverary.—Which are the principal lochs of this county?

ANNA.—Those of Fyne, Cambelton, Tarbet, Etive, Linnhe, Awe, Sunart, and Shiel.

MRS. ROWE.—Loch Fyne is an inlet of the sea, about 34 miles long, and from 1 to 6 broad, which receives and returns a tide on each side of the Isle of Arran, which lies directly opposite its mouth: it is beautifully indented with bays, and surrounded by woodland mountains.

Loch Cambelton is a safe, capacious, and beautiful arm of the sea in the southern extremity of the district of Cantyre, near the town of the same name: it is land-locked on every side, and its entrance is screened by two islands, or

rather isolated hills; from the summit of one of these is a
most extensive view, comprehending the Ayrshire coast,
the Isle of Arran, the Irish Hills, and some of the Hebrides.
This loch abounds with excellent fish, and when enlivened
by numerous pleasure-boats and fishing-smacks, exhibits a
striking and pleasingly variegated scene.

Loch Tarbet is the arm of the sea which, by its inunda-
tion, may be said to form the peninsula of Cantyre.

Loch Etive is an extensive arm of the sea in the district
of Lorn.

Loch Linnhe forms the mouth of the Caledonian Canal
before described.

Loch Awe is a fine inland expanse of water, about 30
miles long, and from 1 to 2 broad, containing many beautiful islands tufted with trees.

Loch Sunart is that arm of the sea which separates the
island of Mull from the district of Morven.

Loch Shiel is an estuary of the sea at the northern extremity of the county, defended on both sides by hills of
the most lofty character; and in this region of alpine wil-
derness, where scarcely any object can be ascribed to the
hand of man, is a monument, erected solely at the expense
of a private individual, to immortalize the spot where
Prince Charles first reared his standard in 1745, when he
made the daring and romantic attempt to recover a throne
lost by the imprudence of his ancestors.

Argyleshire is supposed to have acquired its name from
Argyle (signifying the 'Land of Strangers'), this being the
part where the Scoto-Irish landed in the sixth century from
Dariada, a district in the north-east of Ireland, under three
leaders, Lorn, Fergus, and Angus, the sons of an Irish
chieftain.

Though this county abounds in every description of wild
and romantic scenery, rocks, frightful precipices, and stupendous mountains, apparently piled one upon another, yet

in the high grounds the soil, though little fitted for cultivation, affords good pasturage.—Which of the Hebrides, or Western Islands, are included in this county?

GEORGE.—They are very numerous; the most noted are Mull, Staffa, Icolmkill, Isla, Jura, Col, and Tirey.

MRS. ROWE.—Mull is an extensive tract of land lying to the west of the northern part of the county, presenting a wild and melancholy view of extensive heaths covered with small black cattle, a great number of which are annually exported, and, with fish and a considerable quantity of kelp, are the only objects of commerce. There are many good natural harbours; but the village of Tobermorey is the only one of any importance: it is a modern fishing station at the northern extremity of the island, and contains a custom-house and post-office.

ANNA.—It was in the harbour near this place that the Florida, a Spanish man-of-war belonging to the Invincible Armada, was sunk, after the dispersion and overthrow of its companions, in 1588. It is related that Queen Elizabeth sent a person there to procure its destruction, which he executed in the most perfidious manner; for having first formed an intimacy with some of the crew, he placed some combustible substance in a convenient situation, and afterwards waited a fit opportunity to carry his diabolical mission into effect, when he caused the vessel to be blown up, and nearly all on board perished, among whom were some distinguished Spaniards.

MRS. ROWE.—Staffa, a small island to the west of Mull, is rendered of consequence by its peculiar geological structure, more than one half of it being occupied by handsome colonnades of regular basaltic pillars, which are nearly laid bare by the sea. The rest of the island exhibits the same basaltic appearance, but the pillars are bent and twisted in various directions: they generally rest on an irregular pavement, formed of the upper sides of those which have been broken off. These pillars are of various shapes, and are

generally similar to those used in architecture, having con-
cavities and corresponding convexities, as if for the purpose of adding strength to the structure. But the greatest
curiosity is a cavern in the highest part of the island, called
Finnea-coul, or Fingal's Cave: it is a natural recess of
about 100 yards in depth, lined on each side with tall columns, and overhung by a roof composed of fragments of
the same material. The sea flows into the furthest extremity of it, so that boats may sail into it in calm weather:
it is one of the greatest natural curiosities in the world.

The island of Icolmkill lies off the south-west point of
Mull: this has been termed " the illustrious island, which
was once the luminary of the Caledonian regions, whence
savage clans and roving barbarians derived the benefits of
knowledge and the blessings of religion." It was in the
sixth century the place where Columba, an Irish saint, first
propagated the Christian faith amongst a people formerly
devoted to the superstitions of Druidical paganism. It was
long the cemetery of the Scottish monarchs, and subsequently became an abbacy, and the seat of the bishopric
of the Isles. Numerous relics still remain to attest its
former greatness, among which the Cathedral and Bishop's
palace are the most conspicuous.

On the right of the Cathedral, and near to it, are the remains of the College, some of the cloisters of which are still
visible. In the inclosure adjoining this building, forty-eight
Scottish kings, four kings of Ireland, eight Norwegian
monarchs, and one king of France, are said to be interred.
Icolmkill, popularly termed I, and classically Iona, was the
depository of a vast collection of valuable papers and books,
all of which were either scattered or destroyed at the Reformation.

Isla and Jura are large islands lying considerably to the
south of Mull; the chief object to be noticed in the former
is the Castle of the Mac Donalds, lords of the Isles: it
stands in the centre of a lake. These insular monarchs are

said to have lived in all the pomp of acknowledged sovereignty, being regularly crowned like other kings, with
these exceptions, that instead of being crowned on a throne,
they stood upon a large stone, which had hollows to receive
their feet, and the Bishop of Argyle usually performed the
ceremony. The stone, as well as the ruins of the palace
and offices, are still to be seen. Jura is chiefly remarkable
for its three beautiful conical hills. Both isles are distinguished from the rest of the Hebrides by the comparative
equality of the weather.

The island of Col lies to the north-west of Mull : it contains some horses, sheep, and goats, and has many lochs,
which abound in fish.

Tirey lies to the south-west of Col : it is noted for its
marble-quarry, and for a handsome race of small horses.
This island is well inhabited : the chief employment of the
people is the making of kelp. Here are several lakes,
which cover about 600 acres ; and in them abundance of
fish is found.

BUTESHIRE.

Boundaries.—Surrounded by the waters of the Firth of Clyde.
Town.—1, Rothsay in the Isle of Bute.
Islands.—A, Bute ; B, Arran ; C, Inch Marnoch ; D, Great Cum-
bray ; E, Lesser Cumbray.

MRS. ROWE.—WHAT islands compose the county of
Bute ?

GEORGE.—Those of Bute, Arran, Big and Little Cumbray, and Inch Marnoch, all lying in the Firth of Clyde.

MRS. ROWE.—Bute is about 15 miles long, and scarcely

5 broad in its widest part, and contains the parishes of
Rothsay and Kingarth, the former of which is situated on
the east coast of the island, and possesses an excellent harbour and pier, and has of late years become a fashionable
resort of the mercantile gentry: the inhabitants are chiefly
fishermen.   The Castle of Rothsay is of various kinds of
architecture, and of different æras; but the period of its
original construction is unknown: it was the favourite residence of Robert III., and afterwards the seat of the family of Bute.   This fortress was burnt down by the Earl
of Argyle in 1685.   Rothsay confers the title of Duke on
the eldest son of the King of Great Britain, as it did long
before the Union upon the heir apparent to the Crown of
Scotland.

Kingarth is noted for its church, containing two ceme-
teries, the upper and lower: the latter was allotted for the
interment of females alone.   Near this place is a circular
inclosure, formed of stone, of good masonry, but without
mortar: it is supposed to have been formerly a sanctuary.
The air of this island is generally temperate; snow never
lies long on the ground, nor is it subject to mists and fogs;
but winds and heavy rains sometimes annoy this otherwise
favoured spot.   The face of the country is hilly, but not
mountainous.   It is fertile in corn and pasture; and there
is also a considerable herring-fishery on the coast.

Arran, or *Arr Inn* (signifying the ‘Island of Mountains’),
is much larger than Bute, and lies to the south-west of it.
Its length is computed to exceed 20 miles, and its breadth
about 12.   Lamlash is its principal harbour; but there is
scarcely such a thing as a town or village upon the island.

It is noted for the excellent quality of its whiskey, which
is its chief product.   The hills of Arran are very rocky and
precipitous, and afford some cataracts of great height,
though of inconsiderable extent.   Goatfield (or the ‘Mountains of the Winds’) consists of extensive hills of moor-stone.
Beinbarrain (or the ‘Sharp-pointed Mountain’), Cumnacail-

lich (or the 'Step of the Old Hag'), and Guanon Athol, will yield to none in ruggedness. The caverns, which are supposed to have been formerly the habitations of heroes, are now the retreats of smugglers. The interior of the island abounds with beautiful Highland scenery. Upon many parts of it are to be seen high erect columns of stone, the most early of all monuments; circles of rude stones, commonly called Druidical; and cairns, or sepulchral piles, within which are generally found urns inclosing ashes. Much doubt must ever exist regarding the history of such monuments, and they can only be considered the relics of heathen and Druidical superstition.

Brodwick, or Brothwick Castle, now the seat of the Duke of Hamilton, was taken by King Robert Bruce during his unhappy wanderings through the Western Isles. A natural recess in the bold coast towards Cambelton is still called the King's Cave, from its having afforded shelter to the unfortunate monarch before he had captured Brodwick. The streams of this island are stored with fish, particularly salmon. The climate is cold but healthful, and invalids annually resort thither to drink the whey of goats' milk.

Big and Little Cumbray are situated on the south-eastern side of the Isle of Bute, on the latter of which there is a light-house.

Inch Marnoch is a beautiful little isle, lying south-west of Bute: it contains nothing of note but the ruins of a chapel, dedicated to St. Marnoch, from which it derives its name. These islands, like Bute, are tolerably fertile in corn and pasture, and possess considerable herring-fisheries.

AYRSHIRE.

Boundaries.—Renfrewshire, Lanarkshire, Dumfriesshire, Kirkcudbrightshire, Wigtownshire, and the Firth of Clyde.

Towns.—1, Ayr; 2, Lanes; 3, Irvine; 4, Saltcoats; 5, Fairly; 6, Kingsmells; 7, Kilmarnock; 8, Loudon; 9, Old Cummock; 10, Sheldon; 11, Maybole; 12, Carrick; 13, Girvan; 14, Ballintree; 15, Stewarton.

Rivers and Lochs.—a, the Irvine; b, Ayr; c, Doon; d, Girvan; e, Stinchar; f, Loch Dun.

Islands and Capes.—A, Lady Island; B, Ailsa Island; C, Head of Ayr.

Districts.—D, Cunningham; E, Kyle; F, Carrick.

Mrs. Rowe.—DESCRIBE the boundaries, extent, and chief towns of Ayrshire.

Anna.—This county is bounded on the north by Renfrewshire, east by Lanarkshire and Dumfriesshire, southeast and south by Kirkcudbrightshire and Wigtonshire, and on the west by the Firth of Clyde, forming a large bay: its extreme length from north-east to south-west is 60 miles, and across the centre from east to west it measures 30, but decreasing irregularly, till it becomes about 10 at the south-western extremity, and at the north-eastern it approaches almost to a point. It contains the towns of Ayr, Kilmarnock, Irvine, Stewarton, Maybole, Saltcoats, and Ballintree.

Mrs. Rowe.—Ayr, the capital of the county, is a very handsome town, situated at the mouth of the river of the same name, on the north bank of which stands a meaner town, called the Newtown-of-Ayr, under an entirely distinct government. The mouth of the river forms a harbour. Ayr was erected into a royal burgh by William the Lion about the year 1204; and it must have been a place of some importance, as it was made a principal station for the troops of Edward I. in the thirteenth century. Here are two bridges, respectively termed the Auld and New Brigs. The first is said to have been built by two maiden sisters in the reign of Alexander III., whose effigies are now shown upon a stone in the eastern parapet, at the south end of the fabric: it is very narrow, and is now used only as a foot passage. The New Brig, which is not more than one hundred yards below the old one, was built in the year 1788; and to make room for its erection, a very ancient and elegant cross was removed: it was of a hexagon form, and considered a great curiosity. The fort of Ayr was built by Oliver Cromwell upon a flat piece of ground near the sea, being one of the four edifices of the kind built by the Protector in Scotland. The ramparts of this fortress inclosed the ancient church, dedicated to St. John, the tower of which, with a few fragments of the ramparts, still remain.

Not far from hence stood the Castle, which was built by William the Lion in 1197, for the purpose of aweing the wild men of Galloway; and it was also much celebrated in the history of the war of independence. Here was once a Dominican monastery, which was remarkable in history as the place where Robert Bruce held the parliament that secured his succession. Upon its site Cromwell founded a church, which still contains the same seats and galleries with which it was originally fitted up; and there remains no other memorial of the former edifice but a fountain, called the Friar's Well, which runs through the churchyard into the river. The inhabitants of Ayr carry on a considerable trade in coals and grain; and there is a fishery for cod and haddock on the coast: it also possesses manufactures of cotton, iron, and tambour-work.

Kilmarnock is famous for its extensive and valuable manufactures of gloves, carpets, stockings, nightcaps, bonnets, and a variety of woollen goods. The progress of manufactures during the last century in this part of Scotland, and the intense spirit of activity which seems to have peculiarly characterized the inhabitants of this place, have transformed it from a mean village to one of the largest and most elegant towns in the county, possessing, to all appearance, the attributes of a capital.

GEORGE.—It was here that the Lord Soulis was assassinated in the 15th century by a youth of the Boyd family, who stood on the opposite bank of the Fenwick Water, and shot an arrow from his crossbow with such certain effect, that his unfortunate victim expired on the spot.

Irvine is a considerable port, seated at the mouth of a river of the same name, which, after forming the boundary line between this county and Lanarkshire for some distance, falls into the Firth of Clyde at this place. It exports great quantities of coals, woollen goods, carpeting, muslins, lawns, and linen; in return it receives hemp, iron, deals, ship timber, and corn, from Norway and the Baltic.

Stewarton, on a small river which runs into the Firth of Clyde after joining the Irvine, is noted for the quantity of weaving done in it, and also for a manufacture of bonnets, and French and Quebec caps.

Maybole is generally considered the capital of the southern district of Ayrshire, called Carrick, and is a good-looking town, possessing a degree of massive and metropolitan magnificence seldom discernible in much larger ones: it is indebted for this appearance to its having formerly been the winter residence of many of the noble and baronial families in the neighbourhood, some of whose mansions, with their stately turrets, still remain, and give an air of grandeur and antique dignity to all the surrounding houses. Though but few records now exist of the past glories of this place, yet it is at least evident that it might once boast of many of the proud attributes of a capital. The ruins of the collegiate church, established by Gilbert Kennedy in 1441, and desecrated at the Reformation, are still to be seen in the centre of the town. It was in an

upper room of a tenement in this town that John Knox,
and Quintin Kennedy, Abbot of Corsregal, held their celebrated disputation concerning the reformed doctrine of
the Church: it lasted three days, and was attended by
great crowds of people. The principal business of Maybole is that of cotton-weaving, besides which it possesses
a large manufactory for blankets, and a considerable trade
in shoes.

Saltcoats is one of the principal watering-places in the
county, furnishing accommodation in the season for many
visiters. Vast quantities of salt are made here; and it has
a considerable trade in coals, which are dug near the town,
as well as a manufacture of sail-cloth, a rope-yard, and
docks for building ships, not only for this port, but for
other towns.

Ballintree is situated in the southern nook of the county,
on a level part of the shore, close to the mouth of the little
river Stinchar, and was at no very remote period in a state
of primitive rudeness, which is sufficiently evinced by the
fact that within the last half-century there has not been
a single individual connected with the three learned facul-
ties residing in, or within twelve miles of it.—Which are
the principal rivers of Ayrshire?

ANNA.—The Doon and the Ayr.

MRS. ROWE.—The Dun, or Doon, springs from a lake
of the same name on the confines of Kirkcudbrightshire,
and flows in a winding course directly across the county to
join the sea.

The Ayr rises on the borders of Lanarkshire, and after
crossing the county, falls into the river Clyde near the town
of Ayr. The waters of this stream possess a petrifying
quality, and wood hardened in them makes excellent hones
for razors.

Loch Dun, or Doon, affords excellent sport for the angler,
but is remarkable on no other account, except that it sur-

rounds a Castle which belonged to Edward, the brother of Robert Bruce.

GEORGE.—A few miles north-west of Ayr is an island, called Lady Isle, which affords security and good anchorage for vessels upon this dangerous coast, in consequence of which the magistrates of Glasgow have erected two stone beacons on the north-west part of it.

South of this island, at the distance of 15 miles from the coast, stands the island of Ailsa, or Ailsa Craig: it is a most beautiful rock, of a conical shape, about two miles in circumference, and is covered on the top with heath and a little grass. On it stands an old ruinous Castle, which is said to have been erected by Philip II. of Spain. This island is not now inhabited by any human creature, but affords refuge for an immense number of sea-fowl, particularly the Solan goose: it is also the resort of rabbits and a few goats. It serves as a fine sea-mark for either coming in or going out of the Firth of Clyde.

MRS. ROWE.—Ayrshire is divided into three great districts. Cunningham, the most northerly, is a level and fertile tract, and is separated from Kyle, the central section (which is partly mountainous), by the river Irvine. Carrick, the southerly district, is little else than a vast tract of hills, which division is parted from Kyle by the river Doon. Previous to the year 1770 Ayrshire was in a very rude state,—destitute of roads, lands unimproved, and no manufactures; but it is now in every sense of the word a most important county, being highly productive, either in grain, cattle, the produce of the dairy, or mineral wealth. It possesses also a very large and active manufacturing community, and is endowed with a considerable share of historical and poetical information.

It was in this county that the doctrines of the Reformation were first promulgated in Scotland. Can you name any eminent character who was born in this county?

by Robert Bruce, who granted it a charter for that purpose.

Paisley, on the beautiful river Cart, is a large manufacturing town. The silk and thread gauze made here are so
neat and beautiful, that they have been displayed at Court
in the birthday dresses. The extensive cotton-works at
this town employ not only numbers of women, but even
very young girls; and here are besides considerable tan-,
soap-, and candle-works, and manufactures of ribbons, tapes,
inkle, and sewing thread. The magnificent Abbey for which
Paisley was once famed is partly in ruins; but the chapel,
which is entire, is noted for a remarkable echo, where the
violent shutting of a door produces an effect like thunder;
after which a melodious sound delights the ear, conveying
the idea of celestial harmony. At this town terminates the
northern point of the great Roman road, which stretches
from Carlisle through Dumfriesshire and Clydesdale, in
consequence of which it is supposed to have been an important station for the troops of that illustrious people,
under the name of Vanduaria; and some remains of a camp
or station are still visible.

GEORGE.—Cruickstone Castle, near this town, is the
place where the unfortunate Mary queen of Scots spent
the happy period of her union with the Lord Darnley;
and the favourite yew, which was so often impressed on
her copper coins, is still to be seen.

MRS. ROWE.—Elderslie, a town about three miles west
of Paisley, is chiefly worthy of notice as having been the
paternal seat of William Wallace. The present Castle appears to have been of later erection than the æra of that
hero; but the tree whose branches concealed him on a mo-
mentous occasion from the English, yet survives at a short
distance from it. Though the particular adventures of this
hero cannot now be discovered, yet the vast reputation he
gained has not, after the lapse of six centuries, lost its influence upon the popular feelings of the Scots.

Port Glasgow stands on a flat narrow piece of coast on the south side of the Clyde; and immediately behind the town the hills rise to a considerable height. This place was begun to be erected in 1710, in order to form a sea-port to the town of Glasgow. It has an excellent harbour and pier; and the channel, which is two hundred yards broad, and so deep at high water that the largest vessels can easily be moored without discharging any part of her cargo, lies along its shore. From the quays a magnificent prospect may be seen, the river Clyde (whose outlet to the sea, in consequence of its turning southward, is not seen,) having all the appearance of a fresh-water lake covered with vessels. The trade of this place consists in exporting the produce of the manufacturing districts situated upon the Clyde; and it partakes largely in the herring fisheries of the Firth of Clyde.

Greenock is a sea-port at the mouth of the Clyde, and is a place of great opulence and vast commercial enterprise. It has an extensive foreign trade: the imports are cotton, sugar, rum, grain, wine, and other articles for home consumption; the exports are the manufactured goods of the neighbourhood. It also partakes of the whale fishery, as well as that of herrings in the Firth of Clyde: its own manufactures are trifling, consisting of cordage and sail-cloth, sugar-baking, and some few others. The wealth resulting from successful commerce has caused this place to assume of late years a very fine appearance: the Custom-house, which is the finest public building, would do honour to any city in the world for its pure and beautiful style of Grecian architecture, as well as for the excellence of its materials; and it is a memorable proof of the opulence and public spirit of the inhabitants, that the subscription for its erection was filled up to the amount of 10,000l. in the short space of two days.

Gourock is a considerable village and sea-port, situated about three miles below Greenock, and is chiefly to be

noted for the melancholy catastrophe, the loss of the Comet
steam-packet, which occurred in the vicinity in 1825, by
which a number of unfortunate persons (passengers) lost
their lives.   At one end of this village is a huge stone,
where it is said a saint, named Kempock, formerly kept a
shop for the sale of 'winds' to credulous sailors.—Which
are the principal rivers in this county?

ANNA.—The Black and White Cart, which unite their
streams, and fall into the Clyde near Renfrew.

MRS. ROWE.—This county is noted for having been the
paternal residence of the Stuarts before they ascended the
throne, and still gives the title of baron to the king's eldest
son.   It may be described as being entirely subservient to
the great manufacturing town of the west, as its sea-ports,
villages, and towns are all suited to the convenience and
service of Glasgow, in spinning, weaving, and shipping;
and the beauties of nature are compelled to yield to the
more useful purposes of art.

The most valuable mineral in the county is coal, which
is in some parts very abundant.   The coal mine at Quarrel-
town is undoubtedly one of the most extraordinary masses
hitherto discovered; the thickness of the whole, measured
at right angles to the surface of the bed of coals, is upwards
of fifty feet.   It also possesses several limestone quarries,
one of which is worthy of particular notice: it is an enormous rock projecting from the brow of a hill, which contains the limestone in a mass about ten feet thick.   Several
mines have been driven into this rock, and from their having met in the heart of it, present a very singular subter-
ranean scenery.   Various other minerals have been discovered, particularly what is called the Osmund Stone.—Can
you name any distinguished character who was born in this
county?

GEORGE.—The brave general Sir William Wallace, who
nobly defended his country, and attempted to rescue it
from the English yoke.   He was endowed with great per-

onal strength and courage, possessed an active and pa-
riotic spirit, and by his affability, eloquence, and wisdom,
aintained an authority over the rude and undisciplined
ultitude who flocked to his standard. When arraigned at
Vestminster as a traitor to Edward, and for having burnt
illages, stormed castles, and slaughtered many subjects of
ngland, he indignantly exclaimed, "I never was a traitor!"
o the rest of the indictment he pleaded guilty.

LANARKSHIRE.

cundaries.—Dunbartonshire, Stirlingshire, Edinburghshire,
    Peeblesshire, Dumfriesshire, Ayrshire, and Renfrewshire.
owns.—1, Lanark; 2, Glasgow; 3, Rutherglen; 4, Hamilton;
    5, Bothwell; 6, Shots; 7, Carnworth; 8, Covington; 9, El-
    vanfoot Inn; 10, Lead Hills; 11, John's Castle; 12, Dou-
    glas; 13, Strathaven.
ivers.—a, the Clyde; b, the Avon; c, the Great Canal; d, Dou-
    glas.

[rs. Rowe.—WHAT are the boundaries, extent, and
ief towns of Lanarkshire?

Anna.—It is bounded on the north by the counties of
unbarton and Stirling, on the east by West and Mid Lo-
ian and Peeblesshire, on the south by Dumfriesshire,
d on the west by Ayrshire and Renfrewshire. Its ex-
eme length from north to south is about 43 miles; its
eatest width across the centre of the county from east to
est exceeds 30. The chief places are Glasgow, Lanark,
ouglas, Hamilton, Strathaven, Bothwell, Lead Hills, and
utherglen.

Mrs. Rowe.—Glasgow stands on the north bank of the
rer Clyde, and derives its name from the original gloomi-

ness of its situation in a woody ravine, *glas coed* signifying,
in the British language, 'dark wood'. It is the See of an archbishop, and possesses a University founded by James II.
in 1450. Its library is a spacious and elegant building, the
celebrity of which has been much increased from its possessing the valuable editions of the Classics by Robert and
Andrew Foulis. These patriotic citizens instituted an academy for painting and engraving, and made vast collections
in both those arts. The Cathedral of Glasgow is a stupendous Gothic structure : it was erected in the sixth century,
and dedicated to St. Mungo its founder. It contains two
churches, rising one above another, and has a fine spire
springing from a tower in the centre ; and at the western
extremity another tower projects from one of the corners,
which contains the bells. It was made an archiepiscopal
church at the end of the fifteenth century, and escaped the
fury of the Reformers through the resolution of the citizens, who in 1579 (when a great number of workmen were
assembled to demolish this vast monument of the piety of
their grandfathers,) took possession of it, and threatened the
first individual who should attempt to violate it with instant
death. Glasgow, from its extent, the beauty of its buildings, and its vast commercial importance, may be considered
the second city in Scotland. Its principal articles of trade
were originally rum and tobacco : these are now much declined ; but its cotton manufactures may be said to rival
those of Manchester in cheapness and elegance. It also
boasts of a pottery that emulates the Staffordshire ware in
beauty and neatness. Printing types are well executed
here ; and its glass manufactory has been very successful.
It likewise possesses manufactures of coarse earthenware,
hats, stockings, gloves, ropes, and cordage.

GEORGE.—I have read that the Great Canal in Scotland,
which extends from the river Forth to that of Clyde, is
carried in its course along a distance of nearly 36 miles
over ten considerable aqueduct bridges, and upwards of

thirty smaller ones, and that it is crossed by more than thirty drawbridges. The greatest of the aqueduct bridges is that of the Kelvin, which consists of four great arches of masonry: its height is 80 feet, and it crosses a valley of more than 400 feet in breadth; thus carrying a great artificial river over a natural one in a deep valley, above the bed of which large vessels are seen sailing along at an immense height. This canal is undoubtedly one of the most stupendous works of the kind anywhere to be seen; and for the supply of it there are six reservoirs, which cover upwards of 400 acres of land, and contain more than 12,000 locks full of water.

MRS. ROWE.—However detrimental this bold design may have been to picturesque scenery, it has been of the utmost utility in expediting the communication between the Eastern and Western Seas, as it shortens the nautical distance 800 (and in some parts 1000) miles, and affords a safe and speedy navigation to vessels bound to Ireland, or the western ports of Great Britain, that have been detained in the Baltic, and cannot attempt the voyage round by the North Sea without the danger of shipwreck, or the chance of an advantageous market being lost from delay.

Lanark, situated on the river Clyde, is an ancient town, which, though not very engaging in its external appearance, yet possesses many points of the truest and most fascinating interest, as it was here that the glorious Wallace made (and succeeded in) his first effort to redeem his country from the tyranny of the English. This town is indebted for its burgh privileges to Alexander the Fierce; and it is said to have been of great importance during the period of the wars of competition. Not far distant from this place is New Lanark, which is composed of a series of huge square buildings, connected with one or two streets: the principal of these are extensive cotton-mills, established in 1783, and the remainder are the residences of those concerned in the manufactures; and it is said that no persons are permitted to reside in the village unless they are connected with that branch of business.

Douglas stands on a small stream of the same name, and has a large annual fair held in the churchyard, at which great numbers of shoes are sold, that being the principal manufacture of the place. In the vicinity is Douglas Castle, which was built within the last century on the site of a former one, which was the original seat of the celebrated family of Douglas, whose greatness knew no bounds for the term of 150 years from their first elevation. The chief of this family often went abroad with a train of two thousand armed men, and, emulating royal authority, created knights, had his counsellors, and constituted a parliament. The sepulchral monuments of some of these heroes may be seen in a vault, which, having originally formed part of the church, still stands in the burial-ground of the village.

Hamilton stands in a low situation near the river Avon, and derives some importance from the roads from Glasgow towards England, and from Edinburgh to Ayrshire, passing through it. In 1548 Mary queen of Scotland created it a free royal burgh; but the rights and privileges thus acquired from the Crown were, after the Restoration, resigned into the hands of William duke of Hamilton, who in 1670 restored to the inhabitants its former possessions, and erected it into a burgh of regality dependent upon him and his successors. The present magnificent chateau of that nobleman is surrounded by venerable oaks, and was an extensive pile of but moderate external appearance, till, in 1826, a large addition, of better material and greater architectural grace, was made to it; and it is now considered in every respect one of the best houses in the country. It is situated in the beautiful Vale of Avon, near its confluence with the Clyde.

Strathaven may be said to owe its origin to its Castle, the shattered and haggard walls of which overhang the town: from an early period it was one of the seats of the Hamilton family.

ANNA.—It was here that Anne duchess of Hamilton (daughter of the Duke who perished at the battle of Worcester, and in whom ended the old line of the family,) resided during the period of the Commonwealth; and having been deprived of all her possessions, was supported solely by a faithful domestic, who is said to have employed herself for eight years in spinning, in order to procure the means of subsistence for Her Grace, till the Restoration terminated her misfortunes by reinvesting her in her estates.

MRS. ROWE.—It is also worthy of record, that when fortune again smiled on the noble lady she did not forget her humble benefactress, but showed her gratitude by presenting her with a sufficiency to support her in a state of honourable and truly merited independence.

Bothwell, near Hamilton, is a small neat village, which was formerly of more importance than at present, as may be supposed from the stately ruins of its Castle, which stand on an eminence on the banks of the Clyde, and are said to rank among the most magnificent remains of castellated architecture in Scotland. It was an important fortress in the time of the wars of competition, when Edward I. gave it to Aimer de Valence, whom he had made governor of the kingdom. After the battle of Bannockburn many English officers of rank took refuge in it, and were soon afterwards given up to Bruce by the governor, who took care to make good terms for himself.

GEORGE.—Bothwell Bridge, near this village, is noted in history for having in the year 1679 been the scene of a desperate conflict between the Covenanters under the command of Hackstown of Rathillet, and the Royalists headed by the Duke of Monmouth, who suddenly falling upon the enthusiastic and dissentious rebels, completely defeated them; and four hundred men being slain in the pursuit which ensued, he humanely interfered to spare the further effusion of blood.

MRS. ROWE.—The church, formerly collegiate, is a lofty
Gothic edifice, founded in 1398 by Archibald the Grim,
earl of Douglas. This building is said to be, by a strange
exercise of ancient art, cased all over with stone : upon one
of its windows the Douglas arms are to be seen quartered
with the royal arms of Scotland, probably in consequence
of the marriage of the Earl of Douglas with the heiress of
Bothwell, who was the granddaughter of Robert Bruce.

Lead Hills, though only a small village, is renowned for
being the highest human habitation in Great Britain.
Many hundreds of miners reside in it with their families,
who, though secluded in a great measure from society,
not only obtain a comfortable subsistence, but pay more
attention to the cultivation of the mind than many of their
countrymen whose situation is more favourable for the at-
tainment of knowledge. Besides immense quantities of
lead, these hills yield various kinds of ore, such as the
common plated, steel-grained, and the white lamellated and
fibrous ones, so highly thought of in the cabinets of the
curious.

Rutherglen appears to have been erected into a royal
burgh by King David I., and charters are extant confirming its privileges by Robert Bruce, and James V. and VI.
The Castle (which is now demolished, and its site converted
into a kitchen-garden,) was considered one of the most important fortresses of Scotland. It was in the hands of the
English during the wars regarding the succession, and was
attacked by Bruce in 1309. Edward I. sent his nephew
(the young Earl of Gloucester) to raise the siege, in which
he succeeded ; but it was subsequently taken by Bruce.
The church of Rutherglen is small, but very ancient, and
is famous on account of two transactions, in which the fate
of Sir William Wallace and his country was deeply concerned. It was in this edifice that a peace between Scotland and England was concluded, February 8, 1297 ; and

it was also the place in which Sir John Monteith contracted with the English to betray Wallace.—Name the principal rivers of this county.

ANNA.—The Clyde and the Avon.

MRS. ROWE.—The Clyde, which ranks as the third river in Scotland, springs from the mountainous district in the southern part of the county, and after a north-westerly course through Lanark and Glasgow, becomes an estuary at the place where this county joins those of Renfrew and Dunbarton.

ANNA.—Are there not some cataracts and romantic views on the banks of this river, called the Falls of Clyde?

MRS. ROWE.—Of the three falls two are above and one below the town of Lanark: the uppermost is Boniton Linn, where the river, with violent agitation and a far-extending mist, falls in a foaming sheet into a cascade 30 feet in depth. Just below this fall the water becomes prodigiously rapid; and in one point, in this part of its course, it struggles through a chasm not more than four feet broad. The next fall below is Cora Linn, where the water takes three distinct leaps from rock to rock, forming a rude slope of furious foam. The third fall of the Clyde occurs at Stonebyres, about two miles below the town of Lanark. This is more striking to behold than either of the others: it consists of two precipitous cataracts, falling one upon the other into a stupendous chasm below, from whence the river glides dejectedly away with numberless bubbles of foam upon its surface. A pavilion, erected about a century ago, stands on the opposite bank of the stream, as a sort of station for observing the falls. The great patriot Wallace is said to have concealed himself in the cliffs of this wild retreat whilst meditating the salvation of his country.

The Avon rises on the western side of the county, and pursues a north-easterly course to unite its waters with the Clyde near Hamilton.

GEORGE.—It is a singular fact, that the Clyde, Tweed,

and Annan, each of which falls into a different sea at different sides of the kingdom, find their sources in one clump of rising grounds, in the centre of the county south of the Forth.

Lanarkshire, otherwise denominated Clydesdale, from its being simply the vale formed by the river Clyde, is generally considered the principal inland county in the southern division of Scotland, and the most populous of all, being the great theatre of manufactures and commerce. The Vale of Clyde, which is its third and most poetical designation, is divided into three wards, called the Upper, Middle, and Lower Ward. The first comprehends three fifths of the county, and is a mountainous district. The Middle and Lower Wards are of a much more fertile character. Each of the wards is governed by a sheriff-substitute, appointed by a sheriff-deputy of the county. Its mineral treasures consist of coal, limestone, freestone, iron, lead, and some quarries of lapis lazuli ; but coal of various descriptions is its most valuable mineral production, and for which it is particularly celebrated.—Can you name any noted character who was born in Lanarkshire?

ANNA.—William Lithgow, a celebrated traveller in the reign of James VI. He is said to have been a strange compound of good sense, fanaticism, impudence, and pedantry. He went over a great part of Europe and Asia, and returned home dreadfully maimed and disfigured by the inquisitors of Spain, who were instigated to revenge by his insufferable insolence regarding their religion.

Allan Ramsay, a poet of great merit, famed as the author of the ' Gentle Shepherd,' which has been universally read and admired.

LINLITHGOWSHIRE, or WEST LOTHIAN.

Boundaries.—Stirlingshire, Edinburghshire, Lanarkshire, and the Firth of Forth.
Towns.—1, Linlithgow; 2, Borrowstounness, or Bo'ness; 3, Queensferry; 4, Torphichen.
Rivers.—a, the Almond; b, the Avon.

MRS. ROWE.—WHAT are the boundaries, extent, and chief towns of Linlithgowshire?

GEORGE.—It is bounded on the north by the Firth of Forth, on the east by Edinburghshire, on the south by Lanarkshire, and on the west by Stirlingshire. Its length is about 17 miles, and its mean breadth 7. It contains the towns of Linlithgow, Queensferry, Torphichen, and Borrowstounness or Bo'ness.

MRS. ROWE.—Linlithgow, the county town, is an ancient, large, and regularly built royal burgh, standing on a rising ground near a lake, which is famous for the bleaching quality of its water. This town carries on a considerable trade in dressing white leather, in flax, and in wool-combing. A fort was erected here by Edward I., who made it his residence for one winter. It was taken by the Scots in 1307, but was again in the possession of the English during the wars for the restoration of the Baliol dynasty. This Castle was, with the nave of the church, burnt down in 1424, but was rebuilt soon afterwards in a style of superior magnificence, to the embellishment of which James V. and James VI. greatly contributed. Over the entry of a fortified gateway to the exterior court, which includes both the palace and the church, are the remains of four frames of stone, which formerly contained the four orders of knighthood borne by

Protestant cause in 1572. But he rejected the offer with contempt and indignation, saying he had no authority from Scotland to commit murder in France; he had avenged his own just quarrel, but he would neither for price nor prayer avenge that of another man.

At that period the desolation occasioned by the civil wars was so great, that all natural ties were dissolved in political hatred. Blinded by religious zeal, fellow-citizens, brothers and friends ranged on different sides; that reciprocal good will and confidence which ought to bind men together in society were then extinguished; and even the more sacred ties of relationship were utterly forgotten.

Queensferry is a royal burgh, seated on the Firth of Forth, and is supposed to have derived its name from Margaret, queen of Malcolm Canmore, who probably patronized the inhabitants: it is now nothing more than a village of moderate extent. Its harbour serves as a retreat for vessels in hard gales, and also for the importation of coals: it has also several boats employed in the fisheries.

Torphichen is a little straggling village about five miles directly south of Linlithgow: it was once a place of great distinction, where the Knights of St. John (a powerful body of military ecclesiastics, arising out of the Crusades, and who finally possessed vast wealth, as well as landed property in all the countries of Europe,) had their chief Preceptory, the splendour of which is now only attested by fragments of massive and castellated old buildings. Of the church of this establishment (erected in the reign of David I.) the choir and transepts only now remain: in the interior of the former is shewn the monument of Walter Lindsay, who died in 1588.

George.—History records that this religious edifice, like many others, not only afforded an asylum to fugitives and inmates, but that it had a precinct extending the distance of one mile in every direction from the church yard, and marked by stones with a cross cut on the top, which denoted the

EDINBURGHSHIRE, or MID LOTHIAN.

Boundaries.—Haddingtonshire, Berwickshire, Roxburghshire, Lanarkshire, Peeblesshire, Selkirkshire, Linlithgowshire, and the Firth of Forth.

Towns.—Edinburgh, 1; Leith, 2; Musselburgh, 3; Dalkeith; 4, Roslin; 6, Falls; 7, Middleton.

Rivers.—a, the Esk; b, Galla; c, Leith.

WHAT are the boundaries, extent, and chief towns of Edinburghshire, or Mid Lothian?

It is bounded on the north by the Firth of Forth; on the east by the counties of Haddington, Berwick, and Roxburgh; on the south by Lanark, Peebles, and Selkirk; and on the west by Linlithgowshire. Along its southern border it extends from south-east to north-west upwards of 40 miles: its northern boundary, by the shores of the Forth, is so curved that its mean extent is 27 miles in that direction, whilst from north to south it is about 17 miles. It contains the City of Edinburgh, with Leith, Musselburgh, Dalkeith, and Roslin.

The City of Edinburgh is distinguished by the names of the New Town and Old Town.

been unknown to the Romans, though they had stations at
no great distance from its site; but the rudiments of the
present city are supposed to have been formed in the reign
of Malcolm II., who obtained the whole of the district of
Lothian from Eadulf, a Northumbrian earl; though it is
not noticed in history before the time of Alexander I., when
it was held as a town of the royal demesne. In the reign
of James II. it became the favourite residence of the Court,
and began to assume the dignity of a capital; at which time
it was walled round, made the scene of the principal affairs
of Church and State, and rapidly increased in size and prosperity, which it retained uninterruptedly till the accession
of James VI. to the crown of England. During the reign
of George III. it was extended and improved in such a
style, as to render it not only worthy of the first rank among
Scottish cities, but an object of admiration to all strangers.
The most ancient and preeminent architectural edifice is
its Castle, which stands on a lofty and precipitous rock,
and is accessible only by means of a drawbridge : it not
only overlooks the city, its environs, gardens, the New
Town, and a fine rich country, but it commands a most extensive view of the Forth, the shipping, the coast of Fife,
and some distant hills that border upon the Highlands.
This fortress is supposed to have been built by the Saxon
king Edwin, whose territory extended to the river Forth,
as it certainly did not fall into the hands of the Scots till
the reign of Indulphus, who lived in the year 953.

ANNA.—In this Castle died, in 1093, Margaret the
queen of Malcolm III.; and whilst her remains lay in it
(previous to interment), the fortress was besieged by Do-
naldbaine, uncle to Malcolm, who usurped the throne : the
body was conveyed away by stealth, the concealment of
which was aided by a mist, that continued till it was safely
deposited at Queensferry ; and this was regarded as the
merciful interposition of Providence to preserve the royal
relics from insult.

... William Francis, who said, " Methinks ... would ... devise some means of entering yonder ... with the assurance for you with no greater ... a twelve-foot ladder may afford. Know that my ... the keeper of that fortress, and I, a wild gallant ... in the town below : in order to obtain ... access to her, I used to descend by a ladder ... and precipitous path in these cliffs; and this I ... quently practised, that the darkest night was no ... my retiring. If, therefore, it pleases you ... guide, I will be your guide, and the foremost in the ... peril." Murray assented with joy to the proposal, ... at the head of thirty men followed the directions ... The darkness of the night, steepness of the ... danger of discovery from the watchmen, and ... posts which they had from crag to crag, rendered the ... pace such as might have appalled the bravest ... however arrived safely at the wall, which they ... though the constable (who had been too late ... of the alarm by the sentinels' cry of "Treason" ... vigorous defence, they soon became master of the ... this edifice, was ... ...

MARY REAMY.—The room in which the unfortunate Queen Mary, on the 19th of June 1566, gave birth to James the Sixth of Scotland and First of England, is still carefully preserved; besides that, there is another apartment in this Castle closely bolted, which contains the regalia of Scotland. In 1745 this fortress was besieged by the mountaineers, but for want of artillery they did not succeed in taking it: since that period it has been more useful as a barrack than a fortress. At the opposite end of the High Street is Holyrood House, originally an abbey, founded by David I., and considerably improved by James V.; but it was indebted to the taste of Sir William Bruce, and the munificence of Charles II., for its principal beauties. Beneath the ruins of its chapel repose the ashes of James II., James V., Henry Darnley, and many other persons of rank. In the park (which was first inclosed by James I.) are two vast rocks, known by the names of Arthur's Seat and Salisbury's Crag: these exhibit a wild and romantic scene of precipices, columns, and broken masses, and in some places appear to impend the city. Beneath this pile is a freestone quarry, which produces excellent stone for paving.

ASYL.—The magnificent palace of Holyrood (which had nearly fallen into decay from being uninhabited), after the revolution in France, became conspicuous from being made the retreat of a part of the royal family of that kingdom, who during the usurpation of Buonaparte were compelled to abandon their country, and took refuge in this asylum. In 1830 Charles X., a member of the same family, who had succeeded to the dignity of a sovereign, abdicated his throne, and with his relatives and few remaining friends once more found a protection within the precincts of this venerable pile.

MEN. ROWN.—It also affords protection to insolvent debtors from their creditors.

GEORGE.—Darnley, who was interred in the chapel of this edifice, was the husband of Queen Mary, and the instigator of the murder of her favourite David Rizzio, a deed which, for its violence and cruelty, will ever disgrace the annals of history. This unfortunate man, who had at first

possessed this greatest share of the king's favour, ... time ... to his ... in proportion as he was distin-
guished by the queen. The weak-minded Darnley, ... obedient jealousy ... the interposition of such an upstart, ... ly resolved to get rid of him by violence ... communicated his ... to Lord Ruthven, and requested his assistance. The partiality shown to Rizzio ... Her ... offensive to the Court, and Ruthven, ... abled to ... his own revenge (under pretence of obey-
ing the king's will), readily acceded to his proposals. Ac-
cordingly, on the 9th of March 1566, ... the ... Colonsa of Argyle, and Rizzio were at supper together, the king suddenly entered by a private passage, behind whom was Ruthven clad in armour, who from a long sick-
ness looked pale and ghastly. Such an unusual appearance ... terror in the breasts of all who were present ... the unhappy victim, suspecting that he was the object of their search, retired behind the queen, hoping to find pro-
tection ... reverence due to her person ... nothing could ... the assassins, who with a furious mien and ... commanded Rizzio to leave a place ... which he was, ... Mary vainly employed tears, ... and entreaties to save her favourite; he was torn from her by violence, and before he could be dragged through the next apartment, his body was pierced with ... This royal exercise of mercy was ... ... Rizzio. Thus terminated the career of Rizzio, ... an Italian musician, ... came ... the Piedmontese ambassador to Scotland in 1564 ... finding ... regarded him with particular ... of ... he remained in her dominions. Though Darnley had ... knowledge of Rizzio's murder ... contrivance and completion ...

The next public building of importance is the University, erected within the last century by subscription, on the site of one which was founded by James VI., and which was more calculated for the sober literary characters of those days than for the elegant and refined taste of their successors. About the time of the Restoration it is recorded that the students were much tainted by the fanatical principles of the Covenanters; but since the reign of William III. their sole object has been the advancement of science. Cherished by the munificence of the sovereign, and the faithful adherence of the magistrates, this University has gradually advanced in reputation; and in every branch of science connected with medicine, it is considered to rank very high.

ANNA.—The people of Edinburgh, as well as the Scotch nation in general, are famed for possessing great presence of mind and resolution in situations of danger and difficulty.

MRS. ROWE.—It has been said that even mobs have often conducted their designs with all the address and perseverance of legitimate assemblies, a striking example of which occurred in the year 1736, in the murder of Captain Porteous, commandant of the City Guard, who had ordered his men to fire on the riotous populace, by which some of them were killed; and who, being tried for this act of necessary (or wanton) severity, was condemned, but reprieved. This royal exercise of mercy was considered by the Edinburghers as an insult to the dignity of their city; and inflamed by resentment, they dragged the unfortunate officer from his prison, and hanged him in public; after which the mob dispersed in perfect tranquillity to their respective homes. The principal agents in this outrage were well known; yet no one would impeach them, and by the favour and fidelity of their fellow-citizens, they escaped the vengeful inquiries of the Government.

Leith, though situated at the distance of two miles from the metropolis, forms its sea-port, and is a flourishing place,

The harbour is secured by a grand stone-pier at the mouth of the little river called the Water of Leith, and is accommodated with an elegant drawbridge; and as, owing to the eligible situation of this port for navigation, its commerce is very extensive; its largest vessels are employed in the Greenland whale fishery. The principal exports of Leith are lead, glass-ware, linen, woollen stuffs, &c. in return for which it receives the varied productions of all parts of the world. It possesses also flourishing manufactures of bottle- and window-glass, and crystal; a large one for carpets; likewise soap-works, rope-walks, and iron forges; and it has also an hospital for disabled seamen.

In the year 1560 this place was gallantly defended against the English by the French under Mary of Guise, the queen dowager and regent of Scotland.

At this place landed Mary queen of Scotland, after having been educated in France. She embarked at Calais on the 19th of August 1561; and she was so much affected at leaving France, that she refused to retire to the cabin or taste food whilst that coast was in sight. She was frequently heard to sigh and exclaim, "Farewell, France! Farewell, beloved country, which I shall never more behold!" And although she was received by her subjects with every demonstration of joy, respect, and welcome, yet she was deeply affected, and unable to conceal the concern she felt at the absence of that magnificence and splendour to which she had been accustomed from her infancy.

Musselburgh, a sea-port of considerable importance from its extensive fishery, derives its name from a muscle bank lying in the sea below. It is an ancient burgh of regality, although the precise era of its foundation is unknown; but it was rendered of historical importance in the year 1332, when Randolph earl of Murray, being on his way to check the incursions of the English upon the border, died here.

Dalkeith, on the river Esk, formerly possessed a fine castle, built on a perpendicular rock, inaccessible on all sides, except the east, where it was defended by a fosse. In the year 1577 (when it afforded a shelter to the regent Morton) it received the appellation of the "Den of Lions." Its present magnificent palace was erected on the same spot about the beginning of the eighteenth century, and is the principal seat of the Duke of Buccleuch. The staircase, a conservatory of birds, and the bed upon which His late Majesty George IV. reposed when he visited Scotland in 1822, are exhibited as curiosities to strangers. This town is noted for the number of shops it contains, the greater part of which are devoted to the sale of spirituous liquors.

Roslin was once of much greater importance than at present, which is evinced by its magnificent ruins, and from which it appears to have held at one time high rank among the cities of Scotland. The remains of a small chapel, founded in 1440 by William St. Clare (who lived in magnificence in his castle in the vicinity), are worthy of admiration, and exhibit a beautiful specimen of Gothic architecture. The profusion of its decorations is astonishing, and would be tedious in description; some of them are really sermons in stone, being illustrations of the Bible cut in a most extraordinary style. This beautiful edifice was desecrated by a mob from Edinburgh at the Revolution. Of the Castle, which overhangs the picturesque glen of the river Esk, but little of its ancient grandeur is remaining, as amidst its massive ruins a modern house has been reared, and resembles an insignificant laird of the present day surrounded by the ghosts of his forefathers.

GEORGE.—It was in the neighbourhood of this place that in 1302 the English army, under Sir John de Gave, sustained no fewer than three defeats in one day, from the Scots, who were commanded by Commyn and Fraser.

MRS. ROWE.—Which are the principal rivers of this county?

ANNA.—The Esk, Leith, and Galla.

MRS. ROWE.—The Esk rises in the borders of Peebles-

shire, and pursues a north-easterly course through Dalkeith
to the Firth of Forth, which it enters at Musselburgh.

The Leith springs from the southern part of the county,
and flows parallel with the Esk to the Firth of Forth at
Leith.

The Galla rises in the eastern part, and after a southerly
course for some miles, leaves this county for Roxburghshire.

Edinburghshire, or, as it is more generally termed, Mid
Lothian, in point of natural features bears a strong resemblance to Linlithgowshire, being an inclined plane rising from
the southern shore of the Firth of Forth, interspersed with
hills and valleys, and adorned with pleasing and picturesque
views. The fertility of its soil, and the state of its agriculture, rank amongst the highest in Scotland; and few of
the Scottish counties are richer in mineral productions than
this, as it abounds in coal, limestone, and freestone, all of
which are of superior quality.—What distinguished characters can you name that were born in this county ?

GEORGE.—Dr. John Campbell, celebrated as the author
of several works, particularly the 'Ancient and Modern
Universal History,' the 'Lives of the English Admirals,'
and the ' Present State of Europe.'

Dr. John Gregory, eminent as a physician, but still more
so by his writings in favour of morality. His 'Comparative
View of the State of Man and other Animals,' and 'A
Father's Legacy to his Daughters,' have been universally
read.

John Keill, a mathematician and philosopher. He was
Savilian Professor of Astronomy at Oxford, and wrote
some useful treatises on that subject.

Dr. William Robertson, an eminent historian and divine.
His great works are the 'History' of Charles V.' the
'History of America,' and the 'History of Scotland.' Few
men have surpassed him in the attainments of learning, in
talents as an author, and in exemplary attention in discharging the duties of life.

HADDINGTONSHIRE, or EAST LOTHIAN.

Boundaries.—Berwickshire, Edinburghshire, Firth of Forth, and the North Sea.

Towns.—1, Haddington; 2, North Berwick; 3, Dunbar; 4, Preston Pans; 5, Scateraw.

Rivers.—a, the Tyne,

Lochs, Islands, &c.—A, Bresmennan Loch; B, Isle of Brass; C, Spot Law, and Doon Hills; D, North Berwick Law.

MRS. ROWE.—DESCRIBE the situation, extent, and chief towns in Haddingtonshire.

ANNA.—It is bounded on the north by the Firth of Forth, on the east by the North Sea, on the south by Berwickshire, and on the west by the county of Edinburgh. It measures from east to west about 25 miles, and from north to south 18; and contains the towns of Haddington, Dunbar, North Berwick, and Preston Pans.

MRS. ROWE.—Haddington, the capital, is an ancient and populous town, and has long been the seat of an extensive woollen manufactory, in which, till the time of the usurpation of Cromwell, only the coarser articles were made; about that period an English company (of which Colonel Stanfield was the principal partner,) erected some mills and dyeing-houses, and at an immense expense succeeded in establishing a valuable manufacture of fine cloths. Near the Abbey of this town was the seat of a priory of nuns, founded in the year 1198 by Ada countess of Northumberland, daughter of the English earl of Warren, widow of Prince Henry son of David I, king of Scotland, and mother to Malcolm IV, and William surnamed the Lion. This monastery was dedicated to the Virgin Mary, not a

vestige of it now remains, but the mound on which it stood
was held in great reputation long after its destruction. The
town of Haddington has suffered severely from fire at various periods: in 1244 it was entirely consumed; and although at that time (in consequence of the houses being
built of wood and covered with thatch), towns and cities
were liable to frequent calamities from that denominated
element, it is suspected that the origin of this misfortune was more from design than accident, as in the night
on which Haddington was burnt, Stirling, Roxburgh,
Lanark, Perth, Forfar, Montrose, and Aberdeen, shared
the same fate. In 1355 the merciless Edward III. of England wreaked his vengeance on the Scots (who during his
absence in France had seized upon the town of Berwick
and besieged the Castle), by reducing this and the neighbouring towns to ashes. In 1598 almost the whole town
was again consumed, owing to the negligence of a female
servant, in consequence of which a person was appointed
to go through the streets every night at eight o'clock, who,
after tolling a bell, repeated a few rude rhymes expressive
of these misfortunes, and warning the inhabitants to make
use of greater caution in future; and this custom is still
kept up on the anniversary of the accident. After so many
demolitions it is not surprising that not a vestige now remains of the fortifications, which were once very strong.

Dunbar is agreeably situated on an eminence by the sea-
coast, nearly half way between Edinburgh and Berwick.
Its Castle is of such great antiquity, that the time of its
erection is not known; but it is recorded that it was nearly
consumed by fire in 858, and that in 1073 it was the property of the Earl of March, in which family it appears to
have remained some time.

GEORGE.—In 1337 this Castle was besieged by the Earl
of Salisbury, who was obliged to retire after having remained before Dunbar nineteen days. The Earl of March
being absent, his wife, the grand-niece of Bruce, although

better known in Scottish history by the name of Black
Agnes, commanded the defence. This lady well supported the masculine character she assumed, by vigorously animating the garrison by her exhortations, munificence, and example: when stones were hurled down
against the battlements, which covered her with dust, she
scornfully ordered one of her female attendants to wipe off
the dust with her handkerchief; and when, by the order of
the Earl of Salisbury, an enormous machine, called a Sowe,
was advanced to the foot of the wall, she indignantly ad-
vised him to be wary, and immediately commanded a large
rock to be precipitated upon it, by which means it was instantly crushed to pieces. Finding so stout a resistance,
her opponents endeavoured to accomplish by treachery
what it was impossible to effect by bravery, and accordingly
bribed the person who had the care of the gates to leave
them open: this was agreed to; but the countess was informed of the whole transaction, and appointed some person
to be stationed so as to be able to let down the portcullis as
soon as the first man entered (who she doubted not would
be the commander), and by this means secure him prisoner:
but one of his attendants hastily passing before his general,
was made captive in his place. Agnes viewed this event
from a high tower, and on seeing Salisbury's retreat, cried
out in derision, "Farewell, Montague! I intended that you
should have supped with us, and assisted us in defending
the fortress against the English."

Mrs. Rowe.—The old church of Dunbar, which was built
in the form of a cross, was the first collegiate church in
Scotland, being converted from its parochial condition to
that rank in 1342. This ancient edifice was changed into
a more handsome and modern one in 1819, which contains
one of the most splendid marble monuments in the kingdom, to perpetuate the memory of Sir George Home,
created Earl of March and Dunbar by James VI. The
coast near this town is remarkable for its perilous character,

...part of which, at the mouth of the Tyne, is particularly dangerous; and on Tyne Sands (as they are termed) many a brave sailor has found a watery grave.—Whitekirk.—GEORGE.—In the neighbourhood of this place was fought the celebrated battle of Dunbar, in which Cromwell overthrew the Scottish army in 1650. The cause of this signal defeat has been ascribed to the impetuosity of the Scots; for had they remained still, the hero of the Commonwealth must have been starved into a surrender; but being inflamed by the indiscreet zeal of their clerical leaders (much against the will of their commander), they began an irregular attack, which terminated in a total rout and the loss of a great number of valiant men.

Mrs. Rows.—This town was entirely burnt by the English army which Henry VIII. sent, in 1548, to avenge the obstinacy of the Scots in refusing to permit the marriage of their young queen (Mary) with his son (afterwards Edward VI.). Under the rock on which the ruins of its Castle stand are two natural arches, through which the tide flows. Here are also vast basaltic columns of red gritstone, in some respects resembling those of the Giant's Causeway in Ireland. Dunbar trades largely in malt and grain, also North Berwick was once a sea-port of some importance, but is now inconsiderable, and noted only for the ruins of its old Cistercian Priory, founded by Duncan earl of Fife. A short distance from this place, on a high rock overlooking the sea, stand the ruins of Tamtallon Castle, formerly one of the strongholds of the Douglases, and for some time in the possession of James V., who in 1527 perfidiously obtained it of the person to whom it was intrusted. Preston-Pans is a considerable village, and has long been noted for its salt manufacture; and in addition to its salt-pans it possesses a thriving ... of stone-ware. in passing ... also well known for having been the scene of an engagement in 1745, in which the rebel army obtained a decisive victory over the king's forces, with great carnage, and inspired the wavering to join the standard of disaffection.

MRS. ROWE.—Which is the principal river of this county?

GEORGE.—The Tyne, which rises on the confines of Edinburghshire; and after a north-easterly course through Haddington, it falls into the Firth of Forth a few miles north-west of Dunbar.

MRS. ROWE.—This county possesses no eminences that are deserving of the appellation of mountains: Spot Law, about four miles south-west of Dunbar, Doon Hill in its vicinity, and North Berwick Law, near the town of that name, are the most important hills. Bresmennan Lake, a few miles south-east of Haddington, is a beautiful piece of water, about two miles long: its banks are thickly planted with wood, which rise to a great height on both sides, and afford picturesque scenery. In the mouth of the Firth of Forth is a small island, called the Bass, which is an insulated rock, accessible only on the south-west part of it, and there it requires the aid of a rope and ladder. It is supplied with water by a well at the top; and in the spring it is almost covered with nests and eggs of gannets (or Solan geese). The flocks of these birds are at times so prodigious as to entirely darken the air; and their noise is so great, that people when close together can with difficulty hear each other speak. It has a rabbit-warren, and pasture for a few sheep.

ANNA.—This island is of historical importance, as in 1405 it was the retreat of the Prince of Scotland, afterwards James I., when it was found necessary to send him to France, in order to secure him from the machinations of the duke of Albany. He was kept there till a vessel came to remove him; after which he was seized by the English in passing Flamborough Head, and imprisoned nineteen years. Many of the most eminent of the Covenanters in the reign of Charles II. were confined here; and it was the last portion of Great Britain that submitted to the authority of William III., being defended for James II. of England and VII. of Scotland, by David Blair, who many retired to France, and died there. The garrison, on this occasion, acted for several months in opposition to the newly constituted powers, not only repelling but actually attacking their enemies. They had a large boat, which they hoisted up and down at pleasure, and in which they committed many daring piracies. The failure of their supplies of provision from France alone compelled them to surrender.

MRS. ROWE.—Haddingtonshire is considered both a valuable and interesting county, and forms the eastern portion of the Lothian district. It is chiefly distinguished for its fertility, and the excellence of its agriculture: the land is in many places doubly productive, affording immense quantities of coal, while rich crops of corn are raised on its surface. The high grounds in the southern part of the county (comprehending the northern slope of the Lammermuir Hills, which divide it from Berwickshire,) feed vast numbers of sheep. It has few manufactures, but is rich in relics of antiquity and legendary lore, and possesses many attractions for the poet and historian.—Can you mention any celebrated character who was born here?

GEORGE.—John Knox, whose strenuous exertions in forwarding the work of the glorious Reformation will ever make his memory revered. Zeal, intrepidity, and disinterestedness were the prominent features of his character. His temper, however, was too violent; and the acrimony and vehemence with which he admonished, often irritated where he meant to reclaim.

Andrew Fletcher, a patriotic statesman, who in 1710 took with him to Holland a skilful mechanic, and brought back models of a barley-mill, fanners for cleaning corn, and the art of weaving and bleaching Holland cloth. The barley-mill erected by him was the only one in Britain for forty

MRS. ROWE.—Berwick is not included in any critical

years, and the farmers for corn for the same period. The first bleach-field of the British Linen Company was formed under the patronage of this gentleman in 1750.

Andrew Meikle, father of the mechanic who accompanied Fletcher to Holland, and inventor of the threshing-machine.

George Heriot, founder of the Hospital at Edinburgh.

BERWICKSHIRE.

Boundaries.—Haddingtonshire, Edinburghshire, Roxburghshire, Northumberland, and the North Sea.

Towns.—1, Berwick-upon-Tweed; 2, Lady Kirk; 3, Coldstream; 4, Dryburgh; 5, Lauder; 6, Greenlaw; 7, Dunse; 8, Gavinton; 9, Eyemouth; 10, Ayton; 11, Coldingham; 12, Lammerton.

River.—a, the Tweed; b, the White Adder; c, Lauder; d, Eye; e, Black Adder.

Capes, Districts, &c.—A, St. Abb's Head; B, the Merse District; C, Lammermuir; D, Lauderdale.

Mrs. Rowe.—TELL me the situation, extent, and chief towns of Berwickshire.

George.—This county is bounded on the north by Haddingtonshire; on the east by the North Sea; south by Roxburghshire and Northumberland, from which counties it is separated by the Tweed in its principal course; and on the west by the county of Edinburgh, or Mid-Lothian limits. It measures from east to west about 36 miles, and from north to south 16; and contains the towns of Berwick-on-Tweed, Lauder, Coldstream, Greenlaw, Dunse, and the parishes of Lady Kirk, Hume, Lammerton, Gavinton, Eyemouth, and Coldingham.

Mrs. Rowe.—Berwick is not included in any territory,

but forms a separate district from the county to which it gives name; and though deprived of much of its original importance, is still a considerable town, situated on a gentle declivity close by the North Sea, on the north side of the mouth of the river Tweed. It is totally unlike any other town in Britain; and the most obvious idea which a sight of it is calculated to suggest, is, that it resembles the fortified cities of the Continent on a miniature scale. Berwick was garrisoned for the last time by Charles I., for the purpose of overawing the Covenanters; he himself spent a few weeks in it, and settled a treaty with his Scotch subjects in the year 1639. In 1482 this town was finally wrested from Scotland, and, from a convention between the Governments, was declared free of both countries, though garrisoned by the English. The Castle, which was formerly a strong fortress, is gone to decay. The present church was built by Oliver Cromwell, and (in accordance with the spirit of its founder) has no steeple. Here are the remains of several convents, erected at various periods by Scottish monarchs. Abundance of wool and eggs are exported from this inland, and the revenues received from the salmon-fisheries are very considerable. The chief article of importation is timber from Norway.

Lauder, although a royal burgh, is only a small village, altogether destitute of manufactures, but shares, however, with the general improvement of this part of the country, which is increased from one of the great English roads being conducted through it. Its church was in the reign of James III. the scene of a singular act of aristocratic pride. this infatuated sovereign had caressed a mason named Cochran, earl of Mar, who, with Horshill (called) because a smith, Rogers a musician, and Torfian a fencing-master, assisted him in all his councils. The nobles, upon being summoned to concert measures for repelling some foreign invaders, assembled in this sacred place to agree upon the best way of ridding themselves of such ignorant directors. During this meeting, the unsuspicious Cochran went there, attended by a band of warriors, and in all the pride of royal favour demanded the cause of such an assembly. Cochran was not, however, permitted to return to his sovereign with the intelligence; for these infuriated nobles immediately seized him and his brother counsellors, and hanged them over a bridge in sight of the king and his army. This ancient ecclesiastical edifice was destroyed in 1676 by order of the Duke of Lauderdale, owing to its being situated too near his castle, and another was erected at some distance, which, though in the venerable form of the Cross, is not remarkable for elegance. As the buildings of this town are of an ordinary and somewhat irregular cast, and Nature has spread few charms around, it may be confessed to have no prepossessing appearance.

Coldstream is an agreeable and thriving town upon the river Tweed, near the place where it ceases to be a boundary between the two kingdoms. It formerly received great importance from a ford, but it now derives much more from a bridge erected over its river. Previous to the Reformation it had a rich priory of Cistercian Nuns; but not one fragment of this building now remains. There is a tradition that its abbess sent vehicles to the fatal field of Flodden, and brought away the bodies of the higher orders of the soldiers who were slain, and interred them here.

GEORGE.—General Monk resided at Coldstream at the time he was waiting for an opportunity to enter England in order to effect the Restoration; and during the winter of 1659 (which he spent in it,) he raised a regiment of horse, which was then named, and has ever since been denominated, the Coldstream Guards.

MRS. ROWE.—Without any assistance from manufactures, this town seems to subsist from the thoroughfare which its bridge has occasioned, and from the trade which is supplied by the opulent agricultural country around it.

Greenlaw lies in a valley upon the north bank of the Black Adder, over which there are two bridges. It was formerly seated upon the summit of an eminence about a mile to the south, and its site is said to have altered upon its becoming the capital of the county. In the centre of a square market-place is the Cross, which is a neat Corinthian pillar, surmounted by a lion presenting the coat armorial of the Earl of Marchmont, who erected it. The church is a plain edifice, and its steeple is said to have been formerly used as the county jail.

Dunse is an ancient and populous town, and derives its name from the old Celtic word *dun*, which signifies 'a hill,' its original situation having been on the top of a beautiful little eminence called Dunse Law: but the present town stands at the foot of this hill, and is always considered the emporium of Berwickshire, as it possesses all the attributes of a county town except the privileges and the name. It has no manufactures, but derives considerable employment from weaving for the town of Glasgow. Dunse Castle is a magnificent new house, in what is called the castellated style. It was erected partly upon the remains of one which had been the property of that glorious patriot Randolph earl of Murray: the interior decorations of this building are truly splendid, and some of them curiously beautiful.

ANNA.—The ancient Castle of Dunse was remarkable for having been the head-quarters of General Leslie in 1639, when he lay with the Scottish army on the top of the neighbouring Law: and it is said that the apartment in which he and his officers dined was preserved untouched at the re-edification, and is now used as the butler's room in the Castle.

MRS. ROWE.—Lady Kirk, a few miles to the west of Berwick, is noted only for its church, which was erected by King James IV., and is one of the few Gothic buildings of the kind that survived the Reformation.

GEORGE.—The legend connected with the origin of this

church gives it an additional claim to notice, as it records that when James, at the head of his army, was crossing the Tweed by a ford in the neighbourhood, he suddenly found himself in a perilous situation from the violence of the flood, which had nearly carried him away: in his emergency he vowed to build a church, and dedicate it to the Virgin Mary, if she would deliver him; and this edifice, when constructed, was consequently called Lady Kirk, a name which extended to the whole parish, formerly designated Upsettlington.

MRS. ROWE.—The ford also is of historical importance, from being the passage by which the English and Scotch generally invaded the territories of each other before the erection of the bridge at Berwick, which did not take place till the reign of Elizabeth queen of England. It was likewise a place of conference; and in an adjacent field, called Holywell Haugh, King Edward I. met the Scottish nobility, to settle the dispute between Bruce and Baliol relative to the throne of Scotland.

Hume was once much more extensive than at present, stretching to a considerable distance all round its ancient Castle, upon the ruinous walls of which the present one was built, and is the only object in the village worthy of notice. In the former Castle resided the ancient and powerful family whose name it bears, or rather confers.

ASNA.—This fortress was besieged in 1547 by the English under the Duke of Somerset, when, after having stood out for some time under the command of Lady Hume, it was delivered up on fair terms. It was the station of one of the beacons erected during the last war for the alarm of the country in case of invasion, and partook in the celebrated mistake in 1803, when the chain of beacons were lighted throughout this district, and the militia of a great part of the South of Scotland were roused and collected in the course of a night, as recorded in the well-known novel, 'The Antiquary.'

MRS. ROWE.—During the time of the Commonwealth, when this Castle was governed by a person of the sterner sex, Oliver Cromwell sent a requisition from Haddington for its surrender, to which he received a jesting reply ; but on his taking more serious measures, the garrison thought right to recognise a power which they could not oppose, in more respectful terms.

Lammerton is only of note for its kirk (or church) having been the place where King James IV. was married by proxy to Margaret, daughter of Henry VII. of England; and in that union originated all the blessings now enjoyed by Britain as a united instead of a divided kingdom.

GEORGE.—There is a tradition that the clergyman of this village, in consequence of having favoured the king by dispensing (in his case) with the proclamation of banns, was permitted ever after to exercise his functions without that preliminary ceremony.

MRS. ROWE.—Gavinton is a neat and regular modern village erected within the last century, in place of an old hamlet called Langton. It is situated in the midst of a most beautiful country, a little to the west of the burgh of Dunse ; and derives its present name from Mr. Gavin, the lord of the manor.

Eyemouth is a sea-port village, which takes its name from its situation upon the north side of the confluence of the little river Eye with the sea. Its inhabitants principally subsist by fishing, and there are in it several prosperous establishments for the curing of herrings. It also exports a considerable quantity of grain.

Coldingham is a delightful village, situated in the centre of a fine vale at a short distance from the sea, undisturbed by the clatter of the mechanic or the bustle of the merchant, with each house embowered by its own vine and fig-tree. It has significantly been styled "the birth-place of the goddess of pleasure." It once possessed a monastery, which was established in the seventh century by St. Abb, and is said to have been the first in Scotland. The few remaining vestiges of it are little calculated to give any idea of its former magnificence and extent.—Which are the largest streams that water this county?

ANNA.—The Tweed, with respect to size, is considered the fourth in Scotland, but as regards fame, it is perhaps entitled to precedency on account of its dividing the most important sections of the island for some miles before it joins the ocean at Berwick; and the Lauder, which rises in the north-west, and flows in a south-easterly direction to unite its waters with the Tweed.

MRS. ROWE.—Berwickshire comprises three districts of various local character: the Merse, Lammermuir, and Lauderdale. The Merse extends along the northern banks of the Tweed, and is remarkable for being the largest piece of level ground in the whole of this mountainous kingdom, and so fertile, well inclosed and beautiful, that, seen from any of the slight eminences into which it here and there swells, it has the appearance of a vast garden, or rather of an ornamented farm.

Lammermuir is a hilly region equal in size to the Merse, which it divides from the fertile plains of East Lothian, and may justly be styled a pastoral territory.

Lauderdale is a vale formed by the course of the river Lauder, lying transversely at the west end of the other two districts, and partaking of the character of both, being mountainous in the north where it joins Lammermuir, and level at the lower extremity where it borders on Merse. The principal minerals which this county affords, are freestone, whinstone, and gypsum.—Can you name any celebrated character who was born in the county?

David Hume, a philosopher and historian. He published many tracts; but his most celebrated works are his 'Treatise on Human Nature,' his ' Essays,' and his ' History of England.'

ROXBURGHSHIRE.

Boundaries.—Berwickshire, Edinburghshire, Selkirkshire, Dumfriesshire, and Northumberland.
Towns.—1, Jedburgh; 2, Kelso; 3, Newton; 4, Melrose; 5, Galashiels; 6, Abbotsford; 7, Hawick; 8, Mospaul Inn; 9, Castletown; 10, Roxburgh; 11, Dryburgh.
Rivers.—a, the Tweed; b, Teviot; c, Jed; d, Liddel; e, Galla.

Mrs. Rowe.—DESCRIBE the situation, extent, and places of most note in Roxburghshire.

George.—This county, called also Teviotdale, is bounded on the north by Berwickshire, on the east and south by the English counties of Northumberland and Cumberland, and on the west by the shires of Dumfries, Selkirk, and Edinburgh. From north to south it extends about 36 miles, and nearly as much from east to west. It contains the towns of Jedburgh, Kelso, Roxburgh, Hawick, Melrose, Dryburgh, Abbotsford, and Galashiels.

Mrs. Rowe.—Jedburgh is situated in the centre of the county, on the river Jed, and was well known as a place of importance in the history of the border wars. It formerly possessed a noble Castle, which in 1409 was levelled with the ground by the men of Teviotdale, in consequence of being garrisoned by the English.

George.—In the spring of 1523, this town again suffered from the hostilities between England and Scotland, and although without fortifications, it was for some time gallantly defended by its inhabitants; but after the loss of many lives, they were obliged to yield to superior numbers. The English were so incensed at the resistance they had met with, that they burnt the town, and demolished its ancient and beautiful monastery.

ANNA.—In 1554 another inroad was made into this county by the English, under the command of Sir Ralph Eure; and Jedburgh, with the whole neighbouring country, was laid waste.

MRS. ROWE.—This town is a royal burgh of very ancient erection, and appears to have been a place of note previous to the year 1165. It was formerly called Jedworth, and the common name of Jedhart, by which it is known, seems to be a corruption of that appellation. Its name has led antiquaries to suppose that it was the capital of the people denominated *Gadeni*, who, in the period immediately subsequent to the dissolution of the Roman power in Britain, possessed the central part of the marches between Cumberland and Lothian. Its environs abound in rich woodland scenery, which is principally ascribed to the woods called Jed Forest having never been intruded upon by modern improvers, but permitted to flourish as they pleased, ever since they formed a part of the Sylva Caledonia.

Kelso is situated on the river Tweed, and was called by the ancients Calchow, Kelkow, or De Calco. Its Abbey was founded by King David I. in 1128, and dedicated to the Virgin Mary and St. John the Evangelist. David, during the reign of his brother, Alexander the Fierce, brought over some Tyrolesian monks, for whose accommodation he erected this venerable pile. Innocent II. ratified this royal foundation; and King Alexander III. granted to its abbots the honour of wearing the mitre with pontifical robes, and the privilege of assisting at all general councils, which rendered them independent of episcopal jurisdiction. Although Kelso is not the county town, it is generally considered to be the largest which Roxburghshire can boast of possessing, and is noted for its neatness, and the beauty of its environs, as well as for being the resort of a vast number of affluent people, whose suburban villas give it an air of peculiar comfort and refinement. It possesses a manufacture of stockings and leather, but its greatest dependence is on the money spent in it by its genteel inhabitants. It is also often the seat of the Caledonian hunt, and has well-attended races, which are held upon a course called the Bury Moss, a short way northward of the town. Roxburgh, though once so famous in the annals of history, has scarcely a vestige of its former greatness remaining. It stood on a peninsula made by the meeting of the rivers Tweed and Teviot, where the ruins of its ancient Castle still appear upon an eminence of considerable extent. In the frequent warfares between the two kingdoms, this fortress was considered of great importance, and often changed masters. In the reign of the English king Henry VI. it was in the possession of that monarch.

ANNA.—Was it not at this place that the Scottish king James II. was accidentally killed?

GEORGE.—Roxburgh, being situated in the strongest and most fertile part of the Scottish frontiers, was a military post of great importance; it had been in the hands of the English ever since the captivity of David I. James II. was extremely desirous to recover this town, and the cannon (which was in the year 1460 a novelty of which the king was very proud,) stood in the Duke of Roxburgh's park, at Fleurs. Upon the arrival of the Earl of Huntley, (whose valour and fidelity had won the favour of James,) he conducted him to see his batteries, when unhappily standing near a gun that was loaded, the rude mass composed of ribs of iron bound together by hoops of the same metal, (upon being exploded,) burst asunder and killed the monarch on the spot.

MRS. ROWE.—This melancholy event occasioned great dismay in the camp, and the army was about to abandon the siege, when the heroic widowed queen (Mary of Gueldres) hastened to the soldiers' tents, bearing in her arms her infant, and holding him out to them, conjured them not to leave the place till they had laid it in ruins.

This appeal reanimated the courage and efforts of the Scots, who made a vigorous attack, and obliged the English to surrender.

Hawick stands on the river Teviot, and shared the fate of the other border towns in the destruction resulting from hostile invasions. The last time it suffered was in 1570, when the English, under the command of the Earl of Sussex, laid the town in ashes. Here is a considerable manufacture of carpets, cloths, inkle and stockings; and it has been termed Glasgow in miniature, not only in point of manufactures, but also in regard to the character of its inhabitants, as they possess all that jealousy of the power of their rulers, and propensity to political speculation, which usually characterize the votaries of the sedentary arts; insomuch that on the agitation of the Currency question in 1826, they petitioned the national senate for the proposed change, while all the rest of Scotland was decidedly averse to it; this is ingrafted on the old chivalric border spirit, and gives a very strange cast to what yet remains of that original character.

The village of Melrose is an extremely curious and antique little place in the form of a triangle, with small streets leading out of the corners. In the centre of the triangle stands the Cross, a structure supposed to be co-eval with the Abbey, as it bears all the same marks of antiquity; and a field near the town, called the Corse-rig, is held by the proprietor upon the sole condition that he shall " keep up the Cross." Its Abbey, dedicated to the Virgin Mary, was founded by David I. in 1136, and devoted to the use of a body of Cistercian monks. Its situation is extremely beautiful, and, like all other places chosen in those days for the residences of religious orders, was noted for its seclusion, being sheltered on every side by hills. The fertility of the soil and amenity of the climate, are both indicated by the excellence as well as plenty of the fruit produced in the numerous gardens around the town.

Melrose once boasted of an extensive manufacture of linen, which, however, is now declined.

The loveliest part of the Vale of Tweed is ornamented by the sweet and classic shades of Dryburgh, which, though situated chiefly in Berwickshire, can be more conveniently described here. Its chiefest ornament is its Abbey, seated upon a level, round which the Tweed makes a fine circuitous sweep; it is a beautiful ruin, though more remains of the domestic buildings than of the church : it was founded by Hugh Moreville, constable of Scotland in the reign of David I., upon a site which is supposed to have been honoured by the worship of the Druids. Near the ruins still flourishes a tree, which there is good reason to suppose has been planted upwards of seven centuries.

Abbotsford is sufficiently famous for being the residence of that celebrated literary genius of the nineteenth century, Sir Walter Scott, Bart. The house and woods have been entirely the creation of that great man, and it is astonishing that the exertions of one individual should have done so much in so short a period ; but he who has so easily found means whereby universally to gratify a capricious public, seems to have had equal facility in the formation of this seat.

Galashiels is a baronial burgh, and noted for its woollen manufactures. The whole of this town has been erected within the last fifty years, and is situated a little north of the old village, of which scarcely a vestige remains.—Name the principal rivers of Roxburghshire.

ANNA.—The Tweed, Teviot, Jed, Liddel, and Galla.

MRS. ROWE.—The Tweed enters this county in the north-western extremity, and along the whole northern border divides it from Berwickshire.

The Teviot rises in the south, and flows in a north-eastern direction to join the Tweed.

The Jed rises in the Cheviot Hills, and flowing northerly, joins the Teviot below Jedburgh. On its banks are some caverns supposed to have been strongholds of the ancient border warriors.

The Liddel springs from the Cheviot Hills, and flows south-westerly into Dumfriesshire.

The Galla rises in Edinburghshire, and joins the Tweed near Galashiels.—What hills are there of importance in this county?

GEORGE.—The Peniel and the Cockrow range are the highest; of which the Peniel is most worthy of notice. It may be seen from a great distance; and on its summit the late Marquis of Lothian erected a tower in honour of his immortal kinsman the Duke of Wellington.

MRS. ROWE.—The county of Roxburgh is rough and irregular in appearance, consisting of mosses, hills and mountains, interspersed with narrow valleys, well watered, and fertile in corn. The hills feed great numbers of sheep and cattle. On its borders were the famous Battle, Battable, or Debatable lands, claimed by the borderers of both nations.—Can you mention any celebrated characters who owe their birth to this county?

ANNA.—George Augustus Elliott, Baron Heathfield, a gallant British general, and the noble defender of Gibraltar, where he maintained his station for three years of constant investment by the united powers of France and Spain. The eyes of all Europe were on this garrison, and his conduct justly exalted him to the highest rank in the military annals of the day. His self-denial and temperance afford an excellent example for all young men who wish to tread the paths of glory; and grateful posterity will ever cherish his honoured name.

James Thomson, a celebrated poet, whose works are held in the highest esteem, was also a native of this county. His 'Seasons,' 'Tragedies,' the 'Castle of Indolence,' and his poem on 'Liberty,' will ever perpetuate his memory.

SELKIRKSHIRE.

Boundaries.—Edinburghshire, Roxburghshire, Dumfriesshire, and
    Peeblesshire.
Towns.—1, Selkirk; 2, Ettrick; 3, Newark.
Rivers.—a, the Tweed; b, Yarrow; c, Ettrick.
Lochs.—d, Loch o' the Lowes; e, Loch St. Mary.

MRS. ROWE.—DESCRIBE the situation, extent, and
chief places of Selkirkshire.

GEORGE.—It is bounded on the north by Edinburghshire; on the east by Roxburghshire; on the south by
Dumfriesshire; and on the west by Peeblesshire. It is
about 24 miles long from the north-east to south-west, and
varies in breadth from 8 to 16 miles. The places of most
note in it are Selkirk, Newark, and Ettrick.

MRS. ROWE.—Selkirk is a royal burgh of very ancient
erection, situated at the eastern extremity of the county,
upon a piece of high ground overhanging the river Ettrick.
It had formerly an appearance of meanness, but from the
erection of many handsome edifices it is greatly improved.
The town-house is adorned with a steeple and many ornaments, but the church is devoid of both, being a singularly
plain object. An old thatched house, inhabited by the
poorest class, was the original inn of the town, and is said
to have been used in that capacity by the Scottish monarchs
when they came to hunt in the Ettrick Forest; and it is
certain that the great Montrose lived in it for some time
prior to the battle of Philiphaugh.

ANNA.—It is recorded he was sitting in it and writing
a letter to the king to inform him that he had not a single
armed enemy in Scotland, when he was roused by the noise
of Leslie, the Parliamentarian general, attacking his troops;

he then threw himself upon his horse, galloped down the steep descent towards the plain (where his army was lying), and saw that he had lost the day.

MRS. ROWE.—This town was once particularly noted for a manufacture of boots and shoes, as well as one of inkle; these are, however, greatly declined. It is famous for making a light and agreeable species of bread, called Selkirk bannocks; the loaves were originally composed of barley meal, but are now made of the finest flour.

GEORGE.—History informs us that one hundred of the citizens of Selkirk followed their prince, James IV., to the fatal battle of Flodden Field, from which it appears but few returned: the victorious English, in revenge for their gallant conduct there, reduced their town to ashes; but James V. granted them 1000 acres of Ettrick Forest, the wood to rebuild their houses, and the land as a reward for the valour they had displayed on that memorable occasion.

MRS. ROWE.—Newark Castle, the strongest tower in the county, and situated on an eminence overhanging the river Yarrow, with dark wooded hills rising around it, has an appearance truly striking and romantic. A strange, contorted, dismal-looking tree, grows out of the wall of the barbacan, which the sheriff is said to have used at one time as a gallows.

ANNA.—Newark was the scene of a more dreadful sacrifice of human life than could ever have taken place beneath this piece of timber, after the battle of Philiphaugh, when the Parliamentarian general executed here in cold blood no less than one hundred prisoners, his own chaplain standing by all the time and making the most inhuman jests.

MRS. ROWE.—The place where this atrocious butchery was committed still goes by the name of "Slain Men's Lee;" and to confirm the truth of the almost incredible circumstance, a great number of human bones have been recently found on the spot.

Ettrick is a small hamlet in a vale of the same name,

and is chiefly remarkable for the beauty of its situation, being surrounded with dark and lofty hills, similar to those of the Highlands, and forming one of the most impressive natural scenes in the county.—Which are the principal rivers of Selkirkshire?

GEORGE.—The Tweed, Ettrick, and Yarrow.

MRS. ROWE.—The Tweed enters the county from Peeblesshire, at the north-western corner, and after a short course across the north part, being joined by the Ettrick, leaves it for Roxburghshire.

The Ettrick and Yarrow, after running through a romantic country, unite their streams ere they mingle them with the waters of the Tweed: the scenery at the confluence of these two rivers is singularly beautiful.

There is a lake called St. Mary's Loch, lying at the head of the Vale of Yarrow. It is a beautiful expanse of water, about four miles long and about one mile broad. A smaller one, called the Loch of the Lowes, is connected with its western extremity by a small stream.

Selkirkshire is the least populous county in Scotland, being entirely a pastoral district. Its general aspect is bare, nor does its mountainous character secure to it the compensation of magnificent scenery. It was, not many centuries ago, a Royal hunting forest, and though now divested of wood, is still commonly called "The Forest." Queen Mary was the last sovereign that visited the district for the sake of the chase.—Can you name any distinguished characters to whom this county has given birth?

ANNA.—The celebrated Mungo Park, who fell a sacrifice to his ardour for exploring the deserts of Africa and discovering the sources of its principal rivers

PEEBLESSHIRE.

Boundaries.—Edinburghshire, Lanarkshire, Dumfriesshire, and
Selkirkshire.
Towns.—1, Peebles; 2, Linton; 3, Inverliething; 4, Broughton;
5, Skirling; 6, Crook Inn; 7, Biela Inn.
Rivers.—a, the Tweed; b, the Liething; c, the Lyne.

Mrs. Rowe.—WHAT are the boundaries, extent, and
chief places of Peeblesshire?

George.—This county, called also Tweedale, has on the
north Edinburghshire, on the east Selkirkshire, on the
south Dumfriesshire, and on the west Lanarkshire. It is
from 20 to 28 miles in length, and from 7 to 20 in breadth.
The chief towns are Peebles, Linton, Skirling, Broughton,
and Inverliething.

Mrs. Rowe.—Peebles, from its British name signifying
'shealings,' or dwelling-places, seems to have been a settlement during the earliest centuries of the Christian æra; and
it is evident that it was a place of great consequence prior
to the thirteenth century, as it is recorded that Guillaume
de la Chambre, bailiff of Peebles, signed the bond of allegiance to Edward I., at Berwick, in the year 1296. This
town is situated on the river Tweed, and is but slightly distinguished by commerce or manufacture. This place was
several times plundered and burnt by the English, who left
nothing undestroyed but the churches, the manse, or residence of the clergyman, and the cross; these being held
sacred, escaped the general destruction. The ruins of the
Cross church (or monastery) are worthy the attention of the
curious. This building was founded by Alexander III., and
was possessed by Red or Trinity Friars, an order instituted
in honour of the Holy Trinity, and for the redemption of
Christians who were made slaves by the Turks; to which

purpose a third part of its income was applied, and which
continued till the Reformation, when its revenues were disposed of to different persons.   The chief charms of the
town arise from its salubrity and the celebrated excellence
of its schools: Many genteel families are induced to reside
in it on these accounts.

Linton, on the river Lyne, is inhabited chiefly by
weavers, shoemakers, and other artisans, who work only
for the neighbouring residents, none of them being employed
in manufacturing articles for distant markets.

Skirling is an irregular village situated on the western
frontier of the county, and is famous for its four annual
fairs for horses and cattle.

Broughton is situated near the centre of the county, on
the high road from Edinburgh to Moffat, and is a thriving .
village, remarked by strangers for its neatness, it having
been rebuilt within a few years in the English fashion.

The village of Inverliething, not far from Peebles, is
situated in a sequestered spot, where the river Liething falls
into the Tweed, and till lately was noted only for a woollen
manufacture; but from the discovery of a mineral spring,
invalids have resorted to it for health, and others for the
sake of pleasure; so that from a retired village it is become
a fashionable bathing-place. Various new houses have been
lately built for the accommodation of families visiting the
well, and rapid approaches are making to a system of comfort and elegance that must soon render it one of the most
agreeable summer residences in the South of Scotland.—
Which are the principal rivers of this county?

Anna.—The Tweed, the Lyne, and the Liething.

Mrs. Rowe.—The Tweed rises in the southern part of
the county, and first pursues a northerly course, then suddenly turning to the east passes through Peebles on its way
to the county of Selkirk. At particular seasons of the year
this stream is much resorted to on account of its trout-
fishing; it also affords good salmon.

The Lyne and Liething are tributary streams which flow into that grand receptacle.

The hills of this county are unlike the neighbouring ones, none of them being precipitous and rocky; nor do they rise into peaked or even conical summits. When a range of them is seen from a commanding eminence it suggests the idea of the unbroken waves of the Bay of Biscay during the undulations of a subsiding storm. The highest are the Scrape, from the top of which a view is obtained of the Lothians, the Merse, and the borders of England; and the Hell's Cleuch, in the western part of the county, is upwards of 2000 feet high, on the top of which is a cairn of stones called the Pykestane, which marks the boundary of three parishes.

Peeblesshire contains few natural curiosities, and labours under a deficiency of valuable minerals, such as coal, marl, &c., though small seams of lime, freestone, Fuller's earth and slate are to be met with in some of the sequestered districts. The Dale of the Tweed is the most fertile and important part of the country; it is well watered and feeds numbers of sheep and cattle. There are but few plantations, except round particular houses.

DUMFRIESSHIRE.

Boundaries.—Lanarkshire, Peeblesshire, Selkirkshire, Roxburghshire, Ayrshire, Kirkcudbrightshire, Solway Firth, and part
of Cumberland.
Towns.—1, Dumfries; 2, Lochmaben; 3, Annan; 4, Graitney, or
Gretna Green; 5, Langholm; 6, Sarby; 7, Moffat; 8, Loch-
wood; 9, Dinwoody; 10, Locherby; 11, Gateside; 12, Sanquhar; 13, Lincluden.
Rivers.—a, the Nith; b, Cairn; c, Annan; d, Milk; e, Esk;
f, Castle Loch.
A, Vale of Eskdale; B, Annandale; C, Nithsdale; D, Solway
Firth.

MRS. ROWE.—NAME the boundaries, extent, and chief
places of Dumfriesshire.

ANNA.—The county of Dumfries is bounded on the north
by Lanarkshire, Peeblesshire, and Selkirkshire; on the
east by Roxburghshire; on the west by Ayrshire and Kirkcudbrightshire; and on the south by Solway Firth and a
part of Cumberland. Its greatest length is upwards of 50
miles, and its extreme breadth more than 30. The places
of most note are Dumfries, Sanquhar, Annan, Lochmaben,
Moffat, Locherby, Lincluden, and Gretna Green.

MRS. ROWE.—Dumfries is not only the county town, but
may be considered as the metropolis of the south-western
part of Scotland, and was at an early period a place of some
note. It is pleasantly situated on the river Nith, which, in
consequence of the influx of the tide, is navigable for small
vessels, and renders the town a kind of sea-port. It possesses no important manufactures, though there are some
tan-works; and stockings, hats, linen, and coarse woollen
cloths are prepared in small quantities for home consumption. A weekly market is kept at Dumfries, at which the
following singular custom once existed:—The county

hangman went through the market with a brass ladle or
large spoon, which he pushed into every sack of meal or
corn, and carried it off full. At one time the farmers refused
to comply with this usage, in consequence of which it was
tried in a court of law, and it was found to be a perqui-
site belonging to the office of hangman. The two churches
are remarkably neat buildings: in the cemetery of St. Michael's are several pyramidal ornaments, and on some
grave-stones are inscriptions recording the violence and
infamy of the apostate Sharp, and the bigotry of James II.
Dumfries, like the other border towns, was much exposed
to the inroads of the English, and was frequently ruined
by them. To prevent their invasions, a ditch and mound,
called Warden's Dyke, were drawn from the Nith to Locher
Moss, where watch and ward was constantly kept. On
most of the eminences of those parts beacons were likewise
erected for alarming the country; and all the inhabitants
capable of bearing arms were obliged, on the firing of sig-
nals, to repair instantly to the warden of the marches, under
pain of high treason. This place now derives a melancholy
interest from having been the residence of the poet Robert
Burns, the place where he breathed his last, and where all
of him that could die was deposited; and it cannot fail to
strike the stranger who visits his grave, that while all the
other monuments are left to be overgrown by dust and ob-
literated by decay, Burns's mausoleum (the object of perpetual attention,) exhibits a constant freshness; the door is
ever open, the floor often cleaned, and the evergreens and
flowers around it are, for his sake, unfading and imperishable.

Sanquhar is worthy of notice for its old Castle, a picturesque ruin overlooking the river Nith. In the reign of
Edward I. this Castle was in possession of the English, but
was recaptured by Sir William Douglas, of Douglasdale,
who put the garrison to the sword. The manufacture of
woollen goods, in various branches, has been carried on in
this place with great success.

Annan is a royal burgh, from a charter granted by Robert Bruce, who was lord of Annandale before his accession to the throne. It is an extremely neat and well-built town, situated on the eastern bank of the river Annan, near its confluence with the Solway, and by means of which it is a sea-port, and has an extensive trade in wine and corn. The fisheries on the coast and in its river afford employment to a great number of people. Many military transactions of the border warfare between the Scotch and English, took place in Annan and its vicinity. It was one of the principal residences of those bold and brave men of Annandale of whom it is said, in the History of Scotland, that from their continual irruptions with the English borderers, they became incapable of moderation or the civil submission of peace, even in their intercourse with their Scottish neighbours.

GEORGE.—It is recorded that the Royal Bruce had a castle here, no vestige of which remains but a single stone, which was taken from the rubbish and inserted into the wall of a gentleman's garden : on it is inscribed, "Robert de Brus Counte de Carrick et Seigneur du Val d'Annan, 1300."

MRS. ROWE.—Lochmaben is poetically called "Queen of the Lochs," from its situation in the midst of eight or nine sheets of water, which are great natural ornaments. It is also noted for a considerable manufacture of coarse linen, and in its neighbourhood, (on the river Annan,) for a fine salmon fishery. Its Castle, now in ruins, was once the residence of King Robert Bruce, and was the scene of some of the heroic actions of Sir William Wallace of Ellerslie.

The Cross of Lochmaben is a curious, tall, time-worn stone, which the town council purchased of the laird of Elshieshields, by making over to his heirs and successors for ever the mill and mill lands of Lochmaben, in order that it might be erected as a Cross in their burgh, and remain a proud monument of their taste and public spirit.

Moffat is worthy of note from its possessing two mineral springs, which were discovered in 1633, and have ever since been resorted to from all parts of the kingdom; the water has a sulphureous smell, similar to that of Harrowgate, but not quite so strong.

Locherby is a neat little town, situated in that fertile part of the country where may be seen some of the most lovely scenery in the whole of Annandale; and it has long been famous for its lamb and wool market, though not upon the same scale as at present. The annual fair day presents a scene of animation which is said to be unequalled in the county; the charms of business are there intermixed with manly sports, and it may indeed be justly called the seat of the Olympic games of the south-western province of Scotland.

Lincluden was originally noted for its convent, but about the end of the fourteenth century Archibald the Grim, Earl of Douglas and Lord of Galloway, on account of the alleged profligacy of the nuns, but more probably to establish a more commodious means of providing for the cadets of the House of Douglas, converted the institution into a collegiate church for a provost and twelve beadsmen. The whole is now dreadfully dilapidated, and enough only remains to show that it was erected in a style of splendour, and enriched with much minute decoration.

Graitney lies on the west bank of the Sark, near its junction with the sea. This place has long been famous in the annals of matrimonial adventurers, and is still resorted to by fugitive lovers. A man of the name of Elliott, in the year 1828, was the principal person then employed on those occasions; he resided at the village of Springfield, about a mile from the church, and his charge was regulated by the rank of his employers; half-a-guinea was the lowest fee that he ever demanded. This shameful traffic was founded by a tobacconist of the name of Joseph Paisley, who died in the year 1814. The common term Gretna Green arose from his residence, which was at Megg's Hill, on the common or green betwixt Graitney and Springfield. This self-created priest is generally devoid of literature, principles, morals and manners.—Which are the principal rivers that water this county?

Anna.—The Esk, Annan, and the Nith.

Mrs. Rowe.—These three streams descend from the mountains, and intersect the county in their courses to unite their waters with the Solway Firth, forming three distinct vales, called Eskdale, Annandale, and Nithsdale.

Of the lochs which surround the village of Lochmaben, the principal is that called the Castle Loch, which is a fine sheet of water, skirted by green and fruitful fields, and woods of the true rich and massive hue. Fed entirely by its own springs, it is remarkable, in the eyes of the natural historian and likewise of the epicure, for containing a peculiar and delicious little fish called the *vendise*.

Dumfriesshire, though not particularly noted for its natural features, has many picturesque and delightful views on the banks of its rivers; and, like the rest of Scotland, (though now nearly bare,) was formerly luxuriant in wood. It is traditionally asserted that the laird of Corehead (a village pretty far up Annandale,) lived to boast that he could let a hound slip at his door which would not get out of the woods of his own property till it reached the sands of Solway. Although Solway Moss is not included in this part of the kingdom, but appertains to the county of Cumberland, in England, it is so situated on the borders at the mouth of the Esk, that a few remarks on it here cannot be considered misapplied. It consists of 1600 acres of thin peaty mud, with a crust too weak, in the driest summer, to support a man's weight. In 1771, being swoln by the rain, it burst through the shell of turf which covered it, and spread a black stream of peat over a large extent of cultivated land in the neighbouring valley, which it entirely filled up. On this occasion, large horns of deer and other

substances were ejected.—Has Dumfriesshire given birth
to any great characters?

GEORGE.—This county, being situated upon the borders,
was anciently a fruitful nursery of warriors; and the proprietors of many estates in it form prominent characters in
Scottish history. The names of Bruce, Baliol, Douglas, Johnston, Maxwell, Fleming, and Scott, are sufficient
to bring to remembrance the eminence of the feudal barons,
who anciently possessed a great proportion of this territory.
In more modern times, many active and enterprising characters have sprung from this county, among whom the
celebrated Paterson, who is said to have planned the Bank
of England, and also the Scottish settlement at the Isthmus
of Darien: he was born in the village of Tinwald, and more
than once represented Dumfries in the Scottish Parliament.

KIRKCUDBRIGHTSHIRE.

Boundaries.—Ayrshire, Dumfriesshire, Wigtownshire, and Sol-
    way Firth.
Towns.—1, New Galloway; 2, Kirkcudbright; 3, Dalbeattie;
    4, Mollins; 5, Barly; 6, Creetown.
Rivers.—a, the Orr, or Urr; b, Dee, or Kirkcudbright; c, Fleet.
Lochs.—e, Loch Orr, or Urr; f, Loch Ken; g, Loch Dee; h, Loch
    Cree.
Capes and Firths.—A, Saturness Point; B, Solway Firth.

MRS. ROWE.—WHAT are the boundaries, extent, and
chief towns of Kirkcudbrightshire?

ANNA.—Kirkcudbrightshire, or Stewartry, is bounded
on the north by Ayrshire and Dumfriesshire; on the east
by the latter county; on the south by Solway Firth and
the Irish Sea; and on the west by Wigtownshire, from which
it is parted by the river Cree. From the extreme of its

western boundary to that of its eastern is 48 miles, and
from north to south, in its widest part, it measures upwards of 30.   It contains the towns of Kirkcudbright,
New Galloway, and Dalbeattie.

MRS. ROWE.—Kirkcudbright, the capital, is a well-built
sea-port burgh town of a very pleasing appearance, and its
neighbourhood possesses considerable natural charms in
the way of scenery.   This town has acquired an air of live-
liness and gaiety from having become the residence of
persons of fortune.   It formerly possessed some foreign
trade with the West Indian colonies and America, which
is declined, and it now chiefly subsists on a small manufacture of hosiery, and the resources it derives from its
opulent inhabitants.   Its Castle is a large dirty-looking
edifice, and although it bears the date of 1584, yet its
perfectly entire and strong walls almost lead the beholder
to doubt its being so ancient.   Near the harbour are the
remains of an old battery erected by King William III.
whilst he sheltered in this bay from a storm, when on his
voyage to raise the siege of Londonderry; and in the
vicinity of this bay are also a few remains of a more ancient
piece of fortification, which is said to have been once considered among the strongest and most important in Galloway.   This Castle became the property of John Baliol, by
marriage: afterwards it went to the Douglases, since which
it has been transferred to the town corporation; and from
its having been eventually alienated by them, became private property.

GEORGE.—It was in this edifice that the unfortunate
King Henery VI. resided for some time during his exile
in Scotland; and he embarked from hence with his queen
when they quitted this country.

MRS. ROWE.—New Galloway is one of the most inferior
burgh towns of Scotland; it consists of only one street, and,
excepting a handsome new bridge erected over the Ken,
possesses nothing worthy of notice.

Dalbeattie is situated on a tributary stream of the river Urr, or Orr, which is navigable nearly to the village. The neighbouring country is barren in the extreme, consisting almost entirely of grey granite hills covered with the most scanty herbage, and here and there interspersed with copses of oak and birch. One of the largest and most entire Roman camps in Scotland, called 'the Moat of Urr,' is still to be seen in this neighbourhood; and not far from hence, near the sea-coast, are the remains of the ancient Abbey of Dundrennan, which is not only noted in historical tradition, but worthy of remark for the natural beauty of its situation. Though this building is in a very dilapidated state, yet enough of it remains to evince that it was formerly one of superior grandeur and magnificence.

ANNA.—It is recorded that the last night spent by the unfortunate Queen Mary in her Scottish dominions, was within the walls of this monastery.

MRS. ROWE.—The peasantry of Dalbeattie still point out the rock from which this hapless princess embarked upon her ill-fated voyage to England; it stands in a little creek surrounded by vast and precipitous rocks, and in commemoration of that event is styled 'Port Mary'.—Can you tell me the principal rivers which water this county?

GEORGE.—The Dee, the Ken, the Urr or Orr, and the Fleet.

MRS. ROWE.—The Dee rises in the northern part, and runs first in a south-easterly direction, then turning to the south, after being increased by the Ken, falls into the Solway Firth.

The Ken passes through New Galloway in its way to join the Dee.

The Urr, or Orr, rises from a loch of the same name, and flows southerly into the Solway Firth.

The Fleet lies to the west of the Dee, and after a short course flows into Wigtown Bay.

The principal lochs are those of Ken, Orr, Dee, and Cree, all of which are rich in fish of various kinds, and are surrounded by beautiful scenery.

The Stewartry of Kirkcudbrightshire forms the eastern and larger portion of the ancient and extensive district of Galloway; the great strath of the Dee, continued by the beautiful vale of the Ken, divides it diagonally from the Solway upwards.—The general aspect of this county is hilly, but it has no mountains of any considerable elevation; many parts of it afford excellent pasturage, and numerous flocks of sheep and herds of cattle are fed on it.

WIGTOWNSHIRE.

Boundaries.—Ayrshire, Kirkcudbrightshire, and the Irish Sea.
Towns.—1, Wigtown; 2, Newtown Stewart; 3, Eggerness; 4, Whitehorn; 5, Glenluss; 6, Stranraer; 7, Port Patrick.
River.—d, the Cree.
Capes and Bays.—C, Fairland Point; D, Mull of Galloway; E, Burrow Head; F, Loch Ryan Bay; G, Glenruss; H, Wigtown Bay.

MRS. ROWE.—WHAT are the boundaries, extent, and chief towns of Wigtownshire?

GEORGE.—This county, which is sometimes called Upper or West Galloway, is bounded on the north by Ayrshire, on the east by Kirkcudbrightshire, and on the south and west by the Irish Sea; it measures from Wigtown on the eastern side to Port Patrick on the western upwards of 30 miles, and its greatest breadth from north to south is about 25. Its principal towns are Wigtown, Newtown Stewart, Whitehorn, Stranraer, and Port Patrick.

MRS. ROWE.—Wigtown, the capital, is situated on a bay

to which it gives name; and it is said that no town in the
South of Scotland is so remotely placed as this, being in
the centre of a peninsula and at a considerable distance
from any post-road; in consequence of which it is obliged
to depend entirely upon its own resources. It derives
great advantage from its soil being particularly suited to
the cultivation of wheat, and it has also some manufactures
of plaid and flannel. Many of the buildings of this town
are apparently of considerable antiquity, and although it is
generally thought a dull place, yet such is the wealth of the
surrounding neighbourhood, that it supports a branch of
the British Linen Company's Bank.

Newtown Stewart, on the banks of the river Cree, is an
agreeable and improving village; it has been greatly ornamented by the erection of a bridge over the river, which is
a handsome structure, and connects the main part of the
place with an inferior portion. In consequence of this village possessing a species of municipal government, it is
adorned with a town hall.

Whitehorn is situated to the south of Wigtown, and is a
place of great antiquity, having been a Roman station, and
the capital of a British people called *Novantes.* It was the
first bishop's see in Scotland, and some slight remains of
its Cathedral are yet visible, as well as of a priory founded
by Fergus lord of Galloway. At a short distance from
the town is a place of worship, which is said to have been
the earliest religious foundation in the kingdom.

Stranraer is a sea-port town, situated at the head of the
bay of Loch Ryan, and possesses few charms but that of
being reputed a healthy place; which has caused it to become the retreat of a great number of annuitants. Stranraer
has some trade to the Baltic and Norway for deals and
iron, and possesses a few coasting and herring vessels, as
well as a small manufacture of linens. In the centre of the
town is a tall strong building which was formerly a castle,
but is now used as a jail.

VOL. II.   I

Port Patrick is known as being the nearest point of Great Britain to Ireland; formerly the harbour was a mere inlet fit only for receiving flat-bottomed boats, but now there is one of the finest quays in Britain, and it is indebted to the exertions of Sir David Blair for the erection of a reflecting light-house. It is much noted for its ferry to Donaghadee, in Ireland, from which it is about 20 miles distant. A considerable number of horses and cattle are annually imported from Ireland to this place, where are four elegant packet-boats for the conveyance of the mail, and for the accommodation of passengers ; mail-coaches go regularly from London and Edinburgh to Port Patrick on the one side, and between Dublin and Donaghadee on the other.—Which is the largest stream in this county ?

GEORGE.—The principal one is the Cree, which springs from a loch of the same name in Kirkcudbrightshire, and after separating the two counties, falls through Wigtown Bay into the Irish Sea.

MRS. ROWE.—The principal bays which make their inroads into this county, are those of Wigtown on the east, Glenluss on the south, and Loch Ryan on the north. Wigtownshire mainly consists in two peninsulas, which jutting out from the more continental part of Galloway, are distinguished from it by comparative flatness and greater partial fertility. Luce Bay divides and helps to form these promontories. That part of the county which lies to the west of the Vale of Luce is termed the Rhinns of Galloway, (from *rhinns*, a peninsula,) it being almost completely inclosed by the bay of Loch Ryan. The northern part of Wigtownshire is moorish and mountainous, but the southern point of this wild coast is called the Mull of Galloway, and is the most southerly point of that district. From the remote and peninsulated situation of Galloway, its early history is involved in greater obscurity than that of any other part of Scotland; it has, however, been generally represented, and probably with truth, as a region where primeval barbarity long and powerfully opposed the progress of civilization. At the time when the southern part of Ayrshire made a part of this district, it formed a kind of independent kingdom, and was in perpetual war with the monarchs of Scotland, under its own native princes, or barons. At one time it was attached to England, and Fergus, a lord of Galloway, signed the great Charter in that character ; at a later period Galloway sided in the wars of competition with its native master Baliol,and in the reign of David II. the representative of that unfortunate family found protection, and established a Court in this remote corner of his nominal kingdom. Galloway was at length entirely subdued and brought to acknowledge the authority of the Scottish king, William lord Douglas, about the year 1358.—From its hilly and irregular surface it is in a great measure a pastoral district, and much noted for its cattle, which are its principal article of commerce.

IRELAND.

———◆———

Mrs. Rowe.—WE have now concluded our remarks upon Great Britain, and I shall pursue a similar system in explaining the most prominent features regarding the geography of IRELAND. Have you any knowledge of its ancient appellation?

George.—I have read that Cæsar and Tacitus distinguished it from Great Britain by the name of *Hibernia*; and Orosius gave the same name to the country, though he styled its inhabitants Scoti, which agrees with the appellation of *Scotia*, by which Ireland was long known. Ptolemy, the geographer, called it *Ivernia*. Diodorus Siculus gave to it the name of *Iris*, and Strabo that of *Ierne*, which latter term bears an affinity to the Irish word *Erin*. Archbishop Usher asserts, " that it was not till after the coalition between the Scots and the Picts, in the eleventh century, that both nations, viz. Ireland and modern Scotland, came promiscuously to be called Scotland; and even then, all correct writers, in mentioning the two countries, distinguished them by *"Vetus et nova Scotia, major aut minor, ulterior et citerior."* In the works of foreign authors this island appears to have retained the name of *Scotia* till the fifteenth century.

Anna.—Can you inform us by whom Ireland was first inhabited?

Mrs. Rowe.—It is most probable that Ireland, as well as England, was first peopled by the Celtic, and afterwards by the Belgic tribes; but the correct knowledge of its early possessors, as well as its history, is, like that of all other nations, obscured in fable. It appears, however, clear that this island became a celebrated seat of learning and religion when the greater portion of Europe laboured under the oppression of Gothic ignorance; so great was the number of holy men it produced in the fifth and sixth centuries, that it was dignified with the title of *Insula Sanctorum*, or the Isle of Saints. "Hither," says an Irish historian, "the sciences fled for protection, and here their followers and professors were amply supported;" and the learning, religion and hospitality for which Ireland was so justly celebrated is said to have arisen from its numerous monastic establishments. Notwithstanding all these advantages, any writer who attempts to delineate the peculiarities of this country will experience great mortification in finding that so few books are to be obtained relating to it, when compared with those descriptive of every other part of the British Islands.

GEORGE.—How was Ireland governed previous to the English invasion?

MRS. ROWE.—We learn from Hooker, that "each province had their particular princes; but choice was made by the whole estates of the land of some one of them to be monarch, and he, for the time being, did take and receive homage and fealty of all the others, not in respect that he was a particular prince, but because he was the monarch."

ANNA.—What first induced Henry II. of England to attempt the conquest of this island?

MRS. ROWE.—Henry, viewing with resentment the many depredations which the Irish, united with the Ostmen (a name by which the Norwegians and Danes were then known), were continually committing on the coasts of his territories, determined to attempt the conquest of this island; and about the year 1155 obtained a Bull

from Pope Adrian to authorize his invasion of it whenever a favourable opportunity should arrive.   In 1167
Dermod MacMorogh, king of Leinster, was compelled to
take refuge in England, and having implored Henry to assist him in revenging the injuries he had received from his
countrymen, and sworn allegiance to him, an edict was is-
sued in his favour, wherein Henry II. granted permission
to any of his subjects to aid Dermod in the recovery of his
kingdom. Some time after this event the Earl of Pembroke
(surnamed Strongbow, whose estates were then under attainder,) petitioned his royal master either to restore to
him his possessions or grant him the liberty to seek his
fortune in foreign countries; and, having previously received a promise of King Dermod's daughter Eva in marriage, with a succession to the whole of his inheritance and
property in Ireland as a reward for his services, he determined to undertake the Irish expedition, and consequently
landed at Waterford on the 23rd of August 1171.   The
promised contract of the marriage of Strongbow was ful-
filled soon after his arrival, and he subsequently gained so
much influence in Ireland that Henry, jealous of his increasing power, resolved upon completing the conquest of
this kingdom in person, and on the 18th of October 1172
he sailed from Milford Haven with an army, and soon
after his arrival the feudal title of Lord Paramount of
Ireland, which he then claimed, was acknowledged by all
the petty princes of the island, and ratified by the last native sovereign Rodoric king of Connaught and lord of
Ireland, which title was continued to Henry's successors
till the reign of Henry VIII., who was proclaimed king.

GEORGE.—What is the present government of Ireland?

MRS. ROWE.—His Majesty's deputy is styled Lord Lieu-
tenant of Ireland, who, as well as the Council, is appointed
from time to time by the King, and the former enjoys all
the privileges and exercises all the authority of Royalty

there. The laws of Ireland differ but little from those of England: the national establishment of religion is the same; and in 1802 the Irish Parliament was united with that of Great Britain.—Can you tell me the situation, extent, and divisions of this part of His Majesty's dominions?

GEORGE.—Ireland is one of the British Islands, lying to the west of Great Britain, between 51 and 56 degrees of north latitude and 5 and 11 of west longitude. The Atlantic Ocean bounds it on every side excepting the east, where St. George's Channel, or the Irish Sea, parts it from England and Wales, and a channel about twenty miles broad divides it from Scotland. Its computed admeasurement is about 258 miles from Fairhead in the North of Antrim to the Mizen Head Cape in the county of Cork, and 160 miles from the eastern extremity of Down to the most westerly coast of Mayo. It is divided into four provinces, viz. Ulster, Leinster, Munster, and Connaught, which are again divided into counties, of which Ulster contains nine, Leinster twelve, Munster six, and Connaught five.

ULSTER.

MRS. ROWE.—TELL me the situation of the province of Ulster, and the names of the counties it contains.

ANNA.—It is situated in the North of Ireland, and contains the counties of Antrim, Down, Armagh, Monaghan, Cavan, Tyrone, Fermanagh, Londonderry, and Donegal.

ANTRIM.

Boundaries.—Down, Armagh, Tyrone, Londonderry, and the Atlantic Ocean.

Towns.—1, Antrim; 2, Belfast; 3, Lisburn; 4, Carrickfergus; 5, Connor; 6, Coleraine; 7, Bushmills; 8, Dunluce Castle; 9, Ballycastle; 10, Ballymena; 11, Randalstown; 12, Ballycory; 13, Larne; 14, Glenellen; 15, Clogh; 16, Clogmill; 17, Newtonglens; 18, Castle Cary; 19, Portrush.

Rivers.—a, the Ban, or Banna; b, Maine; c, Kilwater; d, Bush.

Lough.—A, Lough Neagh.

Islands.—B, Rathlin Island; C, Island or Peninsula of Magee; D, Portrush Island.

Capes and Bays.—E, Giant's Causeway; F, Fairhead; G, Red Bay; H, Glenarm Bay; I, Old Fleet Harbour; J, Carrickfergus Bay.

Mountains.—K, the White Mountains.

Mrs. Rowe.—WHAT are the boundaries, extent, and chief towns of Antrim?

George.—It is bounded on the north and east by the Atlantic Ocean, on the south by the counties of Down and Armagh, and on the west by those of Tyrone and Londonderry. It measures from north to south 50 miles, and from east to west 36. Its principal towns are Antrim, Belfast, Lisburn, Carrickfergus, Connor, Coleraine, Bushmills, Dunluce Castle, Ballycastle, Portrush, and Larne.

Mrs. Rowe.—Antrim is situated on the banks of the Six-Mile Water, near its confluence with Lough Neagh. This town is in an improving state, for which it is partly indebted to the linen trade. In the beautiful adjacent district there are many bleach-fields, and the land is very fertile. An elegant Gothic church, with a steeple and spire, has been lately built here.

Anna.—Near this place a furious battle was fought in 1798, in which Earl O'Neill was slain.

Mrs. Rowe.—Belfast is a sea-port, situated near the entrance of the river Laggan into Carrickfergus Lough, over which is a bridge of twenty-one arches and 2560 feet in length. It has a good harbour, which is connected with Lough Neagh by means of a navigable canal. This town is noted for an academical Institution, and its manufactures of cotton, cambric, sail-cloth, and linen; besides which it has glasshouses, and near the bridge are some salt-pans: it also exports great quantities of provisions. This place possesses greater attractions for the merchant than the antiquary, as its commerce is extensive and the wealth and spirit of the inhabitants have been employed in its improvement. In a grove near the town stands a round tower, with nearly a perfect roof.

George.—I have read that on the summit of a hill, not far from the town, amongst other Druidical remains in the Giant's Ring, is a cromlech, which consists of a range of rude pillars, of from two to three and a half feet high; which are covered by a rough stone of seven feet by six and a half: this was formerly an inclined plane; and close by these still remain some fixed stones of considerable size. The altar stands in a circular inclosure one third of a mile in circumference: the rampart which surrounds it is sufficiently wide for two to ride abreast, and it slopes on each side instead of ending in a point, so that a person standing near the altar can only see the inclosure and the sky: in that situation, and alone, he cannot but feel a degree of awe, from the idea of total seclusion; and he must form a high idea of the influence necessary to unite a body of men to execute this work at the remote period in which it was erected.

Mrs. Rowe.—Lisburn is a well-built town on the river Laggan, and is celebrated for its manufactures of damask cloths, cambrics and muslins, as well as for its excellent school. The church has a large square tower, with a taper-

I 5

ing spire, and serves as a Cathedral for the see of Down and Connor.

Carrickfergus, the county and assize town of Antrim, is situated on the north shore of a bay of the same name.

ANNA.—I have read that this place received its name from the following historical event: Fergus, son of an Irish prince named Ferchard, was called into Scotland to assist that nation against the Southern Britons, and being hastily recalled to Ireland, to judge in some controversy, was, on his return, overtaken by a storm in this bay, in which he perished, and it was consequently named Carrick Fergus, or Fergus's Rock.

MRS. ROWE.—On a point of this bay stands a Castle, which is a magnificent object; it was founded in 1178 by Hugh de Lacy earl of Ulster. In the year 1770 the French, under Thurot, made a descent here, and surprised the Castle; but it was soon retaken, and the assault was amply revenged by the capture of the whole squadron. In 1790 it was repaired and made a depôt for arms and ammunition.

GEORGE.—Here King William III. landed when he came to defend the country against the expelled monarch James II., and the stone on which he first set foot is still shown as an object of veneration.

MRS. ROWE.—The church of Carrickfergus is an old irregular edifice, and contains some ancient tombs. This town carries on very little trade, but has some manufactures of linen and cotton, and employs a great number of hands in the fishery of the bay.

Connor was formerly a place of some importance, but is now a small village of white cottages. The see of Connor is united with the bishopric of Down. Some appearance of the foundation walls of the Cathedral still exist, and in the cemetery there is a white church with a steeple, environed by trees. The Kells Water flows beneath the eminence on which this church is built; and near it are the remains of a tower, which is supposed to have formed part of a residence of King Fergus and other princes of early days.

Coleraine is seated on the river Ban, about four miles from its mouth, and is a corporate town and barony of Londonderry. It formerly possessed a Castle, built in 1213. This town is noted for its manufacture of linen, but as a port it is inferior to Portrush, in consequence of the course of the river being so strong that the tide does not ascend far up, nor is its navigation good. It is noted for its salmon- and eel-fisheries. Coleraine has large barracks and a church pleasantly situated.

ANNA.—I have read that salmon are caught by means of a trap of basket-work (like those used in rivers for taking eels,) through which these fish pass, and as it is the nature of salmon to swim always against the stream, they never think of a retreat.

GEORGE.—Near the river Ban is a tumulus, and not far from that is another earthen work boldly situated on the banks of this river; the latter is partly covered with wood.

MRS. ROWE.—Bushmills is a village near the entrance of the river Bush into Ballintrae Bay, and is a place of great resort on account of its vicinity to the Giant's Causeway.

GEORGE.—The Reverend William Hamilton says, "The Causeway is generally described as a mole or quay projecting from the base of a steep promontory, some hundred feet into the sea, and is formed of perpendicular pillars of basaltes, which stand in contact with each other, exhibiting a sort of polygon pavement somewhat resembling solid honeycomb. The pillars are irregular prisms of various denominations from three to eight sides, but the hexagonal columns are as numerous as all the others together. On a minute examination, each pillar is found to be separable into joints, whose articulation is neat and compact beyond

expression; the convex termination of one joint always
meeting a concave socket in the next; besides which the
angles of one frequently shoot over those of the other, so
that they are completely locked together, and can rarely be
separated without a fracture of these parts.   The sides of
each column are unequal amongst themselves, but the contiguous sides of adjoining columns are always of equal dimensions, so as to touch in all their parts.   Though the
angles be of various magnitudes, yet the sum of the contiguous angles of adjoining pillars always makes up four
right ones; so that there are no void spaces among the
basaltes, the surface of the Causeway exhibiting to view
a regular and compact pavement of polygon stones.   The
outside covering is soft and of a brown colour, being the
earthy part of the stone nearly deprived of its metallic
principle by the action of the air and of the marine acid
which it receives from the sea."

MRS. ROWE.—Not far from the Causeway stands Dunluce Castle, on an isolated abrupt rock perforated by the
waves, which have formed under it a very spacious cavern.
This rock projects into the sea, and seems, as it were, split
off from the main land.   Over the immediate chasm lies
the only approach to the Castle, along a narrow wall, which
has been built somewhat like a bridge, connecting it to the
adjoining land; and this circumstance must have rendered
it almost impregnable before the invention of artillery.   It
is supposed to have been founded by De Courcy earl of
Ulster, afterwards enlarged by native chieftains, and finally
by the M'Donalds in the time of Elizabeth.

GEORGE.—A particular chamber in this Castle is said to
be the favourite abode of Mave Roe, a *banshee*, or fairy,
who is said to sweep it every night; but it may be observed
that the winds which rush through that and the other desolate apartments will sufficiently account for the cleanliness
of the room, without the aid of supernatural agency.

ANNA.—When Sir John Perrot was Lord Deputy of

Ireland, he besieged this Castle, it being one of the strongest
fortresses within the realm. It had in it then a strong
ward, whereof the captain was a Scotchman, who, when
the Deputy sent to him to yield, refused parley, and said,
" he would keep it to the last man"; but finding himself
powerfully beset, he requested mercy, which was granted
him, with liberty to depart.

MRS. ROWE.—In 1585 this fort was lost by the treachery of its governor, whom the Deputy had placed in it
with fourteen men, thinking he was of English extraction,
but afterwards found he was a Scotchman. This constable
reposing confidence in his own countrymen, discharged the
English soldiers, unknown to Sir John Perrot; two of these
having confederated with the enemy, drew up fifty of them
in the night by ropes made with withies. Having surprised the Castle, they assaulted the little tower where the
constable was, and a few men with him, to whom they
offered the liberty to depart; but willing to pay the price
of his folly, the constable chose rather to forfeit his life,
and was slain.

GEORGE.—To the west of Dunluce is a fine rock of limestone, as white as chalk; a great quantity of which is
burned in kilns, and used as manure.

MRS. ROWE.—Ballycastle is a sea-port much celebrated
for its beauty and the sublimity of the surrounding scenery.
Its church is finely situated close to the walls of its crum-
bling Abbey. Near the harbour is a long bridge across
the mouth of the river, which is formed by means of the
Carey and Ramoan streams descending from the ravines
and deep glens of the mountains. A large quantity of
kelp is collected here, and burnt on the shore. Its collieries occupy the hills along the coast of the bay for about
a mile; and in the immediate vicinity of the town are two
mineral springs.

Portrush is a village-port with a custom-house establishment and salt-works. Its yellow strand is much admired.

The alternate cliffs of lime, perforated by caverns formed by the waves, and rocks of whinstone and basaltes, furnish a varied line of coast ; but the green summits of the gently swelling hills, which form the back of the cliffs, are generally destitute of trees.

Larne, formerly known by the name of Inver, is situated on a narrow inlet of the sea called Lough Larne. The harbour, though small, is the best port between Belfast and Derry. This town is much frequented as a watering-place, and carries on some trade in provisions, salt and lime. The linen manufacture flourishes here.

GEORGE.—Near this place is Tubbermore Well, the waters of which turn two mills ; and to the north of Larne harbour are the ruins of Olderfleet Castle, which was erected by one of the Bissets, who possessed the property in the reign of Henry III.

MRS. ROWE.—It was here that Lord Edward Bruce, the brother of the Scottish king, landed in 1315, with the design of conquering Ireland ; an attempt that was the cause of much bloodshed throughout the kingdom.—Which are the rivers of this county?

ANNA.—The Ban or Banna, Maine, Kilwater and Bush.

MRS. ROWE.—The Ban, or Banna, rises in the Mourne mountains in Down, and soon becomes a stream of navigable size. It passes Portadown, where it is joined by the Newry Canal, and from thence flows into Lough Neagh, from which it issues in a north-westerly direction; and after dividing this county from Londonderry, falls into the sea near Coleraine.

The Maine rises in the eastern part of the county, and first pursues a westerly course ; then, flowing southerly, it falls into Lough Neagh, below Randalstown.

The Kilwater is a small stream, which, after a short easterly course, falls into the sea at Larne.

The Bush flows in a winding and rapid stream through a rich and varied country to the sea at Bushmills.

Lough Neagh is a beautiful sheet of water, 20 miles in length and 12 in breadth. It is bounded by no less than five counties, Armagh, Tyrone, Londonderry, Down, and Antrim. It contains large quantities of shad, bream, trout, churl or bodach, roach, and pike; and is periodically visited by salmon and eels. Char are also found here. On this lough are two small islands. Blackwater Island is situated at the mouth of the river of that name. Ram Island is about three miles from the shore. On the latter are a round tower and a cemetery.

GEORGE.—I perceive in the map an island on the northern coast.

MRS. ROWE.—It is that of Rathlin. Its length from one extremity to the other is computed at 5 miles, and its breadth at about 2. The channel which separates it from the mainland is called Slunk-na-Marra, and is about 7 miles across. The passage cannot at all times be effected, as the swell of the North Sea currents is very heavy after a breeze or at spring tides. Inhospitable as the situation of this little isle may appear, in the midst of a turbulent and tempestuous sea, its inhabitants are much attached to their desolate home, and, excepting those that are engaged in the fisheries, seldom visit Ireland. St. Columba established a monastery here, which was destroyed by the Danes. Its coasts partake of the beautiful and basaltic character of the Antrim shore, and in several places rise more than 300 feet above the level of the sea. At Doon Point, the basaltic columns have a very curious appearance. On the cliff at the east end of the island, is Bruce's Castle, so called from the gallant Robert Bruce, who fortified it, and successfully resisted his enemies during the civil wars of Scotland. The islanders derive their chief support from the quantity of kelp burnt there, the export of which is considerable. The shores of Rathlin are frequented by a great number of sea-fowl. The peninsula of Magee, improperly styled Island Magee, lies on the eastern coast of this county, and is noted for its basaltic cliffs, called the Gobbins, which are 200 feet high ; and it is said that over these heights were precipitated the bodies of thirty Catholics who had been cruelly murdered by Monroe, the Scottish commander of Carrickfergus Castle in the reign of Charles I. Upon this peninsula is the Giant's Cradle, which is a large stone so nicely balanced that a small force will put it in motion, though the utmost strength of many men cannot overturn it. The Gobbins are frequented by various water-fowl as well as by the gos-hawk. A pair of these birds was formerly the tribute or rent paid for the peninsula, and the festival of hawk-lifting on Midsummer Day was a grand scene of merriment. The whole way northwards from hence to that noted promontory Bengore Head consists of extended views of the ocean on the one hand, and on the other, rocky mountains of considerable height, which are in some places clothed with woods, and with massive columns of basaltes, forming a line of coast the most fantastically beautiful that imagination can conceive.

The county of Antrim contains much diversified scenery, mountains wild covered with heath and bogs, or frowning in abrupt and lofty cliffs, and in some parts fertile plains exhibiting all the mild beauties of cultivation. Its extensive linen manufactures and productive fisheries are its principal branches of commerce. Its mineral productions are limestone, coal, sandstone, crystals, granite, and porphyry.

DOWN.

Boundaries.—Antrim; Armagh; Carlingford Bay; Carrickfergus Bay; the Irish Sea; and Louth.

Towns.—1, Downpatrick; 2, Hillsborough; 3, Dundrum; 4, Newry; 5, Strangford; 6, Newtown Ardes; 7, Rathfryland; 8, Killyleagh; 9, Bangor; 10, Donaghadee; 11, Grey Abbey; 12, Dromore; 13, Gillford; 14, Wellan; 15, Clogh; 16, Killough; 17, Newcastle; 18, Kirkiel; 19, Ardglass; 20, Loughbrickland; 21, Ballinahinch; 22, Warrenpoint.

Rivers.—a, the Laggan; b, Newry, or Narrow-water; c, Newry Canal.

Lough.—A, Strangford Lough or Bay.

Island.—B, Copland Island.

Mountain.— C, the Mourne.

MRS. ROWE.—WHAT are the boundaries, extent, and chief towns of Down?

ANNA.—It is bounded on the north by Antrim and Carrickfergus Bay, on the east and south-east by the Irish Sea, on the south by Louth and Carlingford Bay, and on the west by Armagh. Its length from north-east to south-west is nearly 50 miles, and its breadth about 40. The chief towns are Down or Downpatrick, Hillsborough, Dromore, Dundrum, Newry, Grey Abbey, Loughbrickland, Ballinahinch, Newtown Ardes, Killough, Bangor, Donaghadee, and Warrenpoint.

MRS. ROWE.—Down, or Downpatrick, the county town, is noted for its situation on the southern branch of Lough Strangford, and for its antiquities. This city derives its name from St. Patrick, who founded a celebrated Abbey in it, in which he is said to have been interred, A. D. 493. St. Columb and St. Bridget were also buried here. North of this town is a great doone, or elevated rath, upon which tradition affirms a palace formerly stood. It is surrounded by three ramparts and terraces: its circumference is said to be 2100 feet, and its height 60 feet. Adjoining the Abbey, stood a round tower, which was 60 feet high; when it was taken down, in 1790, there appeared beneath it the foundation of some other stone building of good masonry. Connor was united with the see of Downpatrick in 1442. The land is here rich and fertile; and there is a good race-course about a mile from the town.

Hillsborough is a beautiful modern town, built on the face of a hill ascending to the south. It has an elegant church in the form of a cross, in which is a monument by Nollekins to the memory of Archdeacon Leslie. The general agricultural improvement of the environs of this town owes much of its beauty to the Noble family from whom it derives its name. A short distance from this place is one of the finest maze courses in Ireland; it has a hill in the centre.

Dromore is noted for a large rath on the ridge of a hill just beyond the town, (whence the name *Drum Mor*): from this eminence there is a curious hollowed passage to the river Laggan. It is the see of a bishop. A church and abbey were built here by St. Colman in the sixth century. It possesses a chalybeate spring; but is a retired place, and derives its principal support from its trade in linen.

Dundrum is a village at the head of a bay of the same name. Upon a rock stands the extensive ruin of its Castle, built by the powerful Baron John de Courcy, who first undertook the conquest of Ulster. It was erected for the Knights' Templars, who possessed it in 1313, at which time that order was abolished; and it was granted to the Prior of Down.

GEORGE.—In 1517, the Earl of Kildare, then Lord Deputy, took this fortress by storm from the Irish, who garrisoned it, after driving out the English some time before. It was recovered and repaired by the Magennises, and again taken by the Lord Deputy Gray in 1538, but finally dismantled by Oliver Cromwell's army.

Newry is a large and improving town, situated on the Newry, or Narrow-water, over which it has two stone bridges. Here is also a drawbridge over the Canal, which is navigable for small sloops from Carlingford Bay to Lough Neagh. The new church, with its elegant Gothic spire, is a very ornamental object. The ruins of its old church are conspicuous on the ridge of the hill, on which stood the Abbey, built by MacLaughlin, an Irish monarch, in the 12th century. This edifice was burned in the civil war, but the lay impropriator still enjoys certain civil and ecclesiastical privileges in right of this abbacy. The retreating forces of James II. set fire to this town. It is now, however, in commerce and manufactures one of the most flourishing places in the county.

Loughbrickland stands near a lake noted for its speckled trout as well as the dreadful catastrophe which happened to some Protestants in the great rebellion, who, having been driven upon the ice by their enemies, without any possible means of escaping to the shore, upon its breaking, sunk to the bottom. This town is likewise noted as a place of encampment for King William's army, on their way to the battle of the Boyne; some vestiges of the intrenchment still remain.

Ballinahinch is situated at the junction of four roads, and is noted for an action gained by the king's forces, June 13th, 1798, under the command of General Nugent, against the insurgents of the North, when the town was burnt. Near this place is a celebrated sulphuretted chalybeate spa, and beyond that a beautiful lake. Its neighbourhood is well ornamented and tolerably cultivated.

Newtown Ardes is a handsome town situated at the head of Lough Strangford, near its north strand. The newly-erected parish church, with its steeple and spire, is an elegant building. The old town was built and settled by James Hamilton lord Claneboy and Clanbrassil. It was burnt in the civil war, and the Scottish inhabitants slain:

these were replaced by a fresh colony. A few of the ancient buildings remain: the old Gothic church is venerable;
also a Cross, with the date of 1636 ; and near the town are
the ruins of the Castle of the Montgomeries. This place
is noted for its manufactures of fine diaper and linen, and at
high water the tide flows up to the town.

Killough is a small sea-port, with a harbour that affords
safe anchorage. The shore is extremely agreeable.

ANNA.—In the cliff is a cavern, in which, at the flowing
of the tide, or at high water, there is a continued melodious
echo, responding to the noise of the surge.

MRS. ROWE.—Here are barracks for cavalry, a large and
well-built church, and a mineral spring. In its vicinity
are some ruins, in the castellated style, which seem to have
been occupied at some early period as shops or warehouses
by foreign merchants ; and close to one of the towers is a
building styled Horn Castle, from the quantity of ox-, deer-,
and cow-horns which have been found near it. These
ruins are now called the Castle of Ardglass.

Bangor, the most northerly town in the county, is seated
at the mouth of Carrickfergus Bay, and is much frequented
for sea-bathing. An Abbey, founded in 555, is now a ruin,
close to the parish church, which was built in 1623 and
has a handsome steeple: in this church are monuments of
the Hamiltons, Earls of Clanbrassil, who planted a numerous body of Scots in the lordship of Claneboy, granted to
James Hamilton on the forfeiture of O'Neil earl of Tyrone.
The harbour of Bangor is safe, and there is a good pier,
quay, dock, and basin. It also possesses two cotton facto-
ries, worked by steam-engines. The county militia is frequently quartered here.

Grey Abbey is a retired village on the east side of Lough
Strangford, and celebrated for its monastery, built by John
de Courcy earl of Ulster. De Courcy's monument, and
that of his lady Africa, daughter of the King of Man, are
to be seen here, with their effigies sculptured. The arches

of the Abbey are still fine, but the roof is dilapidated: its well, for the use of the monks, is filled by a fine spring.

Donaghadee is noted as the port of communication with the West of Scotland. Its distance from Port Patrick is computed at eighteen or twenty miles, and steam-vessels perform the passage in two hours and half. The houses towards the shore are built in the form of an amphitheatre, and from their being white produce a very pleasant effect. At the north end of the town is a large bare rath, from the top of which there is a fine view. The new harbour of Donaghadee was commenced in 1821; it comprises seven acres, and is defended by extensive piers. This place is much frequented for sea-bathing, and possesses a handsome bath-house.

Warrenpoint, so called from its being built on the site of a rabbit-warren, is a small port and sea-bathing village, which is rapidly increasing in importance. It possesses a handsome modern church and hot and cold baths. Near it is Sea View, a range of buildings so called from their being erected as lodging-houses for the accommodation of the numerous visitors who in summer frequent this romantic spot. The prospects which it commands of Carlingford harbour, the mountains, and the light-house, are justly admired. Warrenpoint is a post station, and forms a line of communication with the vicinity of Newry and Liverpool, a steamboat and other packets plying between that port, the Isle of Man, and this place.—Which are the principal rivers of this county?

ANNA.—The Laggan, and the Newry, or Narrow-water.

MRS. ROWE.—The Laggan rises near the centre of the county, and first pursues a westerly course, then turning suddenly, flows in a north-easterly direction to the sea at Belfast.

The Newry rises east of the canal, and proceeds southward through the town of Newry into Carlingford Bay.

The highest mountains are the Mourne, which give name

to a beautiful district in the southern part of this county.
They are an extensive range, and over one of the loftiest is
a road leading to Carlingford, which is actually cut through
a stratum of sea shells. The Slieve Croob mountain, about
two miles distant from Ballinahinch, is noted for a remarkable cairn eighty yards in circumference at the base and
fifty at the top ; and at Annaborn, in the immediate vicinity,
is another, with a rude stone chamber in the centre. The
space between this mountain and Ballinahinch is so completely occupied with rocks and hills that it anciently bore
the name of Magheradrol, or Field of Difficulties.

The county of Down is said to derive its name from the
remarkable number of its hills (*donne*, or *dun*, signifying
a hill). It is a very fertile district, though partly encum-
bered with bogs ; the western side, in particular, is in a high
state of cultivation, the whole tract being embellished with
plantations. The banks of the rivers Ban and Laggan
are covered with bleach-fields, and present that cheerful
and pleasing scenery which characterizes a manufacturing
county. Its mineral productions are copper, lead, freestone,
and granite. In the more uncultivated parts of this county
a great number of horses are reared.—Can you mention any
distinguished character to whom this county has given birth?

GEORGE.—Sir Hans Sloane, who was an eminent physician,
naturalist, and botanist. He published the 'Natural History
of Jamaica,' and at his death left his valuable library and
large collection of shells, fossils, and curiosities, to the public, on condition that Parliament should pay to his heirs
£20,000, which sum was considerably under their real
value.

ARMAGH.

Boundaries.—Tyrone, Monaghan, Louth, Down, and Lough Neagh.
Towns.—1, Armagh; 2, Lurgan; 3, Charlemont; 4, Blackwater;
    5, Jonesborough; 6, Mahon; 7, Newtown Hamilton; 8, Tan-
    deragee; 9, Keady; 10, Portadown; 11, Rich-hill; 12, Tynan.
River.—d, Blackwater.
Mountains.—A, the Fewers.

Mrs. Rowe.—WHAT are the boundaries, extent, and
chief towns of Armagh?

George.—It is bounded on the north by Tyrone and
Lough Neagh, on the east by Down, on the south by Louth,
and on the west by Monaghan. It measures from north to
south 32 miles, and from east to west 20. The chief towns
are Armagh, Keady, Charlemont, Portadown, Rich-hill,
Jonesborough, Tanderagee, Newtown Hamilton, and Tynan.

Mrs. Rowe.—Armagh is an archiepiscopal see, and the
capital of the county. It stands on the side of a fine hill, at
the foot of which the river Callan flows in its passage to the
Blackwater. On the summit of this eminence stands its
ancient Cathedral, which is cruciform, and its tower rises
above the intersection of the transept with the nave. This
city became an archbishopric in 1142, but the erection of
this grand edifice dates from about 1260. From our knowledge that St. Patrick founded the church of Armagh in the
fifth century, from the important character of its history
and antiquities, and from the distinguished conduct of many
of its prelates in religious and civil affairs, as well as from
its conspicuous and elevated situation, it is rendered an object of peculiar interest. This place became early the
centre of our northern civilization, and its chief seat of
learning and religion. Its first chronicles, its churches, and
the city itself, were destroyed by the Danes. Here were

buried many distinguished princes, Brian Boroimhe and others. Archbishop Usher ranks amongst its most celebrated prelates; and the palace of Armagh has long been regarded as a beautiful residence. The Augustine priory of St. Peter and St. Paul was held in high estimation as a monastic foundation. Its new church, with its stately spire, college, library, observatory, and curious market cross, are among its many public buildings worthy of particular notice. This city has long been the favourite residence of many eminent persons, and it also ranks high for its manufacture of linen, which is its principal article of trade.

GEORGE.—I have read that in consequence of the opposition of Archbishop Dowdal to the wishes of the Government in establishing the Protestant worship, the primacy was, about the time of the Reformation, granted to Browne, Archbishop of Dublin.

MRS. ROWE.—Since which the metropolitan pre-eminence has been maintained by both prelates, with a slight variation in the title, the Archbishop of Armagh being styled Primate of all Ireland.

Keady stands near the river Callan, and is noted for its lead-mines on the estate of the Earl of Farnham. The bleaching-grounds and mills on and near the Callan are numerous, and assist in giving an air of prosperity to this part of the county.

Charlemont is a market and corporate town and a military depôt. Its fort and barracks are worthy of observation, and the manufacture of linen is considerable in its vicinity.

Portadown is a well-built town on the western side of the Ban, over which is a handsome stone bridge; and a little above this place the Newry canal joins the river, and thus forms a communication with Lough Neagh. Here is a good market for grain, which, with the manufacture of linen, gives a degree of activity to this little town.

Rich-hill is a beautiful little village, noted for the two handsome columns erected in the picturesque grounds of Sir Capel Molyneux, Bart., in honour of the order of St. Patrick and the Volunteers of Ireland.

Jonesborough is a fine sporting station, and its church closes the prospect of the most romantic mountains which surround a widely elevated plain, consisting principally of a deep red moss. Near it is Piedmont, formerly Lord Clermont's, and above the crags and desolate tops of the hills are to be seen shells of numerous houses which were burned by the insurgents in 1798, and which the then Noble proprietor did not permit to be repaired.

Tanderagee is a small market-town, seated on a high hill which commands a fine prospect of several fertile valleys. Its church is a handsome Gothic structure, and close to it stands a delightful mansion, built upon the site of O'Hanlan's castle. This town is seated in the centre of the linen manufacture, and the Newry Canal passes it.

GEORGE.—Near this place is Point's Pass, noted for having been the scene of many battles in the feudal times.

MRS. ROWE.—Newtown Hamilton, is a small village in which, according to tradition, the great O'Neil was slain in an encounter with a chieftain of Louth, in consequence of the latter singeing the beard of the former at a banquet where he was his guest; this town possesses a neat church, and near it are intrenchments, supposed to have been a camp of Cromwell's army; also at a short distance are the remains of a fortified castle and barracks which appear to have been formerly the only safe retreats in this mountainous neighbourhood. Much of the land in this district is bare and unproductive.

Tynan is a small town, seated on an eminence near a river of the same name. It possesses a handsome church and lofty steeple, and in the churchyard is a curious oblong stone, of about 18 inches square and 4 feet long, set upon a large block of stone and capped with another divided into square compartments, on which are some vestiges of sculpture ; near this place stood the ruins of an ancient castle.—Which is the principal river that waters this county ?

ANNA.—The Blackwater rises on the confines of Monaghan and flows in a north-easterly direction, through the towns of Blackwater and Charlemont, in its passage to unite its waters with those of Lough Neagh.

MRS. ROWE.—The highest mountains are the Fewers, a wild, barren, but romantic district well worthy the notice of those who seek for picturesque scenery ; and the admirers of Dean Swift will be gratified in tracing many spots mentioned in the works of that eccentric man, especially Hamilton's Bawn, Gosford Castle, and Draper's Hill. The Slieve Gullen, in the vicinity of Jonesborough, rivals the loftiest mountain in England or Wales. On its summit is a cairn of stones which form the roof of a cavern that at first view appears to be natural, but upon examination affords evident proof of its being the work of art. The apartment is difficult of entrance, but it is large within, and as there is a flagged way to the edge of the lake at the foot, it seems to have been intended for other than sepulchral purposes ; it is popularly said to be the abode of sprites and elves. Rocks, caverns and glens are the prominent features of the summit of this mountain, without any appearance of calcareous matter, and the bold prospect which it affords will repay the fatigue of the ascent, as well as furnish the awful and impressive pleasure of contemplating bold promontories and rugged cliffs, bared by tempests, and arresting the floating meteors, which furnish, throughout, ample resources for the religious and philosophic mind. The nothern part of the county of Armagh consists of most extensive bogs of extraordinary depth and a remarkably black soil; consequently it affords no scenery worth mentioning : but in the immediate vicinity of the city an abundant population finds employment in well inclosed and well cultivated fields; in the mountainous district the hand of industry or the eye of taste has scarcely yet penetrated. The manufacture of linen affords the principal source of employment to the inhabitants of this county. Its mineral productions are lead and iron.

MONAGHAN.

Boundaries.—Tyrone, Armagh, Louth, Meath, Cavan, and Fermanagh.

Towns.—1, Monaghan; 2, Carrickmacross; 3, Castle Shane; 4, Castle Blaney; 5, Glasslough; 6, Drum; 7, Clones; 8, Tedawnet; 9, Emydale; 10, Ballybay; 11, Ballytrean; 12, Inniskeen.

Mountains.—A, The Fewers.

Mrs. Rowe.—WHAT are the boundaries, extent, and chief towns of Monaghan?

George.—It is bounded on the north by Tyrone, north-east and east by Armagh, south-east and south by Louth and Meath, and south-west and west by Cavan and Fermanagh. Its greatest extent from north to south is 40 miles, and its extreme breadth 28, though in some places it does not exceed 15 miles. Its chief towns are Monaghan, Carrickmacross, Clones, Castle Blaney, and Glasslough.

Mrs. Rowe.—Monaghan, the county town, is an ancient place. Its first abbey, which was destroyed, was of very early date; it was rebuilt for Conventual Franciscans in 1462, but again demolished, and its site is now occupied by a castle of Lord Blaney's. It has several public buildings worthy of notice, amongst which are its cavalry barracks,

K 2

the diocesan school of Clogher, its church, and a handsome
market-house erected by lord Rossmore in 1792.

Carrickmacross is a market-town possessing a good endowed school and a neat modern church. It has manufactures of soap, leather, and hats. Near it are some small
lakes.

Ballybay is a neat village, and in it are two beautiful
small lakes.

Clones, formerly called Cluaneois, is a market-town; its
numerous antiquities attest its early importance. Its abbey
was founded by St. Tigernach, who is said to have fallen a
victim to the plague in 548; this edifice was of the Augustine order, and was rebuilt by the English in 1212, when
its castle was also erected; the abbey is said to have been
once episcopal; near its ruins are to be seen some curious
burial-places with ornamented tombstones, and in its
cemetery stands a round tower with walls four feet thick.
Contiguous to it is a large tomb or stone coffin, with some
ancient inscriptions on it. In the vicinity of this town are
many Danish forts; and at a short distance is the magnificent demesne of Dawsongrove, with its handsome mausoleum and several picturesque lakes. The forest of Bel-
mont affords some very fine scenery, and near to it is a
celebrated medicinal well called Grana-buy-more. In
Clones are two Danish raths, one with a table top, and
one on the summit of a hill near, of an immense size.
The handsome modern church in this town is worthy of
notice.

George.—I cannot understand the meaning of the word
rath; is it a general name for mounds of earth which are
to be seen in various parts of the British Isles?

Mrs. Rowe.—Sir Richard Colt Hoare says, that Ireland
presents a great variety of these earthen works, by which
is to be understood banks or mounds of earth raised in
various shapes and applied to different purposes; but the
Irish writers have not sufficiently distinguished their cha-

racters, as they have applied to them the general term
rath, and attributed their formation to the Danes. The
word *rath* appears to be a corruption of *road*, which in
the Danish language signifies a council, and which is inter-
preted by Lhuyd, in his Irish English Dictionary, "a village, a prince's seat; also, an artificial mount, or barrow."
Sir Richard Colt Hoare proceeds to class these earthen
works in the following order.

1. A mound of earth formed in the shape of a cone, en-
circled generally by a slight ditch. These tumuli, he consi-
ders, were originally raised by the Celtic or Belgic tribes
who inhabited Ireland, and for sepulchral purposes, as many
of them have been opened and found to contain ashes,
bones, urns, and other ornaments, and in a great degree
corresponded with those discovered in England, which
proves that the respective inhabitants of the age made use
of the same modes of burial when these mounds of earth
were thrown up. Some are flat at top, but as the surface appears too small to have answered any military purpose, he
concludes they also where sepulchral.

2. A large circle surrounded by a raised agger of earth
and a slight ditch. There are many of these works in Ireland, and frequently two near each other; the name of *rath*
more appropriately belongs to these, as from their dimensions and slight elevation, they were calculated for those
conferences and meetings which the word literally implies,
and the circumstance of finding two adjoining each other
seems to strengthen this supposition; and as no such elevated form can be found amongst the great variety of barrows
which the chalky downs of the West of England present,
we may conclude these are not sepulchral.

3. High raised circular tumuli with more than one
fosse; these are evidently military works, as are likewise,

4. Those with ramparts and outworks. The most common plan of these is a high circular mound with a square
or oblong work attached to it; the whole surrounded by

one ditch or more. This mode of fortification was adopted also in Wales, and from their frequent demolition and speedy reedification, Sir Richard Colton Hoare concludes that the buildings upon them were made of wood, or they could not have been so quickly destroyed and restored. There is a greater similarity in the military works of Ireland than in those of England or Wales; neither are they so complicated in their form, or so stupendous in their proportion. Common tradition ascribes the foundation of these mounds to the Danes, and no doubt a great proportion of them are not older than the occupation of the nothern and eastern coasts of Ireland by the Ostmen. But some must be of the earliest Scandinavian date, particularly the Giant's Ring, near Belfast, and the Rough Fort, near Templepatrick, which have Druidical remains incorporated with them; others argue for their Celtic and Belgic origin, as the word *rath* is of Celtic derivation.

GEORGE.—In some parts we read of small mounds placed singly, while in others they are said to be placed in lines of communication for miles together.

MRS. ROWE.—Many of those smaller mounds have been proved to be tumuli, or sepulchral monuments, but where there is a line of them to be found for miles together, they were evidently for exploratory purposes, or chains of military posts, of which the one on the road from Belfast is a remarkable instance; but we must resume our geography.

Castle Blaney is a pleasant town, with a handsome church. Its castle is the residence of Lord Blaney, and in the grounds is a lake on which are many islands.

Glasslough is an agreeable village; to the west of it is a remarkably high hill, on the summit of which are the remains of a fort, memorable in the rebellion of 1641.

The county of Monaghan possesses no river of importance, nor are there any loughs in it worthy of note. It is a hilly county, well cultivated and populous, and the plantations surrounding the many handsome residences of gentlemen give a cheerful effect to the scenery. The linen manufacture is extensively carried on, and is its principal source of support. Its mineral productions are lead, antimony, ironstone, marble and coal. The principal lead ores are to be found at Castle Blaney and near to the church at Clontibrett.

CAVAN.

Boundaries.—Monaghan, Fermanagh, Leitrim, Longford and West Meath.

Towns.—1, Cavan; 2, Belturbet; 3, Ballyconnel; 4, Kilmore; 5, Virginia; 6, Coronery; 7, Cootehill; 8, Ballyayen; 9, Bally Jamesduff; 10, Ballyhays; 11, Swadlinbar; 12, Baillieborough; 13, King's-court.

Rivers.—a, the Erne; b, Woodford.

Loughs.—A, Lough Ramor; B, Lough Shecklin.

Mrs. Rowe.—WHAT are the boundaries, extent, and chief towns of Cavan?

Anna.—It is bounded on the north by Fermanagh and Monaghan, east by West Meath, south by Longford, and west by Leitrim. Its greatest extent from north-west to south-east is 55 miles, and from east to west it measures 36. The principal towns are Cavan, Belturbet, Ballyhays, Kilmore, Swadlinbar, Baillieborough, King's-court, and Virginia.

Mrs. Rowe.—Cavan is situated on a small river of the same name. Though the capital of the county, it possesses little worthy of note besides its royally endowed school, a modern church, and barracks for horse-soldiers. An abbey for Dominican Friars was founded here in 1300. The vi-

cinity of this town is enriched with many beautiful mansions and picturesque scenery, particularly that of Earl
Farnham, which justly claims admiration.

Belturbet is an ancient town seated on the river Erne
at its entrance into the upper lake of Lough Erne. It has
a handsome church with a tower and steeple, beyond which
are the remains of a fortification; and near the bridge are
the remains of its castle. In this town are barracks.
Great quantities of linen are manufactured here and in the
neighbourhood.

Ballyhays, though now only a small village, must formerly have been of considerable note. Its mansion-house
is a curious specimen of Irish feudal splendour, besides
which it has several antique buildings. Near to it is the
enchanting little village called Butler's Bridge, and not far
from that stands Drumlane Priory, which was founded in
the 6th century, and dedicated to the Virgin Mary. It
was long esteemed as a sepulchral place of great sanctity,
though, perhaps, more celebrated as the birthplace of St.
Maidoe, a noted legendary personage. It is probable that
the round tower, which stands close to one corner of this
sacred edifice, is the most ancient building. What remains
of the priory serves for the village church, though little
better in appearance than a large barn.

Kilmore is remarkable for possessing the smallest cathedral in the island, and with Ardagh, in the county of
Longford, forms a bishopric.

GEORGE.—Lough Outer is situated near this town, and
on one of its small islands are the ruins of an ancient castle,
which was the prison of the good Bishop Bedell during the
rebellion in 1641.

MRS. ROWE.—The finest trees, in a variety of shades, are
to be seen on the many beautiful islands of this lake; and
the deep recesses and romantic scenery of these sequestered
islets were well suited to the many superstitious rites which
were formerly celebrated on them.

Swadlinbar is a neat village, which has long been celebrated for its spa, containing sulphur, earth, sea-salt, and
fossil alkali. Near it are the ruins of a church.

Baillieborough is situated on a branch of the river Blackwater. Its castle stands on the side of a lough, at a short
distance; and near it is a chalybeate spring. The view
from the church is good, and not far from it, on the summit of a hill, is a pool long celebrated for its medicinal
qualities. This natural spring deserves the attention of the
geologist and medical student.

King's-court is a village of modern erection, rising fast
into a thriving town, and clearly exemplifying the good
effects of patriotism. In the immediate vicinity of this
place are several deep glens and valleys, within which flow
rapid streams, affording many romantic scenes. Not far
from hence is a narrow dale, in which the mineralogist will
find much amusement.

Virginia is a pleasant village on the northern side of
Lough Ramor, and is the favourite residence of persons
who resort to this lake for the enjoyment it affords to the
angler.—What are the names of the rivers of this county?

GEORGE.—The Erne or Earn, which derives its source
from Lough Gounagh, on the borders of Longford, and
flowing northward through Belturbet, enters Fermanagh,
and expands into a lake; and the Woodford, which rises on
the borders of Leitrim, and pursuing a north-easterly course
through the village of Ballyconnel, after crossing the western part of the county, falls into Lough Erne.

MRS. ROWE.—Are there any loughs in Cavan worthy of
notice?

ANNA.—Those of Ramor and Shecklin are the largest.
The former is studded with islands which were once clothed
with foliage, but though now destitute of trees, yet they
possess the ruins of several old castles; and it contains various kinds of fish. The latter is said to be 7 miles long,
and in some parts 4 broad. On the northern banks of this

lough are several sporting-boxes erected by gentlemen, the grounds of which are extremely well wooded, whilst on its southern verge, amidst lofty hills and fertile corn-fields, may be seen the ruins of the ancient Castle of Ross. This lough is celebrated for its trout.

MRS. ROWE.—Cavan, though an inland county, yet possesses more water and more diversified scenery than any other district in the island, with the exception of Kerry; for, although there are no elevations deserving the name of mountains, yet it is rugged and uneven, and pleasingly intersected with many beautiful lakes. This county was one of the most celebrated in ancient feuds and wars, and from its natural securities and fastnesses (woods and bogs being less accessible to foreign enemies,) retained its primitive manners and customs to a later period than most other parts of the country. It is rich in mineral stores, and the principal source of employment for its inhabitants is derived from its manufactures of linens and muslins.

FERMANAGH.

Boundaries.—Donnegal, Tyrone, Monaghan, Cavan, and Leitrim.
Towns.—1, Enniskillen; 2, Church Hill; 3, Belleek; 4, Donough; 5, Lisneskea; 6, Tempo; 7, Ballycassidy; 8, Kinawly; 9, Newtown Butler; 10, Wattle Bridge; 11, Bellcoo.
Rivers.—a, the Clodagh; b, the Erne.
Loughs.—Erne or Earn, A, Upper Lough; B, Lower Lough.
Bay.—C, Donnegal.

MRS. ROWE.—WHAT are the boundaries, extent, and chief towns of Fermanagh?

ANNA.—It is bounded on the north by Donnegal and Tyrone, on the east by Monaghan, on the south by Cavan,
and on the west by Leitrim. From north to south it
measures 35 miles, and from east to west about 25. The
principal towns are Inniskillen, Belleek, Church Hill, Newtown Butler, Wattle Bridge, Donough, and Bellcoo.

MRS. ROWE.—Enniskillen, or Inniskillen, is pleasantly
situated on a strait which connects the two divisions of
Lough Erne. It appears like a town in the midst of waters,
and presents a range of buildings extending a considerable
way on both sides the river, over which there is a lofty
stone bridge. The Enniskillen dragoons distinguished
themselves in the war of the Revolution, and the town was
successfully maintained against the besieging army of
James II. Near the bridge part of the military works still
remain. In this town are handsome barracks, a superb
royal-chartered school-house, and an ancient castle. In the
vicinity of this place is Florence Court, a noble demesne of
Earl Enniskillen's. It is seated at the foot of lofty mountains, which, from the peculiarity of their strata, look like
fortified ground. At Daughtons, not far from Enniskillen,
are some curious caves. The manufacture of linen is carried on to a considerable extent in this town.

Belleek is a small but well-built town, finely situated on
the south of the great channel by which Lough Erne discharges itself into the bay of Donnegal. Here the waters
roll furiously over a bed of rock, forming in their course
two fine cataracts, when they pass under a lofty bridge, and
from thence continue to flow rapidly for some distance
under perpendicular and well-wooded rocks, which afford
some very beautiful scenery both above and below the
bridge.

Church Hill is a village which derives its name from its
handsome church with a square steeple, standing on a hill.
Near it are the ruins of some castles.

Newtown Butler is a village noted for its beautiful

church. The Earl of Lanesborough derives the title of baron from this place.

Wattle Bridge is a village on the banks of the Fin, near which are the fragments of a Druidical temple; also a church dedicated to St. Mary, and two small loughs.

Donough is a small village situated on a stream which flows into Lough Erne. Near it are a small lough and the ruins of an ancient church.

Bellcoo is a neat village seated on a considerable stream that runs into Lough Cane, and from thence to Lough Melvin. The well called Davugh Phedric is noted as a cold bath, and nearly equal to Holywell in temperature. Near this place are the ruins of a church.—Which are the principal rivers of this county?

ANNA.—The Clodagh runs westerly from Lough Erne till it loses itself in Lough Cane; issuing from thence it flows north-westerly, and after parting this county from Leitrim, falls into Donnegal Bay; and the Erne, which flows in a westerly direction from the northern part of Lough Erne into the same bay.

MRS. ROWE.—The great glory of this county is Lough Erne. It extends 20 miles in length, and is divided into two lakes, called the Upper and Lower Lake; these are connected by a narrow strait, the waters of which form a rapid current under the walls and bridge of the town of Inniskillen. On the left, towards the north, are to be seen some castellated ruins. The river soon after assumes the form of a lake; and Davenish Island presents a very naked appearance, being totally destitute of wood; its soil, however, is very rich, and produces most abundant crops of corn. On this island is a fine round tower, remarkable for its superior workmanship; its height is said by Twiss to be sixty-nine feet to the cornice, the conical top fifteen feet more, the circumference forty-eight feet, the thickness of the walls three feet five inches, and the diameter of the inside nine feet two inches: the walls are built of hewn stone,

each stone about a foot square within and without, and with
scarcely any cement; the roof is of the same materials, in
the form of a cone, and finished with one large stone shaped
like a bell. Near the top are four windows opposite to the
cardinal points; the centre stone over each window is decorated with a human head. The doorway faces the east,
and is about nine feet from the ground; over it is a pointed
window, larger than those in the stories above, which are
square-headed. The usual projections for the reception of
the different floors are very evident within this turret, and
the smooth and well-joined surface of the interior walls does
great credit to the ancient masons who erected it. The
most easterly building on this island is a Gothic church,
which is large and beautiful, with a noble carved window
over the high altar; next to this window, to the right,
about ten feet above the ground, is the following inscription,
the letters and points of which are raised: "Matheus
O'Dubagan hoc opus fecit Bartholomea O'Flannagan Priori
de Dominis, A.D. 1449." Round this inscription is a frame.
Contiguous to the round tower is a vaulted building of hewn
stone, which ends in a point, and is called St. Molaise's
House; near to this is his bed, in the shape of a stone coffin,
in which he used to pray. Tradition records that pains in
the back are relieved by lying in this bed.

GEORGE.—I have read that St. Laserian, called also
Molaise, built a celebrated monastery, under the invocation
of the Virgin Mary, in Daimh-inis, or the Ox's Island.
This saint died A.D. 563, and was succeeded by St. Natalis,
son of Ængusius, king of Connaught. A number of abbots are mentioned to have succeeded him, to the year 1462,
when the Prior O'Flannagan died. In the years 822, 834,
and 961, this abbey was plundered by the Danes, and in
1157 and 1360 it was much hurt by fire.

MRS. ROWE.—It is said to have been a remarkably
curious building, and the workmanship of it extremely
good. Many other islands on both parts of this lough ex-

hibit very ancient monastic ruins, and the various beauties
of this noble expanse of water, with its numerous islets and
indented shores, delight the eye; whilst the scenery, particularly towards the beautiful residence of the Earl of Ross,
afford a picturesque view and romantic subject for the pencil of the tourist.   This view presents a very different
appearance when seen at the commencement and at the
close of the day, owing to the natural moisture of the
country being raised into vapour by a meridian sun, con-
densed by cold winds rushing in through extended valleys
through the day, and settling in the dells or fringing the
mountain tops in the still repose of evening, or rising like
a curtain at the influence of the morning beam.   The surrounding woods abound with game, and on the surface of
the lough myriads of aquatic fowls are constantly sporting.
Its waters afford numerous species of excellent fish, particularly perch, and it has been asserted that no spot in
Europe exceeds this as a place of diversion to the fowler
and angler.

By means of this lough and river the county is navigable
in its whole length.   Its general surface is mountainous,
interspersed with extensive boggy tracts, which rendered it
almost impregnable in early times, and travelling is still
difficult in many places.   The linen manufacture and raising
of cattle form the principal trade.   Its mineral productions
are very unimportant, but in the boggy parts sea-shells are
often found mixed in strata of white clay fifteen feet below
the surface.

TYRONE.

Boundaries.—Donnegal, Londonderry, Lough Neagh, Armagh, Monaghan, and Fermanagh.
Towns.—1, Clogher; 2, Augher; 3, Newtown Stewart; 4, Strabane; 5, Ballymagorry; 6, Dungannon; 7, Ormagh; 8, Cookstown; 9, Stewartstown; 10, Mountjoy; 11, Altmore; 12, Aughnacloy; 13, Trillic; 14, Moy.
Rivers.—a, the Derg; b, Mourne; c, Common.
Mountains.—A, the Spenin.

Mrs. Rowe.—WHAT are the boundaries, extent, and chief towns of Tyrone?

Anna.—It is bounded on the north by Londonderry, on the east by Lough Neagh and a part of Armagh, on the south by Armagh and Monaghan, and on the south-west, west, and north-west by Fermanagh and Donnegal. It measures about 45 miles from north to south, and in the broadest part from east to west, about 50. Its chief towns are Ormagh, Clogher, Dungannon, Cookstown, Newtown Stewart, Strabane or Strathbane, Aughnacloy, and Moy.

Mrs. Rowe.—Ormagh (signifying 'chief's residence',) is the county-and assize- town, and is pleasantly situated at the junction of the rivers Drumraw and Common. It formerly possessed an abbey, of which no vestiges now remain, though there are ruins of its ancient castle. This town was burnt in 1748, but has been neatly rebuilt, and the adjacent district possesses a flourishing linen manufacture. Its principal buildings are a neat stone church, a free-school, barracks, the county gaol, and infirmary.

Clogher is now only a small village, in the southern part of the county, though it is an episcopal see of high antiquity. The see of Louth was united to this in the 11th century, and its cathedral now serves as a parish church. The

Druids are supposed to have dwelt in this place in early times, and its ancient abbey was destroyed by fire in 1396. The bishop's palace and demesne are worthy of note.

Dungannon is a town of note, situated on a canal which passes Coal Island, the mines of which are constantly worked. By means of this canal a communication is obtained through Lough Neagh with Lisburn, Belfast, Newry, &c.

GEORGE.—This town was the ancient residence of the O'Neils, chieftains of the north, one of whom was created Earl of Tyrone, or Tirowen, and though leader in the rebellion against Queen Elizabeth, yet retained his provincial rank as a native prince, by the double art of the courtier in doing homage to the queen, and of the warrior in repelling the English forces from his territory.

MRS. ROWE.—His castle was some time after destroyed by the troops of Ireton. Its monastery, founded by the O'Neil family, was soon after granted to the Earl of West Meath, by whom it was assigned to Sir A. Chichester: vestiges of this building still remain. This town possesses a modern church and several public buildings.

Cookstown is situated on a river of the same name. It consists principally of one long well-built street bordered by lofty trees, nearly one mile in length. It has a good market and carries on the linen manufacture. The cultivated vale through which the Cookstown river flows, is bounded by lofty hills. A neat Gothic church was erected here in 1820.

Newtown Stewart stands on the banks of the Strule, near its junction with the Mourne. Not far from its church are the ruins of its ancient castle, and in its vicinity is the splendid mansion of Baron's Court, which is considered one of the finest in the kingdom. The park is also celebrated for its timber. In an island on the lake are the picturesque ruins of a castle, and the mountain scenery of this neighbourhood is truly romantic.

Strabane, or Strathbane, is a large town situated near
the confluence of the rivers Fin and Mourne. It has a
handsome stone bridge across the river, and in it are also
good barracks.

ANNA.—In 1615 James Hamilton, Baron Strabane, built
the town, castle, church, and school-house; and in the time
of James I. and Charles II. this family and the Clanbrassil
branch seated at Tullymore, Carnysure and Coronery, acquired great possessions throughout the North of Ireland.

MRS. ROWE.—Near this place are the remains of the
once elegant ruins of Corock Abbey for Franciscan Friars.

Aughnacloy is an agreeable market-town near the Blackwater stream, in which are to be found excellent trout.

This place is a thoroughfare from several of the principal
towns of the county to those in Armagh and Monaghan.
Near it are the ruins of Lismore Fort, once of considerable
strength; and in the vicinity of Aughnacloy is a noted spa.

Moy stands near the Blackwater river, and is noted for
its monthly fairs for horses and cattle. Its church was
built in 1819, and is a fine stone structure with a handsome
steeple.—Which are the largest rivers of this county?

GEORGE.—The Derg, Mourne, and Common,

MRS. ROWE.—The Derg rises from a lough of the same
name in the county of Donnegal, and after a short north-
easterly course, joins the Mourne.

The Mourne finds its source in the southern part of the
county, and flows northerly till it unites its waters with the
Fin, from whence it flows on under the name of Foyle to
Lough Foyle.

The Common rises in the centre of the county, and joins
the Mourne near Ormagh.

The northern parts of this county may be considered
mountainous, particularly towards Strabane, where the
Spenin range extends into Londonderry: other parts of it
are rugged and uneven, but none very high. It is completely an inland county, and from the lands being divided

into small parcels, has an increased population, which gives much cheerfulness to its general aspect. Its principal articles of commerce are linen and linen thread. Coals are the only mineral yet discovered, though it is conjectured that iron exists in many places, as there are numerous chalybeates.

LONDONDERRY, or DERRY.

Boundaries.—Antrim, Lough Neagh, Tyrone, Donnegal, Lough Foyle, and the Atlantic Ocean.
Towns.—1, Londonderry; 2, Newtown Limavaddy; 3, Culmore Fort; 4, Ballykelly; 5, Kilrea; 6, Moneymore; 7, Castle Dawson; 8, Maghera; 9, Garvagh; 10, Dungiven; 11, Clady; 12, Magherafelt; 13, Dawson's Bridge; 14, Ballaghy.
Rivers.—a, the Foyle; c, the Mayola; d, the Roe.
Loughs.—A, Lough Foyle; B, Lough Neagh.

Mrs. Rowe.—WHAT are the boundaries, extent, and chief towns of Londonderry?

Anna.—It is bounded on the north by Lough Foyle and the Atlantic Ocean, on the east and south-east by Antrim and Lough Neagh, on the south by Tyrone, and on the south-west and west by Tyrone and Donnegal. It measures from north to south 37 miles, and from east to west 35. Its principal towns are Londonderry, Kilrea, Magherafelt, Dungiven, Newtown Limavaddy, Clady, Dawson's Bridge, Ballaghy, Moneymore, Maghera, and Ballykelly.

Mrs. Rowe.—Londonderry, or Derry, is seated on the river Foyle, and is surrounded by ramparts about a mile in circumference. This city is a place of great antiquity, the see of a bishop, and forms a county in itself, distinct from that of which it is the capital. St. Columb is said to have founded an abbey here in 546. It was colonised by Londoners, to whom James I. granted a charter. Its Cathedral was erected in 1633, and is a noble Gothic edifice, with a lofty square tower. The wooden bridge, built in 1790 by Mr. Cox of Boston in America, is remarkable for its curious construction; it is 1068 feet long and 40 broad, and has a drawbridge for the admission of vessels. Its harbour is safe and capacious, and its quays are commodious. The King's Stores form a fine range of buildings, and amongst the guns may be seen the Walker, a piece of ordnance ten feet in length, bearing the date of 1642. This city is celebrated for the gallant and successful defence which its inhabitants made under the direction of Mr. Walker, a clergyman, when it was besieged by the army of James II. in 1690.

GEORGE.—I have read that Colonel Lundie, who was appointed governor of Londonderry by King William III., was secretly attached to the cause of James II., and prevailed upon the officers of the garrison to send messengers to the besiegers with an offer of surrender; but the inhabitants being apprized of their intention, shot one of the officers whom they suspected, and boldly resolved to maintain the town. The courage of the new-formed garrison (under their reverend leader,) fully compensated for the weakness of their fortifications and the want of artillery: several attacks were made and repulsed with resolution. All the success that valour could promise was on the side of the besieged; but they, after some time, found themselves exhausted by continual fatigue, and to add to their calamities, they began to feel the miseries of famine and disease. General Kirke, who had been sent from England with supplies, in vain attempted to come to their assistance, being prevented sailing up the river by a boom which had been thrown across it, and the batteries of the enemy. For a long time these unfortunate people were compelled to subsist upon horses, dogs, and all kinds of vermin; and even this loathsome food began to fail them. Kirke, upon hearing that the exhausted garrison had resolved upon making proposals for capitulation, determined to make one desperate effort, in order to supply them with the means of subsistence. Accordingly, three victuallers, with a frigate to cover them, sailed up the river, in order to throw some provisions into the town. The eyes of all were fixed upon these vessels; the besiegers eager to destroy them, and the garrison as resolute for their defence. The foremost of the victuallers broke the boom upon the first attempt, and was stranded by the violence of the shock; upon this a shout, which reached the camp and the city, burst from the assailing party, who advanced with fury against a prize which they considered they must inevitably secure, whilst the smoke of the cannon on both sides wrapped the whole scene in darkness. To the astonishment of all, the victualler was seen in a short time emerging from her danger, having got off by the rebound of her own guns, and she led up her little squadron to the very walls of the city. The joy expressed by the inhabitants at this unexpected relief was only equalled by the rage of the disappointed enemy, who were so dispirited that they with precipitation abandoned the siege in the succeeding night. The siege lasted 105 days, during which the garrison lost upwards of 10,000 men, and the besieging army about 8,000.

Mrs. Rowe.—The linen manufacture flourishes here, and the imports and exports of Londonderry are considerable.

Kilrea is a small town noted for its market for linen, the manufacture of which flourishes in the neighbourhood.

Magherafelt is noted only for its endowed school and handsome church and spire.

Dungiven is a market-town, built in a rich valley watered by the beautiful river Roe, which is joined by two tributary streams near this place; the approach to it is by a road cut through a mountain. The Sept of O'Cahane was once powerful amidst the high range of hills in its vicinity, and a native chieftain of that name, who built a friary here, was, with his seven sons, interred in its ancient cemetery. Here is still a spacious mansion, though somewhat dilapidated. Its church is cruciform; and in this town is an extensive bleach-green.

Newtown Limavaddy is a very handsome town, situated on the banks of the Roe, and surrounded by beautiful scenery, and in its vicinity the manufacture of linen is considerable.

ANNA.—Dr. William Hamilton, who was esteemed for his learning and accomplishments, and whose letters on the north-east coast of Antrim give a correct idea of the extreme beauty and magnificence of the scenery of the North of Ireland, was inhumanly murdered by the insurgents, when rector of this town.

Culmore Fort, situated on Lough Foyle, on the borders of the county of Donnegal, was the scene of an act of treachery when taken by Sir Cahir O'Doherty in the beginning of the 17th century.

GEORGE.—This barbarous man pretended to be desirous of contracting an intimacy with the English of these parts, and particularly with the governor of this fortress, whom, with his wife and child, he invited to a feast. When there, he imperiously said to the former, "You must quietly surrender to me Culmore Fort, or yourself, wife, and child shall die." Immediately a band of armed kerns rushed into the room and were ordered by Sir Cahir to execute him. Through the entreaties of Lady O'Doherty he was dissuaded from his murderous intention; but turning to the general's wife, he said, " Madam, go instantly to Culmore with these armed men and procure for them a peaceable entrance into the fort." The terrified lady immediately undertook this perilous mission, and repaired to the castle with the rebels. Upon her arrival, telling the sentry that her husband had broken his leg, she gained admittance for herself and the whole party, when the garrison was murdered, and though the governor's life was spared, yet his reputation was utterly ruined.

MRS. ROWE.—Clady is a pretty village, built on the banks of the river Fanghan. Near it stands the ruin of O'Cahane's Castle.

Dawson's Bridge is a village on the Mayola river, near where it falls into the north-west bay of Lough Neagh. From this place a good road communicates by the bridge at Toome Ferry with the county of Antrim.

Ballaghy is a village pleasantly situated in the midst of mountain scenery of the most romantic description. In its vicinity are some beautiful seats and diversified grounds.

Moneymore is situated in a vale formed by the Slieve Gallen mountain. This place has been very much improved by the Drapers' Company of London, to whom it belongs. It possesses a church and two free-schools.

Maghera is a small town pleasantly situated in the beautiful vale of Mayola. It has a fine church, built of stone in 1820; part of the doorway of its old church now remains, and is curiously sculptured; besides which it possesses a Lancastrian school and barracks. The Braeface, a tract of land on this side of Carntogher mountains, is adorned with pretty cottages and fine hawthorns, which bush is esteemed sacred by the peasantry, who dread the enmity of its evil sprites, in case it is lopped or cut down. Here are also some moats and raths.

Ballykelly is a small place in the northern part of the county, noted for its linen manufacture and its church, which is a singular object.—Which are the principal rivers of this county?

ANNA.—The Foyle, which is a continuation of the Mourne, flows northwards into Lough Foyle; and the Mayola, which rises in Tyrone and flows in an easterly direction till it empties itself in Lough Neagh.

MRS. ROWE.—The principal lough is that of Foyle, which may be more properly termed an inlet of the sea.

Off its mouth is the Tounds Bank, and the sands stretch along the left of the channel into the bay; but the channel itself is not obstructed, and there are five fathoms water close to the city of Londonderry.

The mountainous scenery of Derry presents neither roughness nor green herbage, but something between the two which may be defined uncultivated vegetation, while the lower parts are inundated with water, and have in some places been converted into bogs. The arable land is seldom divided to any extent, and the scenery is but little enriched by the elegancies of cultivation. Limestone abounds here, and on the coast there is a limestone rock, where there is a remarkable cavern called the Robbers' Cave; it contains apartments in which, some years ago, a banditti concealed themselves and their booty, and were extremely trouble-some to the neighbourhood. Iron ore has also been found, and small veins of lead and copper. At a small village on the north coast there is a famous rabbit-warren, and the linen manufacture is carried on in most parts of the county.

DONNEGAL, or TYRCONNEL.

Boundaries.—Fermanagh, Londonderry, Tyrone, and the Atlantic Ocean.
Towns.—1, Donnegal; 2, Raphoe; 3, Killebegs; 4, Letterkenny; 5, St. John's Town; 6, Ballyshannon; 7, Pettigo; 8, Lifford; 9, Whitecastle; 10, Greencastle; 11, Cortyhack; 12, St. Helen's; 13, Dunglo; 14, Naren; 15, Ardrea; 16, Convoy; 17, Kilmacrenan; 18, Dunfanaghy.
Rivers.—a, the Fin; b, Eask, or Esk; c, Swilly.
Loughs.—A, Lough Derg; B, Lough Finn; C, Lough Swilly.
Mountains.—D, Barnsmore; E, Derryveagh; F, Slievelong; G, Slievenaught.
Islands.—H, Tory or Torry Island; I, North Isles of Arran; J, Raglin.
Capes and Bays.—K, North Cape; L, Cape Telling; M, Cape St. John; N, Donnegal Bay; O, Mulroy Bay.

Mrs. Rowe.—WHAT are the boundaries, extent, and chief towns of this county?

George.—It is bounded on the north and west by the Atlantic Ocean, on the east by Londonderry and Tyrone, and on the south by Fermanagh and Leitrim. It measures from north to south 60 miles, and from east to west 42. The chief towns are Donnegal, Raphoe, Killebegs, Letterkenny, Convoy, Kilmacrenan, and Ballyshannon.

Mrs. Rowe.—Donnegal, the capital, is situated in the southern part of the county, at the mouth of the river Esk. The surrounding scenery is picturesque, and, with the ruins of an old castellated mansion, the river, and bridge, affords a good subject for the pencil. Immediately adjoining the town is a small port, and not far from that are the remains of a Franciscan Monastery, founded in the year 1474 by Odo Roe, son of Neal Garbh O'Donnell, prince of Tyrconnel, who died in 1505. The construction of this edifice

was exactly after the Egyptian manner of building, and it
appears to have contained places for depositing valuable
effects in times of danger. In a building over it are evident
marks of a regular Roman pediment. By means of its bay
this town carries on some trade.

Raphoe is a small town, the see of a bishop, founded by
St. Eunan in the 9th century. Its cathedral has been handsomely repaired, and its episcopal residence, which was
formerly a castle, and besieged in 1641, is now a beautiful
mansion. St. Columb founded an abbey here, and a
round tower once stood upon the hill contiguous to it.

Killebegs is situated in the south-western part of the
county, and has an excellent harbour, which is of considerable advantage to the fishery, as great shoals of herrings
visit this coast. It also possesses an ancient Castle, and a
Franciscan house founded by Mr. Sweeney, which, with
the beautiful scenery of the coast, are objects of interest
to the tourist.

Letterkenny is a small market-town on the river Swilly,
noted for its picturesque mountain scenery.

GEORGE.—It is also memorable for having been the scene
of an engagement in the 17th century, between the parti-
sans of Oliver Cromwell and Ebher M'Mahon, a Popish
bishop and general, who, with his sword in one hand and his
crosier in the other, headed his men to the charge, but lost
both his cause and his life.

MRS. ROWE.—Convoy is a small place, situated between
the rivers Swilly and Fin, and is only remarkable for having
in its neighbourhood a kind of magnesian stone, that might
be applied to many purposes in architecture, being as easily
cut as a piece of wood; it bears the fire so well that it
would answer for crucibles: the country people use it as
bowls for tobacco-pipes.

Kilmacrenan is the name of a barony in the northern
part of the county, and is noted for containing some ecclesiastical ruins, founded by St. Columb, part of which form

the parish church; and in the midst of an inaccessible district in its vicinity is the rock upon the summit of which, from the earliest Milesian times, the chieftains of Tyrconnel are said to have been inaugurated, with savage solemnities, by the abbots of Kilmacrenan, successors of Columbkill.

GEORGE.—It is also of note for being the place where, in the reign of James I., Sir Cahir O'Doherty concealed himself with a numerous force, designing the most general rebellion that had ever existed in Ireland. A reward of 500 marks having been offered by the lord deputy for this outlaw's head, a Scotchman named Ramsay, whose inclosure Sir Cahir had attacked, driven off his cattle, murdered his wife and children, and reduced his once happy cot to a mass of smoking ruins, being rendered desperate by a spirit of revenge, and having discovered this rebel's retreat, applied the fire to his levelled matchlock, and before the report began to roll its echoes through the woods and hills, the ball had pronounced the death-warrant of his inhuman victim. The panic-struck followers of Sir Cahir immediately deserted the lifeless body of their leader and fled through the mountains.

Ballyshannon is a beautiful and romantic place, built on heights both on the north and south side of the river Erne, over which it has a magnificent bridge of fourteen arches. Some ruins of the once famous Castle of the O'Donnells, the turbulent feudal chieftains of Tyrconnel, are to be seen here. Its noted salmon-leap is a fall of a wide body of water, which, though only twelve feet in height, is very beautiful. Large quantities of fish are usually taken, and the fishery is farmed of the proprietor: the curing-house stands on a rock in the centre of the stream. The views of the sea, beheld between the hills and rocky banks of the river, are grand, and the harbour below the town is good; besides which it has handsome barracks and a neat church. In its vicinity are several Danish raths, and near it, in a secluded but picturesque situation, are the ruins of Asheroe Abbey.

Ballintra is a small town, noted only for having in its immediate neighbourhood a truly romantic demesne called Brown Hall, in which a rapid torrent forces its obscure course through the earth, with the hollow sound of subterraneous cascades.

Dunfanaghy is a village seated on a cove of an extensive harbour called Sheephaven, at a short distance from North Cape. Near it is Horn Head, where, in the roof of a cave of the cliffs, which are sixty-two feet high, there is a natural perforation. This funnel is called M'Swine's Gun, and the surge of the Atlantic Ocean, when impelled in boisterous weather into this cavern, issues forth at the summit of the cliff with a roar, which is heard at a great distance, and often exhibits a curious waterspout of some elevation. Near this is the ancient Castle of M'Sweeney, now repaired and inhabited.

Naren is a village situated on a promontory on the western coast of the county. Off this shore is seen the island of Enniskill, on which is an ancient chapel in ruins, and a holy well. Its founder, St. Conal, is said to have been slain here in 599.

Dunglo is a sequestered fishing-village, situated in the Rosses, at the head of a creek, and chiefly known as the market for the supply of the town and island of Rutland, which, being one of the North Isles of Arran, is seen from this haven. Its only buildings are a church and a mill.

Lifford, the assize-town of the county, is romantically situated on the river Foyle, and its vicinity is embellished by many handsome seats. Its principal buildings are the jail, erected in 1825, its church, court-house, and county-infirmary.—Which are the principal rivers of this county?

ANNA.—The Fin, Esk, and Swilly.

MRS. ROWE.—The Fin issues from the lake of the same name, and runs parallel to the great road which traverses the county longitudinally from Fintown to Lifford.

The Esk issues from a lake about three miles in length

and one in breadth, hemmed in by Ross mountain and other
steep ridges; it then takes its rapid course through a ravine
between the high slopes of Barnsmore and a heathy precipice on the opposite bank.

The Swilly springs from the centre of the county, and
after a north-easterly course, falls into the south end of
Lough Swilly, at Letterkenny.

Lough Derg is an expanse of water situated in the
southern part of the county, amidst a wild waste of moors
and sombre mountains.

GEORGE.—It is remarkable for its purgatory, founded,
as reported, by St. Patrick, in a small island about 130
yards long and 50 broad. The purgatory itself consists of
a cave 16½ feet long by 2 wide, and so very low that a
tall man cannot stand erect in it. Around it are the remains of several chapels and holy circles, dedicated to
different saints. This asylum of superstition is of great
antiquity.

ANNA.—I have read that pilgrims who visited this place
were obliged to go round the sharp and stony rocks of
these abodes of devotees on their bare knees, and that they
were compelled to remain on the island nine days, breaking
their fast but once a day with oatmeal and water, and
lodging on straw without pillow or pallet.

MRS. ROWE.—Besides this there are many small rocky
islands on this lake, whose tufted brown summits give a
wildness and sublimity to the scenery.

Lough Swilly is a large gulph in the northern part of the
island, and the scenery around it is delightful.

Lough Fin is about two miles in length, and is situated
nearly in the centre of the county. It produces an abundance of fish.

The mountains of this county are very considerable; the
highest ranges are the Barnsmore, which extend quite across
from the south-western corner into the neighbouring county
of Tyrone.

The Derryveagh reach along the western coast.

The Slievelong are in the south-western part of the county, and the Slievenaught are in the peninsula formed by the Loughs Foyle and Swilly.

GEORGE.—I have read that through the precipitous and almost inaccessible Barnsmore range, Nature has made an extraordinary gap, on each side of which are abrupt and almost perpendicular elevations; and amongst numerous water-worn chasms are to be seen tufts of heath and yellow-blooming furze, with here and there a stunted oak or birch, which give an appearance of vegetation to this sublime and alpine picture.

MRS. ROWE.—Near this pass is a castellated ruin, which is said to have been erected in the reign of James II., and in which the impartial historian Rapin compiled his voluminous History of England.

ANNA.—I perceive by the map there are several islands on this coast, the largest of which are those of Tory, the North Islands of Arran, and Raglin off Cape Telling.

GEORGE.—It was off Tory Island that Sir John Borlase Warren encountered a French fleet with troops and Irish rebel chieftains on board, in October 1798, and by capturing them all, crushed the hopes of the French army that had landed at Killala, and broke the spirits and cause of the rebels who had joined them.

MRS. ROWE.—This island is about nine miles distant from the shore, and is an interesting spot; its name is said to be of Punic origin, being a corruption of Thor Eye, which denotes that it was anciently consecrated to Thor, the Scandinavian deity that presided over stormy and desolate places. On it are the ruins of a fortress said to have been built by Erick of the Red Arm, one of the Norwegian sea lords, whose roving rule extended around these isles and coasts; also a tower and several chapels, the erection of which is ascribed to St. Columbkill: and in a portion of the burial ground several ancient saints are said to have

been interred. Its inhabitants seldom visit the mainland,
and it is recorded that when a fishing-boat belonging to it
was driven into Ardes Bay a few years back, the men in it
were actually so astonished at the sight of trees that they put
some leaves and small branches of them into their pockets
to convey home to their friends as objects of curiosity.
In August 1826, this island was visited with a calamitous
storm, which destroyed all the corn and potatoes then
growing on it, and filled up all the freshwater springs : its
inhabitants were by it reduced to a state of want and dependence upon public generosity, and were much indebted
to the benevolence of the Bishop of Raphoe, to whom the
island appertains.

The island of Rutland, which is the largest of the North
Isles of Arran, consists of 180 acres, and is situated off a
creek, which runs up to Dunglo. It affords an excellent
shelter for vessels engaged in the fisheries, which have
here a secure roadstead in three fathoms' water. Rutland
is its chief town, and is noted for its fisheries, particularly
that of herrings. This place is well provided with warehouses, and has a handsome quay as well as a dockyard.
Of the numerous bays which intersect this coast, Mulroy
is a deep land-locked arm of the sea, which presents a variety of the most beautiful scenery: in some places it resembles a placid lake, winding through mountains without
any apparent outlet ; in others a broad and magnificent
river opening into a fine harbour, in which a navy might
ride in safety. Formerly its shores were covered with timber, and the oak, ash, and hazel still adorn its declivities.
This county, now known by the name of Donnegal, or Tyrconnel, was anciently inhabited by the Rhobogdii and
Venieni. The whole of its western coast consists of a range
of mountainous rocks, which in some places extend to the
sea: between the mountains in the interior are extensive
tracts of bog, in which are the remains of immense forests
buried deep in the bosom of the vale, though at this time

the tourist travels for miles without a single tree to solace his eye. One part of the county presents a view of most singular appearance, consisting almost of an uninhabited waste of heath, with masses of granite protruding from the sides of the mountains, whilst here and there, wherever a little soil can be found, are small patches of cultivated land, with cabins formed of dry sandstone, cement being unthought of.

In Innishowen Barony, a peninsula formed by the loughs Foyle and Swilly, as already mentioned, are to be seen numerous Druidical remains and some traditionary fragments of Ossian, as well as the site of the ancient Tura, so famed in the historical romances that form the basis of MacPherson's modern Fingal. The mineral productions of this county are sandstone, lead, and iron; emery has also been found here. The manufacture of linen is carried on in some parts of it.

LEINSTER.

Mrs. Rowe.—TELL me the situation of the province of Leinster, and the names of the counties it contains.

Anna.—Leinster is situated in the eastern part of Ireland, and contains the counties of Louth, Dublin, Meath, West Meath, Longford, King's County, Queen's County, Kildare, Wicklow, Kilkenny, Carlow, and Wexford.

LOUTH.

Boundaries.—Armagh, Down, Meath, Monaghan, and St. George's Channel.
Towns.— 1, Louth; 2, Dundalk; 3, Carlingford; 4, Ardee, or Atherdee; 5, Dunleer; 6, Collon; 7, Drogheda; 8, Clogher; 9, Dillons Town; 10, Lurgan Green; 11, Warrenpoint.
Rivers.—a, the Dee; b, the Laggan.
Bays.—A, Carlingford Bay; B, Dundalk Bay; C, Drogheda Bay.

MRS. ROWE.—WHAT are the boundaries, extent, and chief towns of Louth?

GEORGE.—It is bounded on the north by Armagh and Down, on the east by the Irish Sea, on the south and south-west by Meath, and on the west by Monaghan. It is the smallest county in Ireland, measuring only 26 miles from north to south, and 12 from east to west. Its chief towns are Louth, Dundalk, Castletown, Carlingford, Ardee, Dunleer, Collon, and Drogheda.

Louth was once a town of importance, from which the county took its name. St. Patrick is said to have founded an abbey here, the site of which was afterwards occupied by a priory for canons regular; but there are no vestiges of either building, and the place is now reduced to a small village.

Dundalk claims an ancient foundation from its bay and harbour in the Irish Channel, which were of great importance in the early history of Ireland. It is situated at the very extremity of what is called the 'English Pale,' and was consequently exposed to frequent hostilities. It formerly presented a mass of strong castles, towers, and castellated mansions of the English barons, erected for the purposes of defence, and some remains of these may still be traced. A part of the ancient monastery for Crouched

Friars now forms its hospital; besides which it has ruins of a house for Grey Friars, and a curious square tower. The erection of its spacious Sessions-house was completed in 1822, and this truly classical specimen of architecture is said to have been built after the model of the Temple of Theseus at Athens. On the summit of a hill to the west of the town are the remains of a fine old Danish station and rath; and at a short distance from this stands an old church enveloped in ivy: here is also a Catholic cemetery of great sanctity. Dundalk is celebrated for its manufactures of muslins and cambrics, and is most advantageously situated for an extensive coasting trade, its harbour being commodious and very safe for shipping: it is also noted for its distillery of whiskey.

Castletown is a small village standing on the side of Dundalk hill, and is distinguished for its Castle, an ancient edifice with towers and battlements, partly repaired, and forming the offices to the more modern mansion of the Earl of Roden, in which are preserved some curious antique portraits of Henry VIII. and Anne Boleyn. This castle was taken in the 14th century by Edward Bruce, and on the side of the hill towards the river there are some earthworks which are apparently vestiges of those times. Upon the peninsula of Balrichan, in its vicinity, are several Druidical remains. Amongst them are the ruins of a castle with a subterraneous cave; a massive stone called the Giant's Load, which is twelve feet long and six feet square, resting on three upright stones; mount Albani, an earthen camp with a tumulus; also Castle Rath, and the tower of Ballug.

Carlingford is a place of great antiquity, and is seated on a bay which is capable of receiving the largest vessels, but so full of rocks as to be extremely dangerous: this place when first founded consisted entirely of castles or fortified mansions, erected for the protection of the 'English Pale' against the incursions of the unconquered northern Septs. The origin of its principal castle has been

attributed to King John: it was well situated to defend
the narrow pass, which, like another Thermopylæ, has high
and abrupt mountains above, with an impetuous sea dash-
ing beneath it. This edifice is now a mere mass of ruins,
triangular in its shape, and seated on a solid rock: its walls
are eleven feet thick.   On the south side of the town are
the picturesque ruins of an ancient Dominican Abbey,
founded by De Burgh in the 14th century; and at the foot
of a high mountain in the vicinity is a limestone quarry,
mixed with basaltes, crystallizations of pyrites, shells, &c.
From the situation of this town, the sun is lost behind
the hills for several hours after sunrise and before sunset.
Among the rocks of Carlingford Bay are found the finest
green-finned oysters, for which this place has long been
celebrated.

Ardee, or Atherdee, is seated on the river Dee.   This
town was formerly walled round, and its gloomy yet venerable jail once formed part of an extensive fortress : it also
possessed a house for Crouched Friars, and a Carmelite
Friary ; the church of the latter was destroyed by an army
of Scots when many of the townspeople were sheltered
within it.   Here is Castle Guard, which is supposed by
some to have been a sepulchre, or more probably, from its
construction, a place of meeting: it is 90 feet high,
the circumference at the base 600 feet, and 140 at the table
top, with the remains of two concentric octagonal buildings, and a wide and deep trench round it, which is well
planted.

Dunleer is a village situated on the high north road ; it
has good inns but exhibits less commercial spirit and importance than might be expected in such a thoroughfare.

GEORGE.—In its vicinity are some monastic ruins, which
form a singular and interesting group.   The precincts of
a small churchyard contain two perfect stone crosses,
and one imperfect; two chapels, and a large round tower
which maintains its usual position to the north-west of the

church. The loftiest of the two crosses is said to be of one
entire stone, and is called St. Boyne's Cross, which is the
most ancient religious relic now extant in Ireland. The
ornamental figures on it at once show the uncivilized age
in which they were engraved: there is also an inscription
on this cross in the old Irish character, equally inelegant
with the figures, some letters of which evidently form the
word Muredach, who was for some time king of Ireland,
and died A.D. 534, about 100 years after the arrival of
St. Patrick. This abbey continues to be a burial place
of note.

MRS. ROWE.—Collon has long been of note from its
contiguity to the highly celebrated Abbey of Mellifont; it
is also worthy of notice as every road, hedge, and cottage
in it give evident proofs of what can be done by modern
improvement in Ireland. Its Gothic church has a fine
spire, and is surrounded by trees, which, with the neat white-
washed houses, stone bridge over the river that runs
through the town, and large bleaching-green on its banks,
have a pleasing effect. It also possesses an extensive manufacture of cotton stockings.

ANNA.—A weekly market was granted to this town by
King Henry III. in 1229, with freedom from all tolls and
customs throughout the kingdom; and Edward III., in
1349, gave the inhabitants liberty to erect a gallows, pil-
lory, and tumbril (or ducking-stool).

GEORGE.—Mellifont Abbey is said to have been erected
in 1142 by Donough M'Corvoill (or Carrol,) prince of
Uriell, for monks of the Cistercian order, with which St.
Bernard furnished it from his own abbey at Clairvaux.
Christian O'Conarchy was its first abbot, and in 1150 he
was made Bishop of Lismore. In 1157 a great synod was
held here for the purpose of consecrating the church, at
which were present the Archbishop of Armagh, the Apo-
stolic Legate, and divers other princes and bishops. Many
rich grants were made to the abbey on this occasion. Its

founder was buried here in 1168; and in 1189, Murchard O'Carrol king of Uriell died, and was buried near the former.

MRS. ROWE.—Uriell, or Orgiel, comprehended anciently the present counties of Louth, Monaghan, and Armagh, the sovereignty of which was generally invested in the family of O'Carrol.

ANNA.—In the year 1203 King John granted a new charter to this abbey, confirming to them their former possessions; but in the year 1306 all its temporalities were seized, and vested in the king's hands, on account of the endless disputes for the chair of the abbacy: in consequence it was decreed in 1322, that no person should be received into it before he had verified upon oath that he was not of English descent.

MRS. ROWE.—Kings Edward III. and Henry IV. confirmed all the grants made from time to time to this abbey, and Richard Conter, who was its last abbot, had a pension granted to him for life. The abbots of this religious house sat as barons in parliament. In 1617 these extensive possessions were granted to Sir Gerald Moor, who resided here, and made it a magnificent seat, and at the same time a place of defence, as it bordered immediately upon the Irish rebels. On the 24th of November, 1641, it was assailed by a strong party. The garrison, which then consisted only of fifteen horse and twenty-two foot, made a vigorous defence; but their ammunition being exhausted, the horse forced their way through the Irish camp, and were followed by the foot to Drogheda. Only eleven were taken, which number were sacrificed in revenge for the 120 of the Irish who fell in the field of battle. Two inconsiderable buildings now mark the site of this once sumptuous Cistercian Monastery. Small, however, as are the remains, they still claim the tourist's attention.

Drogheda is a large, populous, and well-built port, situated on the river Boyne, but its liberties south of the river are in East Meath. It has an excellent harbour, in which vessels of large size may ride in safety; and its commerce and coasting trade are considerable. The town is seated in a valley, with a steep range of hills to the north. St. Peter's church and spire of hewn stone, its barracks, and the ancient steeples of the abbeys, transpierced by wide arches in the direction of the cardinal points, are worthy of notice.

GEORGE.—In 1650 this town was besieged by Oliver Cromwell, who, with a ferocity sufficient to tarnish the most heroic valour, entered it by storm, and indiscriminately butchered men, women, and children.

ANNA.—On an eminence in a valley on the banks of the Boyne stands the obelisk which commemorates the decisive victory gained by King William against the forces of James II., July 1st, 1690.

MRS. ROWE.—Drogheda is historically celebrated. It gallantly resisted all the efforts of the Irish under Sir Phelim O'Neil in 1641; and the present prosperity and trade of the place rank it amongst the chief towns of the kingdom. It is likewise noted for its excellent salmon-fishery.

GEORGE.—It was near this town, in a Dominican Friary, that King Richard II. received the personal homage and fealty of several Irish princes.

MRS. ROWE.—Which are the principal rivers of this county?

ANNA.—The Dee, which enters it in the west from Meath, and takes an easterly course till it meets the Laggan, where it falls into the sea; and the Laggan, which rises in the northern part of Meath, and flows south-easterly through this county.

Louth, though the smallest county in the kingdom, ranks amongst the most fertile and best cultivated. It is bordered by precipitous broken hills to the north, and is embellished by a considerable growth of ash-trees, which in

many parts surround the villages or border the roads. It
is fortunate that this tree is so much favoured by the
Irish, as its pendent and elegant branches are pleasing to
the sight, and its wood of constant utility to agriculturists.
On the salt-marshes a large number of cattle and sheep are
fed. Sea-fowls, such as wild geese, barnacles, and gulls,
also frequent the coast.

DUBLIN.

Boundaries.—Meath, Kildare, Wicklow, and St. George's Chan-
nel.
Towns.—1, Dublin; 2, Blackrock; 3, Swords; 4, Balruddery; 5,
Kilgoblin; 6, Bray; 7, Dundrum; 8, Lucan; 9, Newcastle;
10, Rathcoole; 11, Inniskerry; 12, Donnybrook; 13, Lusk;
14, Balbriggan; 15, Naul; 16, Howth; 17, Clontarf; 18,
Chapel Izod; 19, Dunleary or Kingstown.
Rivers.—a, the Liffey; b, the Grand Canal.
Cape and Bay.—A, Howth Head; B, Dublin Bay.
Islands.—C, Black Rock; D, Ireland's Eye; E, Lambay Island;
F, St. Patrick's Isle.

MRS. ROWE.—WHAT are the boundaries, extent, and
chief towns of Dublin?

ANNA.—It is bounded on the north by East Meath, on
the east by the Irish Sea, on the south by Wicklow, and
on the west by Kildare and East Meath. It measures
from north to south 30 miles, and from east to west 18,
though in some parts it does not much exceed 10. Its
chief towns are Dublin, Blackrock, Swords, Donnybrook,
Finglass, St. Douloughs, Malahide, Howth, Rathfarnham,
Balbriggan, Lusk, Rush, Bullock, Dalkey, Glassneven,
Naul, Chapel Izod, Lucan, and Dunleary or Kingstown.

MRS. ROWE.—Dublin, the metropolis of Ireland and an archbishopric, is a large, populous, and handsome city, seated near the mouth of the river Liffey, about a mile from the bay of Dublin, which is a semicircular basin eight miles in diameter. This bay is celebrated for the beauty of its shores, and is said to bear a near resemblance to that of Naples. On the north side of it the harbour is divided by a stupendous stone pier, which stretches about three miles from the shore, and is terminated by a lighthouse, which, like another Eddystone, seems to rise out of the sea, from whence a flag is seen to fly at the flow of the tide, which is the only time that the sand-bank, called the Bar, can be crossed with safety. This harbour is sheltered by the hill of Howth, and the entrance to the city is defended by extensive moles. The Liffey divides Dublin into two nearly equal portions, which may be denominated the north and south divisions. The old town stands on the latter side of the river, and contains many ancient public buildings. On the north side is a regularly built new town, and its best streets are not intersected by close lanes and small ancient houses, as in the southern division. It possesses all the modern public erections, as well as the residences of the nobility and gentry, and some of the chief avenues of the metropolis. This place must at an early period have been of considerable importance, as by the 10th century it was styled the most noble city of Dublin; and long before Ireland became a portion of the British dominions, it was in possession of the Danes, who surrounded it with a wall and other fortifications.

GEORGE.—Henry II., after he had subdued the island, ordered a palace to be erected here, in which he held a parliament in the year 1175, when he granted his first charter to the city, holding out great encouragement for colonizers from England to settle in it. He also gave a grand Christmas entertainment in this edifice to several petty princes who had submitted to him.

ANNA.—In the reign of William III., A.D. 1689, James II. made his public entry into this city, and was received by the Papists with shouts of joy and superstitious ceremonies; and the following year, after the memorable battle of the Boyne, this misguided prince, despairing of future success, returned hither, and shortly after quitted the island.

MRS. ROWE.—Dublin, from its situation and importance, ranks high among the cities of Europe, and in magnitude and the number of its inhabitants it stands second in the British dominions. Of its numerous public buildings, the national bank (formerly the parliament-house), the two cathedrals, the churches, custom-house, hospitals, museum, barracks, and bridges are worthy of admiration.

GEORGE.—Immediately opposite the post-office stands a fluted Ionic column, surmounted by a colossal statue of Lord Nelson. On the pedestal are inscribed the words Trafalgar, St. Vincent, Nile, and Copenhagen, with the dates of those actions. Its entire height is 134 feet, and it was erected in 1808.

MRS. ROWE.—The Phœnix Park is a royal inclosure, so called from a Corinthian column surmounted by a phœnix, erected by Lord Chesterfield in 1745. It is about 7 miles in circumference, and is pleasingly diversified by woodland and rising ground. In it is the lord-lieutenant's country residence, which is a handsome building. It also contains the royal military infirmary; the Hibernian school, established by Lord Townsend for the maintenance and education of soldiers' children; a chalybeate spa, surrounded by pleasing walks; and the Wellington Testimonial, an obelisk 205 feet in height, resting on a pedestal 24 feet high and 56 square, on the sides of which are basso-relievos representing some of the Duke of Wellington's victories. The obelisk bears the names of the battles won by the noble duke.

GEORGE.—This park was formerly a part of the extensive possessions of Kilmainham, where Richard Strongbow

founded a priory of Knights Templars. Philip king of
France viewed with jealously the increasing power of this
military establishment, and its general dissolution took
place there about the year 1312. The example of Philip
was quickly followed by our Edward II. This order, from
their first establishment in 1118, had gained possession of
sixteen thousand lordships.

Mrs. Rowe.—Dublin is justly celebrated for its manufactures of tabinets, silks, cottons, worsteds, and fustians;
and the proximity of this great capital to the sea gives it
an enviable superiority in commercial importance.

Blackrock is beautifully situated in Dublin Bay, and it
derives its name from some rocks, which are apparently a
few large blocks of stone, overgrown with sea-weed. It is
the most celebrated sea-bathing place in the vicinity of the
capital.

Swords is a post-town much celebrated for its antiquities,
of which various portions still remain. Its Monastery was
converted into a palace for the Archbishop of Dublin, but
is now in ruins. In it was a round tower, detached from
the walls of the church, and of a ruder construction than
many of those erections in Ireland. It is now noted for its
well-attended annual cattle- and horse-fair.

Donnybrook is seated on the river Dodder, and is celebrated for its great annual fair, which lasts six days. In
this village are several cotton-printing mills, and its ancient church deserves notice.

Castle Knock is noted for the ruins of its Castle, which
was built on a commanding height by the English invaders
in the reign of Henry II. At Dunsink, a little beyond this
village, on an eminence, is an observatory.

Finglass is noted for a mineral spring, formerly much resorted to. Its church, erected in 1609, occupies the site
of an abbey.

St. Douloughs is remarkable for its ancient church, sup-

posed to have been erected in the 9th century, in which
and the two succeeding centuries, this and other churches
resembling the cells of Grecian temples, were built in this
kingdom.   These edifices were only 40 feet in length, and
were adorned with rude columns.   Near this is a holy well,
dedicated to the Virgin, which is the resort of numerous
pilgrims.

Malahide is a village near an inlet of the sea, and is
noted for its Castle, built on a beautiful peninsula.   It is
an extensive pile, and commands a grand sea-view.   Its
manor and royalties extend far along the shore.   A cotton
manufacture has long been established here.

Howth is an improving port romantically situated on the
promontory known by the name of the Hill of Howth, the
highest point of which is 567 feet above high-water mark.
Here the mails and packets are landed from Holyhead,
without passing the bar of Dublin Bay.   Howth harbour
is the station of the steam-packets commanded by officers
of the royal navy.   Besides the lighthouse, which stands on
the point called the Bailey, here are some fine ruins of an
ancient abbey, and a race-course made by Lord Howth.

Rathfarnham is a village noted for being the place where
the military road commences, which, after passing the central part of the mountainous district of Wicklow, forms a
communication between Dublin and the interior and south-
western parts of Ireland.   It was executed after the rebellion of 1798, and terminates at the barracks of Agava-
nagh.

Balbriggan is a thriving town on the coast, having a good
pier.   In this place is a remarkable vein of alabaster and
micaceous spars, intermixed with copper and sulphur
streaks.   In the vicinity is the ruin of Bremore Castle, and
on the coast still remain some of the towers and ivy-clad
walls of the chapels of Balclungan Castle, which was destroyed by the parliamentarian army; also an ancient ce-

metery. The cotton manufactures of Balbriggan are considerable, and some exceedingly fine stockings made here bear a high price.

Clontarf is a sea-bathing village, situated on a delightful strand and surrounded by fine groves, parks, and villas. The mode of bathing here is dissimilar to that used in England, where bathing-carts are employed : here bathing-boxes are placed on the shore and watched by their owner; in these the bathers equip themselves, and then walk into the water. Baths are also erected in various parts near the north wall, &c., for the accommodation of visiters, and the sea-water is conveyed from hence to baths in the capital. A battle was fought here in 1014 against the Danes, in which the heroic Irish monarch Brian Horn was killed; and near this place Alan archbishop of Dublin was slain in a revolt occasioned by the son of the Earl of Kildare.

Lusk is celebrated for its fine round tower, and ancient church, in which are several monuments and a curious vestige of antiquity, supposed to have been an idol of the Danes.

Rush is a fishing-village noted for curing ling, a large quantity of which is exported.

Bullock is a delightful sea-bathing village, and is much frequented in summer. An ancient and picturesque Castle stands on the cliff, and in a delightful glen was lately to be seen a rocking-stone, or cromlech, supposed to have been placed there by the Danes.

Dalkey is a beautiful village celebrated for its ancient castles, the remains of two of which are still standing. On a hill in this place is a cromlech, and near that a Druidical circle. A sound or channel, of sufficient depth of water for ships of burthen, separates it from an island of the same name. This issues from a mountain which rises immediately above the village.

Glassneven is noted for being the residence of Tickell the poet, but the site of his house is now occupied by the

botanic garden of the Dublin Society.   In the south-west
corner of the churchyard is a tablet to the memory of Dr.
Delville, the intimate friend of Dean Swift.

Bray is a sea-bathing town, standing on a river of the
same name, which is celebrated for its trout, and offers excellent diversion to the angler; whilst the wooded glens
and awful precipices on its banks, with the romantic scenery of its vicinity, are well suited to amuse the contempla-
tive mind.   In this place are infantry barracks, and the
remains of an old Castle, near which a battle was fought in
1690 between the forces of James II. and William III.
About a mile and a half distant is Bray Head, which rises
807 feet above the level of the sea; its summit may be
reached without much difficulty.   Pebbles found on the
shore beneath it are much prized when cut and polished.
Along the coast are several Martello towers.

Naul is noted for a remarkable glen, abounding with
craggy precipices, in the centre of which is the Roches cascade, and from it issues a stream that separates this county
from Meath.   The ruin of the ancient Castle of Naul is
finely situated.

Chapel Izod is pleasantly situated on the Liffey, and is
noted for the mansion in which King William III. resided
several days.   This edifice afterwards became the country
abode of the viceroys of Ireland.   It is also celebrated for
the growth of strawberries, and from hence the capital is
supplied with that delicious fruit.

Dundrum is a populous village, noted for its goats'
whey and enchanting scenery.   Its old Castle stands on a
hill, which overlooks a beautiful glen.   Not far from hence
the road passes through the Scalp, which is so conspicuous
from Dublin Bay.   It is a remarkable chasm in a mountain
which appears to have been rent asunder by an earthquake:
some have supposed it was cut by human effort, forgetting
that Celtic and northern tribes never performed such works.
The width of this defile is just sufficient for the passage of

the road to Wicklow, the charming scenery of which is admired by every lover of nature.

Lucan stands on the Liffey. In it are several manufactories, iron-works, calico-printing mills, &c. The vicinity of this town is picturesque, and it is much resorted to on account of its sulphuretted chalybeate spring, resembling that at Harrowgate in Yorkshire.

Dunleary, or Kingstown as it is now called, in consequence of the visit King George IV. made to this place in 1821, is a celebrated sea-bathing village. It is well built, and the pier adds greatly to its attractions; it also possesses a convenient harbour, and is the resort of many pleasure-parties from the capital.—Name the principal rivers of this county.

ANNA.—The Liffey rises in the county of Wicklow, and by a circuitous course runs into Kildare, where it passes through the Leinster Aqueduct, under the Grand Canal, and is afterwards precipitated from the rocks of Leixlip, forming a most beautiful waterfall called the Salmon Leap, and from thence it glides through an improved and agreeable country to the city of Dublin, near which it empties itself into the bay.

GEORGE.—Besides this stream, the commerce of the county is greatly accelerated by means of the Grand Canal, which extends from Dublin by the Shannon harbour, near Banagher, to Ballinasloe: a branch proceeds by Portarlington to Athy, were it joins the Barrow. It was with great difficulty that this great work was effected, as, besides having to cut through hard and rocky strata, and construct aqueducts over the valleys and rivers, it had to be carried through a long tract of turf-bog, which, from its fluid-like consistency, filled up the cut whenever the digging ceased. This difficulty was in time surmounted, and the canal itself has proved such a drain to the bog as to enable the land-owner to reclaim a great extent of it and bring it under cultivation.

MRS. ROWE.—There are no mountains of any particular height in this county, if we except the Hill of Howth, which is a remarkable peninsula joined to the mainland by a narrow isthmus : it was anciently called *Ben Hader*, which signifies ' The Birds' Promontory.'

ANNA.—Tradition records that on this hill once stood an edifice styled Dun Criomthan, or the palace of Criomthan, who was the chief or king of the district, and that in the days of the Roman Agricola he made many descents upon the coast of Britain.

MRS. ROWE.—Opposite to this hill is a small island called Ireland's Eye, which is a rugged but picturesque rock. About three leagues north of this is Lambay Island, on which there are large quantities of rabbits. During the summer this island is much frequented by parties of pleasure, and on Trinity Sunday a great number of persons visit a spring on it, traditionally called Holy Trinity Spring. Here also are the ruins of a dwelling-house and fortress, which were erected in the reign of King John, who made a grant of the island, with peculiar privileges, to the ancestors of the celebrated Archbishop Usher, among whose descendants it has ever since remained. Vast quantities of kelp are made here, and the coast abounds with oysters, crabs, and lobsters ; and north of Lambay are three small rocks called the Skerries Islands. One of them, named Holm Patrick, is said to have been the residence of St. Patrick. Between these islands and Rush is Lough Shinney, which possesses a good pier and harbour.

The character of this county offers to the tourist a complete epitome of the whole island. In the northern district are many bogs, and in some spots trees are wanting ; but in various points the most beautiful scenery opens to the view, presenting numerous villages with highly ornamented mansions and villas, interspersed with a variety of ancient and ivy-clad architectural remains. Extensive salt-marshes spread towards the coast. South of the Liffey the land is

principally destitute of tillage; but here the wild uncultivated heaths, rocky mountains, winding glens, and sombre
landscapes, that extend on every side, afford to the picturesque eye ample compensation.

Its ancient inhabitants were the Voluntii and Ellani;
after them came the Danes and Ostmen. In later times
this county was always within the English Pale.—Can you
name any great men who were born in this county?

GEORGE.—Dr. Thomas Parnell, an eminent divine, and
intimate friend of Swift, Gay, Pope, and Arbuthnot. His
elegant poems have ever been admired.

Sir Richard Steele, a distinguished moral and political
writer, the friend of Addison, and one of the editors of the
Tatler, Spectator, Guardian, and Englishman; author of
several plays, and an excellent little tract called the 'Christian Hero'; but his prudence by no means kept pace with
his abilities, being frequently involved in the greatest pecu-
niary difficulties.

Dr. Jonathan Swift, a celebrated wit, whose works have
been universally read; but while his genius and imagination
delight, his strong propensity to indiscriminate satire and
moroseness is intolerable. Three years before he died he
experienced that most dreadful of all calamities—insanity;
and he appeared to have had a presentiment of the change
he should undergo, having previously made his will and left
the bulk of his fortune towards building an hospital for
idiots and lunatics at Dublin.

James Usher archbishop of Armagh, who was, at an early
period of his life, so eminent for his virtues and learning
that he was ordained both deacon and priest when under
the age usually required, which was a remarkable exception
to the canonical rule in his favour. He suffered severely
during the rebellion in the reign of Charles I., being plundered of all his possessions except his library; after which
he came to England, and notwithstanding his difficulties,
published many valuable works, among which his 'Sacred

Chronology, or Annals of the Old and New Testament,' is
the most noted, and is the chief chronological authority of
the learned.

MEATH, or EAST MEATH.

Boundaries.—Louth, Monaghan, Cavan, West Meath, King's
    County, Kildare, Dublin, and St. George's Channel.
Towns.—1, Trim; 2, Ratoath; 3, Kells; 4, Slane; 5, Navan;
    6, Nobber; 7, Dunleek; 8, Julian's Town; 9, Moynalty;
    10, Ladyrath; 11, Old Castle; 12, Kilcarn; 13, Skryne;
    14, Tarah; 15, Dunshaglin; 16, Summerhill; 17, Clonard;
    18, Longwood.
Rivers.—a, the Boyne; b, Blackwater.

MRS. ROWE.—WHAT are the boundaries, extent, and
chief towns of Meath?

GEORGE.—It is bounded on the north by Cavan, Monaghan, and Louth, on the east by St. George's Channel and
Dublin, on the south by Kildare and King's County, and
on the west by West Meath. From north to south it
measures 35 miles, and from east to west, in the widest
part, about 45. The most important places are Trim,
Ratoath, Kells, Slane, Navan, Tarah, Nobber, Clonard, and
Grange.

MRS. ROWE.—Trim, the county- and assize-town, is
pleasantly situated on the river Boyne, on the banks of
which are the ruins of the castle where John lord of Ireland resided; also the abbey founded by St. Patrick, and
afterwards rebuilt by De Lacey lord of Meath. Not far
from hence are to be seen the grand and picturesque ruins
of Newtown Abbey. Trim formerly possessed a mint, and
was the seat of the Irish Parliament till nearly the close of

the 15th century. It was a walled town, and made a gallant defence against Cromwell. Amongst its public buildings are a handsome modern church, a court-house for holding the assizes, barracks, and a pillar of the Corinthian order, erected at the expense of the county in 1817, in honour of the Duke of Wellington. By means of its river it carries on a considerable trade, and has a manufacture of coarse linen. Near this place is Laracor, where Dean Swift resided for many years.

Ratoath is a village noted for its unadorned rath, with a single tree growing on its summit, which makes it a conspicuous object across the level plains of the county. Close to it are the foundations of an abbey, on the site of which stands the church. Here is also a well, dedicated to St. John, which is surrounded by trees, and is the resort of the peasantry towards the end of June.

Kells is a very ancient town, pleasantly situated on the Blackwater river. It was early fortified by the English. In it is a round tower; also a curious stone cross, much decayed, but very richly decorated with figures of men, beasts, flowers, &c. At the back of the town is another small tower, and near that a small stone building arched with flags, which is called Columbkill's Cell, and is supposed to be the first Christian oratory erected here. The church is a modern edifice, and contains a stately monument to Sir Thomas Taylor and his lady. A handsome pillar stands near the town, which was erected by the Marquis of Headfort as a means of employing the poor during a year of scarcity; and in its vicinity is the noble mansion belonging to that nobleman. This town has very little trade.

GEORGE.—Not far from hence is Castle Kieran, where, about the year 540, St. Kieran built a cell for himself; near which a fine spring issues from a rock; to this water many salubrious qualities are ascribed, and it is much resorted to by the Catholics on the first Sunday in August.

The tradition of the country attributes its miraculous power to the order of that Saint, who blessed it.

Slane is a pleasant village on the river Boyne, on the banks of which are some extensive flour-mills, and about half a mile from this place is a fine ruin of its Abbey and the hermitage, which are supposed to have been founded by Eirr, a Bishop of Slane. Its castle and picturesque domains are well watered by the river. George IV. visited this mansion in 1821.

George.—In the vicinity of Slane is a celebrated tumulus, in which is a curious cave lined with large slabs of stone. It is said to have been used by the Druids as a temple or heathen cell, and is supposed by some antiquaries to have been the mausoleum of the chief of a colony of Belgæ established here in remote ages.

Mrs. Rowe.—Navan is a market-town, pleasantly situated at the confluence of the rivers Blackwater and Boyne. Its church is a beautiful modern structure. This town was walled by Hugh de Lacey. On the site of a house for regular canons are its barracks, and in the abbey yard are some curious tombs with sculptured figures. It has a communication with Drogheda by means of a canal, and carries on a considerable trade in corn. Two miles from hence is an episcopal palace, built of limestone found in a quarry in its neighbourhood. In the burial-ground of Abraccan church may be seen a tablet in memory of Bishop Pococke the traveller, and the tomb of Bishop Montgomery with rudely sculptured figures ; and on an eminence not far from hence is a round tower remarkable for a cross engraved on the keystone of the doorway. This singularity argues in favour of the supposition that these famous towers were dedicated to religious purposes.

Tarah is seated on a high hill commanding the adjacent plain, and tradition asserts that it derives its name from the palace of Ollamh Fodha, a prince who reigned here at the time of the Republic of Rome. At Tarah the Irish princes were formerly crowned, and here the triennial assemblies of the States took place till the middle of the 6th century. It formerly possessed a convent of Augustine nuns, founded in 1240, but its church is now its principal object. The vicinity of this village is adorned with many neat mansions.

ANNA.—On the south side of the hill on which this place stands is a moat, or fort, thrown up by Turgesius; and from this strong position the rebels were driven with great loss in May 1798.

MRS. ROWE.—Nobber is celebrated for being the birth-place of the celebrated blind bard, O'Carolan, in 1760.

Clonard stands on the Boyne, and is noted for having in its church an antique font, which formerly belonged to an abbey founded here in 520. This village gave name to a bishopric, which is now incorporated with the see of Meath. Here was also a nunnery.

Grange is a village noted for having in it a cavern, well worth the attention of the antiquary. It is in the form of a cross, and is supposed to have been dedicated to some superstitious rites of the Druids.—Which are the principal rivers of this county?

ANNA.—The Boyne and the Blackwater. The former rises in the county of Kildare, and after entering Meath, pursues a north-easterly course through Trim and Slane; from thence flowing due easterly, it divides this county from Louth, and falls into the sea below Drogheda.

GEORGE.—On the banks of this river a battle was fought between the troops of William III. and James II. in 1690. The contending armies came in sight of each other on op-posite sides of the river, where the water was so shallow that a man might walk through it, which place is known by the name of the Pass of the Boyne. King William no sooner arrived here than he rode in sight of both armies, and being seen by the enemy, a cannon was instantly dis-charged against him, which slightly wounded him in the

shoulder and killed some of his followers. A report of his
having been slain was soon propagated; but the king
no sooner had his wound dressed than he rode through the
camp and undeceived his soldiers. Early on the following
morning he gave his army orders to force a passage over
the river, which they did in three places under a furious
cannonading. The battle then commenced with unusual
vigour, and James's troops, after an obstinate resistance,
were compelled to fly with precipitation. That unfortunate
monarch, viewing the flight from an eminence, is said to
have exclaimed, when he saw his own troops repulsing the
enemy, "Oh, spare my English subjects!" but when he
found the day was likely to turn against him, he quitted his
post, while his men were still fighting, and escaped to
Dublin.

Mrs. Rowe.—It is said that O'Regan, a renowned Irish
general, was so disgusted with this act of cowardice in his
master, that he was heard to say, "If the English would
change commanders, the conquered army would fight the
battle over again."

In this battle King James lost 1500 men and King William about 500.

The Blackwater flows from Lough Ramor, in the county
of Cavan, and pursues a south-easterly course through
Kells to unite itself with the Boyne at Navan.

This county, sometimes called only Meath, by way of
pre-eminence, is an inland district, except between the
counties of Louth and Dublin, where it borders for a few
miles on the Irish Channel. Its mouldering piles of ruined
castles and abbeys, frowning over the landscape in gloomy
grandeur, with the modern mansions and highly cultivated
demesnes of many noblemen, have a picturesque effect, and
numerous parts of it are calculated to afford a rich reward
to the researches of the antiquary. Its principal manufacture is coarse linen cloth, and it has quarries of limestone,
potter's clay, and vitrescent stone.

period of Irish history. This abbey was given to an alder-
man of Dublin at the general dissolution of monasteries,
one of whose successors permitted the friars to assemble
here again, with a splendour nearly equal to their former
state, and to have in it a large establishment for the reception of those who chose to resort hither for shelter, and it
is asserted that within the walls of Multifarnam was first
concerted that rebellion which broke out in massacre A.D.
1641.

Mrs. Rowe.—Kilbeggan is a market-town situated on
the river Brosna, over which it has a good bridge. Its
abbey and monastery, with their possessions, were surrendered to King Henry VIII. It is a place of considerable
trade, and possesses a good stone church.

Moat-a-Grenoge is noted for being the scene of a skir-
mish, in which the forces of James II. were defeated, in
1690. Beyond this town are the ruins of some castles.

Athlone is divided by the Shannon, and is partly in this
county and partly in Roscommon. Over the river is an
ancient bridge, and in the town were formerly several monastic foundations. Its extensive barracks, two churches,
(one of which is very ancient,) its castle, chalybeate spring,
and floating bridge, are all deserving of notice. By means
of the Grand Canal, Athlone carries on a good trade with
Limerick and the adjacent districts. In its vicinity is a
wier for eels.

George.—The ancient fortress which commanded the
passage of the Shannon was burnt in 1641, when the town
was also destroyed.

Mrs. Rowe.—This important pass was vigorously defended by the forces of James II. after the battle of the
Boyne; but at length the English, under the command of
General Ginckle, resolved to ford the river in the face of
the enemy, who were driven from their works, and the
town surrendered at discretion, A.D. 1691. Ginckle was,
in consequence, created Earl of Athlone.

Fore (or Foure) is seated on the north side of a hill, near Lough Lene. It is said to have been anciently a town or university of literature, its name signifying, in the Irish language, the "Town of Books," and Lough Lene, the "Lake of Learning," together with an island in it bearing the like name, which is said to have been the retiring-place of the learned who taught here. Its numerous ecclesiastical remains prove that it must have been, at an early period, of great importance. It possesses the ruins of three parish churches, one monastery, and a church or cell of an Anchorite, the only one of this religious order in Ireland. An inscription still existing in a ruined chapel under the hill bears testimony that a hermit resided here as late as the year 1616.

GEORGE.—Near this place is a tumulus, which appears to be sepulchral: it *is* surrounded by a fosse of the same description, but not so neatly executed, as those on the downs in Wiltshire.

Leny is a village in the vicinity of Loughs Hoyle and Deriveragh, between which is Wilson's Hospital for the support of sixteen old men and the education and maintenance of sixteen boys, natives of the county. This building is supposed to stand in the centre of Ireland. Its revenues are large.

Ballinalack is a village pleasantly situated on the Inny. In its neighbourhood formerly stood the ruins of an abbey, founded shortly after the English invasion by Sir Geoffrey Constance, but these beautiful vestiges of monastic architecture were entirely demolished in 1783.

Kinnegad is a market-town famous for its cheese. In its vicinity are several ancient castles.—Which are the principal rivers of this county?

ANNA.—The Foyle, which flows from Lough Ennel, and running northerly through the town of Mullingar, loses itself in Lough Iron; and the Brosna, which has its source in King's County, and flows northerly into Lough Ennel.

MRS. ROWE.—At a short distance from the town of Fore is Lough Lene, the waters of which penetrate under the rock on the north side, and reappear on the opposite side of the hill near the town, where they turn a mill. On this lake are three wooded islands. It produces good trout and pike, but its shores are flat and uncultivated. At a short distance from this is a raised earthenwork, commonly called the 'Fort of Turgesius,' from the name of a Norwegian chieftain who, according to Giraldus, invaded Ireland in 838, and with the assistance of the Danes, who flocked to his standard, conquered the natives, and was proclaimed monarch of the kingdom. But the spirit of the Irish at length revived, and Melachin prince of Meath, in a time of apparent peace, overcame the usurper. The circumstances of this adventure are thus related by Giraldus: —The Norwegian chieftain having requested the daughter of Melachin king of Meath in marriage, he, knowing the ferocious disposition of the tyrant, dared not to hazard a refusal, but pretended to accede to his proposal, and promised to send his daughter, attended by fifteen young females, to a certain island in the province of Meath, at an appointed time. Melachin is said to have selected that number of the most beautiful and resolute youths, and ordered them to proceed to the place of meeting habited like women, and each to conceal a sword under his garment. Thus accoutred they met Turgesius, and, immediately throwing off the disguise they had assumed, they drew forth their secret weapons, and put the Norwegian and his companions to death, thus saving the honour of the royal father and his daughter, and delivering their country from the hands of a most oppressive tyrant. It is said that this circumstance took place upon an island in Loch Iroh, in the western district of the county.

Lough Ennel is a large expanse of water lying between Mullingar and Kilbeggan. It is beautifully spotted with islets, whilst a promontory of rocks fringed with trees runs into it, and its banks are, in the eastern part, decorated with many gentlemen's seats.

Lough Deriveragh is situated in the northern part of the county, and is united to Lough O'Whel, or Hoyle, by the river Inny.

In the early period of Irish history, East and West Meath formed a distinct province, and had its own petty sovereign. Henry II. conferred it upon Hugh de Lacey, when he invested him with the principal command of the city of Dublin, which important trust he soon found himself unequal to retain. This province was at length degraded into the counties of Meath and West Meath. The latter is small and entirely inland ; though mostly flat, yet in some parts it is pleasingly intersected with hills, many of which are finely wooded, and, with its lake scenery, offer picturesque subjects for the pencil, particularly in the vicinity of Belvidere. It possesses some linen and woollen manufactures, but is almost destitute of mineral productions.

LONGFORD.

Boundaries.—Cavan, Leitrim, Roscommon, and West Meath.
Towns.—1, Longford; 2, Granard; 3, Lanesborough; 4, St. John's
Town; 5, Ballymahon; 6, Kenagh; 7, Barry; 8, Rathoan;
9, Newton Forbes; 10, Roesduff; 11, Edgeworth's Town;
12, Ballynamuck.
Rivers.—a, the Shannon; b, the Cromlin, or Camlin.
Lough.—A, Lough Ree.

Mrs. Rowe.—WHAT are the boundaries, extent, and chief towns of Longford?

Anna.—It is bounded on the north by Leitrim and

M 5

Cavan, on the east and south by West Meath, and on the west by Roscommon. It measures about 25 miles from north to south, and 22 from east to west; and its chief towns are Longford, Edgeworth's Town, Granard, Lanesborough, Ballymahon, St. John's Town, and Ballynamuck.

Mrs. Rowe.—Longford, the capital of the county, stands on the river Camlin, which is navigable from hence to the Shannon, and consequently increases the commercial importance of the town. It formerly possessed an abbey, founded by Idus, who was its first abbot, and a Dominican Friary, erected in the 15th century. It is now only distinguished for its barracks and well-endowed school. A manufacture of linen is carried on here.

Edgeworth's Town is a considerable and improving village, noted for being the residence of the celebrated literary family from whom it derives its name. Its handsome church, with a cast-iron spire covered with slate, after a design of the late Mr. Edgeworth, is deserving notice; and in its vicinity are some quarries of slate.

Granard is a handsomely built market-town, consisting of one street about half a mile long, at the end of which, upon a singular hill called the Moat of Granard, stands its Castle. This eminence is supposed to be artificial, and from its summit commands a view into six surrounding counties. The abbey, which was founded here for Cistercian monks in 1250, was burned by the invading forces of Edward Bruce. Annual prizes for the best performance on the Irish harp are given in this town, and here the manufacture of linen is carried on to a considerable extent. About two miles distant is the beautiful ruin of Larra Abbey, said to have been founded by St. Patrick; and in the vicinity of this place are several loughs, on which are some pretty islands that contain many grand vestiges of monastic opulence.

Lanesborough is a handsome market-town on the banks of the Shannon, over which it has a stone bridge. A few miles above this place the Royal Canal enters the river, and at an equal distance below, the Shannon forms that beautiful expanse of water called Lough Ree. Lanesborough possesses a handsome church and cavalry barracks, and carries on an extensive trade in corn. In its vicinity is the great hill of Rathline, the summit of which commands a fine view; and at the village of the same name is a very ancient Castle, which was dismantled by Cromwell.

Ballymahon is a well-built town situated on the river Inny. From the vicinity of this place to the Shannon and canal, it is enabled to carry on a considerable trade. Its environs are pleasing.

St. John's Town is a small village in the centre of the county, surrounded by many pleasing and picturesque views.

Ballynamuck is a village in the north-western part, noted for having been the place where the invading French army and the misguided rebels surrendered to Lord Cornwallis in 1798.—Which are the principal rivers in this county?

George.—The Shannon, with Lough Ree, forms its western boundary, but its source will be described in the 'County of Clare'; and the Camlin, which rises in the centre of the county, and after taking a westerly course, falls into the above-mentioned river.

Mrs. Rowe.—There are several loughs bordering on this county; the most considerable is that of Ree in the southern part, which, for some distance, divides the counties of Roscommon and West Meath. On it are several small and well-wooded islands. It yields an abundance of various kinds of fish, and its banks afford some agreeably picturesque views.

A great proportion of Longford is one continued bog, almost destitute of timber. Though it possesses less to interest the traveller than many other parts of the island, yet he will here perceive the rapid effects of industry from the manufatuxe of linen. It produces slate and flag stone.

—Can you name any eminent character who was a native
of this county?

GEORGE.—At Pallaice, near Ballymahon, is the house
where Oliver Goldsmith was born, whose varied life affords
an instructive lesson. He was a poet, historian, and natural philosopher, but excelled as the former, and his 'Deserted Village' deserves the approbation of true taste.

KING'S COUNTY.

Boundaries.—West Meath, Meath, Kildare, Queen's County, Tip-
    perary, Galway, and Roscommon.
Towns.—1, Philipstown; 2, Banagher; 3, Ballycumber; 4,
    Clara; 5, Birr; 6, Tullamore; 7, Killiogh; 8, Balliboy; 9,
    Miltown; 10, Newtown; 11, Maystown; 12, Shinroan; 13,
    Clorolish; 14, Moneygawl; 15, Geashill; 16, Frankford;
    17, Fearbane; 18, Edenderry.
Rivers.—a, the Brosna; b, Fervoylagh; c, the Grand Canal.
Mountains, &c.—A, the Slieve Blonier; B, part of the Bog of
    Allen.

MRS. ROWE.—WHAT are the boundaries, extent, and
chief towns of King's County?

ANNA.—It is bounded on the north by West Meath, on
the east by Kildare and Queen's County, on the south and
part of the west by Tipperary, and on the remainder of the
west by Galway. It measures from north to south 45 miles,
and from east to west, in its widest part, about 40. Its
chief towns are Philipstown, Tullamore, Geashill, Frank-
ford, Banagher, Balliboy, Eglish, Birr, Clara.

MRS. ROWE.—Philipstown, the capital of the county, is
a remarkably well-built and paved town: it received its
name from Philip king of Spain, consort of Queen Mary,

KING'S COUNTY.

QUEEN'S COUNTY.

The vicinity of this town is in a progressive state of improvement, from the judicious planting and cultivation across the Silver river, in concert with the introduction of the linen manufacture.

Balliboy is a village on the Silver river, which issues from Lough Anna, on the shore of which is the ancient ruin of Killinany Castle: this water separates King's County from Queen's County: near it is Pallas Lough, and it is a romantic but generally dreary and unprofitable district.

Eglish is a sequestered and thinly-inhabited barony of King's County. Near the church is a handsome seat, and at Castle Eglish is a fine bleach-green.

Birr or Parson's Town, on the western verge of the county, received its name from the family of Parsons who settled here. It is a commodious and modern-built town, with regular streets. In one of its squares on a Doric column 25 feet high is a statue of the late Duke of Cumberland. It possesses a handsome modern Gothic church. The Earl of Ross is the proprietor of this place, and has an excellent castellated residence adjoining it. Considerable improvements are taking place in the vicinity of the town; and there are also the remains of some very strong fortresses in the neighbourhood.

Clara is a beautiful town on the banks of the Brosna, near which they are adorned with bleaching-greens. The chief objects of note in and adjoining this place are its church and the ancient Castles of Erry and Kilcourcy, the latter being the name of the barony. In 1821, one of those extraordinary phenomena, termed moving bogs, occurred in the vicinity of Clara, when the bog of Kilmaleady flowed in an uninterrupted course for three miles. The linen manufacture is carried on here to a considerable extent.

Fearbane is pleasantly seated on the same river, and is noted for its antiquities. In the vicinity of this place are the ruins of Clonmacnoise, which have long engaged the attention of antiquarians: it is celebrated as the burying-

place of numerous princes, chieftains, and priests; and contains many tombs on which inscriptions in the Irish and
learned languages may be traced. These splendid remains
are seated on a rising ground in the midst of delightful
scenery, on the banks of the Shannon.

GEORGE.—I have read that the landed property of this
Augustine monastery was so great, and the number of cells
and ecclesiastical edifices subjected to it so numerous, that
almost half Ireland was said to belong to it; and though it
was held in superstitious reverence by the princes and natives, and esteemed the Iona of Ireland, yet it was frequently
plundered and burnt by the Danes.

MRS. ROWE.—It is said that Columba, a native of Ireland, left his own country in resentment about the year 565,
and vowing never to make a settlement within sight of that
hated island, founded a monastic establishment at Iona in
the Hebrides, and there he died at an advanced age and
was interred, from whence the island took the name of
Y-Columb-Cell, or the Isle of the Cell of Columba.

Edenderry is a market-town situated near the Grand
Canal, and is inhabited principally by Quakers. In it are
the remains of an ancient castle and a monastery: it also possesses a handsome church and tower.—Which are the
principal rivers of this county?

ANNA.—The Brosna rises in the north and pursues a
south-westerly course to the Shannon; and the Fervoylagh,
which rises near the centre of the county, and after a circuitous course, falls into the Barrow river.

MRS. ROWE.—The Slieve Blonier mountains extend
through a range of 15 miles, and form a natural boundary
between the south-eastern part of this county and that of
Queen's County. In them is to be seen a large pyramid of
white stones which is said to be the emblem of the Sun-fire
amongst the Celtic nations, from whence arose their ancient
name of Bladhma, or Beal-di-mai, the necromancy of Baal's
day. Through these mountains there is but one steep,

narrow, and craggy pass, leading into Tipperary. It is called Glandine Gap, and is not more than 5 feet wide. By some, it is, as well as the Pass of the Shannon, termed the Irish Thermopylæ.

This long and narrow county, bordering in some degree upon the Shannon, and traversed by the canal which unites the Irish Channel with that river, is flat and often boggy, especially in that district called the Bog of Allen. Many parts of it are rapidly improving in cultivation and civilization, and the manufacture of linen is the staple employment of its inhabitants. Its mineral productions are iron ore, ochres, with limestone and potter's clay.

QUEEN'S COUNTY.

Boundaries.—King's County, Tipperary, Kilkenny, Carlow, and
    Kildare.
Towns.—1, Maryborough; 2, Ballinakill; 3, Portarlington; 4,
    Mountmellick; 5, Mountrath; 6, Ballyadams; 7, Killeshill;
    8, Durrow Castle; 9, Dunmore; 10, Burros; 11, Cape Town;
    12, Balliroan; 13, Stradbally; 14, Emo; 15, Timohoe; 16,
    Lea.
Rivers.—a, the Nore; b, the Barrow.

MRS. ROWE.—WHAT are the boundaries, extent, and chief towns of this county?

ANNA.—It is bounded on the north by King's County, which, with Tipperary, forms also its western boundary; Kilkenny and Carlow the southern, and Kildare the eastern. It measures from north to south 32 miles, and from east to west 28. Its chief towns are, Maryborough, Ballinakill, Portarlington, Mountmellick, Mountrath, Emo, Timohoe, Stradbally, and Lea.

MRS. ROWE.—Maryborough, the county- and assize-town,

is situated in a delightful country. It (as well as the county,) received its name from Mary queen of England, in whose reign it was made a borough, and received many other privileges and immunities. Its Castle was dismantled by Cromwell, and, although a ruin, still has its constable. In the town there are barracks, and it also possesses a small cotton manufactory. Rathean Common, in the vicinity of this place, is noted for a battle fought in the 3rd century between the people of Leinster and Munster, and the bones of the slain are at this time frequently dug up.

Ballinakill is situated in the southern part of the county, and possesses a handsome modern church with a steeple. Its Castle, which was, after repeated sieges, stormed by the forces of Cromwell, is an interesting old fortress.

Portarlington is divided by the river Barrow into two unequal parts, the larger being in this, and the smaller in King's County. This town is well built, and has always been noted for superior schools for the education of youth of both sexes, particularly in the French language. Portarlington was originally colonised by French emigrants, who were compelled to abandon their country upon the revocation of the edict of Nantes; hence French names are common in various parts of Ireland. It possesses a handsome church with a lofty spire, and there is in its vicinity a celebrated and much frequented spa.

Mountmellick is a well-built and agreeable market-town, inhabited chiefly by Quakers, who support an excellent school in it. It stands on the banks of the Owinass river, near where it runs into the Barrow, and carries on a considerable trade in wool-combing, tanning, malting, as well as the manufacture of cotton goods.

Mountrath is situated on the river Nore, and is noted for its woollen manufacture, besides which it has a cotton factory.

Emo is situated in the nothern part of the county, and is principally noted for being in the vicinity of the Rock of

Dunamase, or Dun-na-maes, which signifies, in the Irish
language, the "Fort of the Plain." It was certainly a place
of great curiosity, which nature and art had combined to
render of the most formidable strength before the use of
artillery was known; and though now almost in ruins, yet it
offers to the antiquary a very good specimen of the military
manners of former times. This rock was inaccessible on
all sides except the eastern, and on its summit was a castle
in which many Irish princes resided. In the year 1167 it
was the principal residence of Dermod MacMurrogh, king
of Leinster. From him it descended to Earl Strongbow;
and from him, in the 13th century, to the Pembroke family.
Not far from hence is a small fortress called Shean Castle,
standing on the summit of one of the high conical hills which
are so frequent in this part of the county : it is still habitable,
though its walls were demolished in the civil wars.

Timohoe is noted for its Castle, now in ruins, having stood
a siege in the civil wars. Its area is filled with cabins of
the peasantry : close to it stand the remains of an ancient
round tower, the entrance to which is ornamented with a
chevron or zigzag moulding, a circumstance which denotes
its origin. About a mile from this place are three ancient
moats.

Stradbally is a market-town, with a handsome church and
good chartered school for educating, clothing and appren-
ticing sixty boys. It is situated in a delightful and fertile
country, and in its vicinity is Dun-clin-poic, or Dun of Cli-
poke, an insulated rock with curious caves. Near it is a
tombstone with a Druidical inscription.

Lea is noted for the remains of a Castle which was famous in the wars of the 13th century : it stands on an eminence by the side of the river Barrow, which formerly filled
the ditch encompassing its walls.

The rivers which water this county are the Nore and
Barrow, which will be fully described in the 'County of
Kilkenny.'

Queen's County presents a variety of objects to the antiquary, whilst it exhibits in many parts the effects of
modern improvement, as a considerable part of its boggy
soil has been brought under cultivation. Its principal mineral productions are coal and iron ore.

KILDARE.

Boundaries.—Meath, King's County, Queen's County, Carlow,
    Wicklow, and Dublin.
Towns.—1, Kildare; 2, Naas; 3, Monastereven; 4, Athy; 5,
    Kilcock; 6, Leixlip; 7, Harris Town; 8, Claine; 9, May-
    nooth; 10, Cloncurry; 11, Kill; 12, Kilkea; 13, Castle
    Dermot; 14, Kilcullen.
Rivers.—a, the Liffey; b, the Rye.
A, the Bog of Allen; B, the Grand Canal.

MRS. ROWE.—WHAT are the boundaries, extent, and
chief towns of Kildare?

ANNA.—It is bounded on the north by Meath, on the east
by Dublin and Wicklow, on the south by Carlow, and on the
west by King's County and Queen's County. The places of
most note are Kildare, Naas, Monastereven, Athy, Kilcullen, Ballitore, Leixlip, Maynooth, Celbridge, and Kilcock.

MRS. ROWE.—Kildare, the capital of the county, is a
bishopric pleasantly situated on a rising ground, and remarkable for its monastic remains. The Abbey is a very
fine ruin, consisting of a part of the tower and a considerable portion of the walls. The north side of the steeple was
knocked down by a battery of Cromwell's army. In the
south wing are two statues in alto relievo, one of which is
that of an ancient knight of the Fitzgerald family, clad
in armour, the other a bishop with his pastoral staff and

mitre, which is supported by monkeys. The nunnery was founded by St. Bridget about the year 500. This lady was much celebrated for her virtues and her miracles, and the monastic annals of the town record the extraordinary in-stance of a sacred fire having been preserved here from the time of the Druids by nuns of this order. It appears that the Archbishop of Dublin, Henry de Loundres, extinguished this fire in the 13th century, but it was rekindled and continued in good preservation until the dissolution of the religious houses. Of this fire many wonderful tales are told; espe-cially, that although it consumed great quantities of fuel, yet the ashes never increased. The place where this relic of heathen superstition was preserved is still in existence, and is now called the Fire House. Close to these ruins is a round tower 132 feet in height, with a light battlement in pretty good preservation, being one of the best specimens of the kind in Ireland. There were also in and near this town two other religious establishments, one for Grey Friars, erected in 1260, the other for White Friars, in 1290.

GEORGE.—A celebrated abbot who was at the head of the latter convent in 1320, is said to have swayed the councils of the whole island. He was well versed in divinity, phi-losophy, rhetoric, and the canon and civil law; and was ge-nerally called the "burning light, the mirror and ornament of his country."

MRS. ROWE.—The modern name of Kildare is derived from *Chille-dair*, or the Wood of Oaks, comprehending the middle part of the present county, where was a large forest, in the centre of which was a plain sacred to heathen super-stition : this is now called the Curragh, and is a fine unequal down of short pasture, containing about 3000 acres, which forms one of the finest race-courses in the king-dom. The king gives plates to be run for here in April, June, and September. George IV. honoured this place with a visit in September 1821.

GEORGE.—Giraldus Cambrensis records an account of a

stupendous monument of stones which was situated on this plain, and which, according to vulgar and fabulous tradition, was transferred from the extreme parts of Africa by the giants, from whom it took the name of Chorea Gigantum. It is also said to have had a second removal from Ireland to the plains of Wiltshire.

MRS. ROWE.—The tumuli dispersed over this plain prove most evidently that it was inhabited in very early times, and it is supposed that if they were properly opened, their contents would throw a great light on Irish history. Kildare suffered severely in the last rebellion.

Naas was formerly a town of great note, in which parliaments were held, and it was honoured by being a residence of the kings of Leinster. On the arrival of the English in 1690 it was fortified, and many castles were erected; but from the ravages of time and the civil wars, in which this town has ever been an object of severe contest, it now bears only the marks of its former splendour. The Grand Canal passes within two miles, and there is a cut from it to this place, and the corn-market here is conducted on an extensive scale. At the foot of the rath at Naas was a cell for Augustine hermits, founded in 1484, and in the centre of the town is a ruin of a monastery which owes its origin to the family of Sir Edward Eustace, lord chancellor.

ANNA.—Not far from this town are the ruins of Jigginstown House, built by the unfortunate Earl Strafford, and intended as a residence for the lord-lieutenant; but upon the attainder of that nobleman it fell into decay.

Monastereven is a market-town on the Barrow, and is noted for the demesne of the Marquis of Drogheda, which occupies the site of a celebrated abbey founded by St. Abban, who granted it the privilege of a sanctuary; and here was kept the consecrated bell of St. Evan, which on solemn trials was sworn to. The park is beautifully laid out, and

contains a fine lake, skirted by a mountain.   The abbot of
this establishment sat as a baron in parliament.

Athy is a market-town on the same river, at which pas-
sage-boats arrive daily by the Grand Canal.   The county
assizes are held here and at Naas alternately.   A monastery for Crouched Friars was founded here in the reign of
King John, and one for Dominican Friars in 1250.   At
Doondun, a village at a short distance, are extensive coal-
pits, which claim notice from exhibiting rocks of whinstone
resting on a stratum or column of basaltes, 40 feet below
the surface, and beneath which are strata of slate and iron
ore.

GEORGE.—On the brow of a hill, at a short distance from
this place, is the Moat of Ardskull, where the Scots under
Edward, the brother of Robert Bruce, obtained a victory
in 1315.

MRS. ROWE.—At Rheban, two miles distant, is a square
intrenched mound, and the remains of an ancient city; and
in the neighbourhood are several ancient raths, which prove
these parts to have been the scene of battle in early history.

Kilcullen, or Kilcullen Bridge, so named from its having
a bridge over the river Liffey, and to distinguish it from
the old town, is noted for the battle in which general Dun-
das defeated the insurgents in 1798.   Its ancient church
called New Abbey, was built by Sir Rowland Eustace in
1460.   In 1764 the steeple of this church fell, and these
ruins, in which may be seen monuments of the Eustace
family, gave name to the modern mansion of New Abbey.
Three miles beyond the bridge is Old Kilcullen, which was
once fortified with a wall and seven gates, only one of which,
with a handsome arch, is now standing.   Here are also the
ruins of an abbey with several antique remains; and at
Calverstown, in the vicinity of this place, a tomb was opened which contained a human skeleton in a sitting posture,
with an earthen urn, or bowl, as if for provisions.   This

is supposed to have been a Danish chieftain. Near this, at Castle Martin, is a curious chapel and mausoleum, which was occupied, during the insurrection of 1798, as a barrack.

Ballitore is a beautiful village, situated in a vale on the banks of the river Gris. It is a colony of Quakers, with houses remarkable for elegant simplicity, and highly cultivated gardens. Near this is Belan House, erected on the site of an old castle which was demolished by Cromwell, and in which is still preserved a bed that both King William and King James slept in, in the year 1690.

Castle Dermot, formerly Tristle Dermot, or Disart Diarmuda, derived its name from St. Dermot, who founded a priory here in the year 500. This town stands on the river Lane, and was once of great importance. Parliaments were held in it in the 14th and 15th centuries. It was strongly fortified, and the Dermods, kings of Leinster, had their residence in this ancient town, which once possessed a mint. It contains some very interesting antiquities, but, as a modern town, it is of little note. In its vicinity are some beautiful seats.

Leixlip is a village romantically situated on the north bank of the Rye, near its confluence with the Liffey. The groves and rocks of this glen are extremely beautiful, and at the end of the town, on an eminence, stands its ancient castle commanding a fine view of the river.

Maynooth is a handsome town, and noted for its Roman Catholic college. In it is a Protestant chartered school, founded in 1750 by the Earl of Kildare; and also an ancient castle of the Fitzgeralds.

Celbridge is a modern-built village, with a fine stone bridge across the Liffey. It possesses a newly erected elegant church, and extensive manufactures of cottons and woollens are carried on here. At the south end of the village are the remains of a magnificent abbey, now repaired and converted into a habitation. Not far from this place is Castle Browne, which has been recently purchased for a society of Jesuits.

Claine is a village on the banks of the Liffey, over which is a stone bridge. It also possesses the ruins of an abbey, and at a short distance is a small but prosperous town, built by Captain Brook in 1780, in which a cotton manufactory is established; and about half a mile from thence, at a place called Cott, is a strong sulphureous spa.

Kilcock is a market-town situated on the Royal Canal, and is chiefly noted for the numerous traditionary tales which are, even to this day, recorded by the natives with superstitious conviction of their causes and effects. Amongst the rest, they assert that St. Columbkill rested at an inn in this place one night, and requested to be awoke as soon as the cock should crow the next morning, having made a vow to rise at that time; but chanticleer happening to sound his trumpet unusually early, so offended the holy man, that he condemned all the race, and prayed that they might never crow again. And it is believed by some of the natives that no cock has ever been heard to crow at Kilcock since that time. From this circumstance it is supposed to have derived its name.—Which are the principal rivers of this county?

Anna.—The Liffey, which has been already described, and the Rye, which rises on the borders of Meath, and flows easterly to join the Liffey near Leixlip.

Mrs. Rowe.—The Bog of Allen, so named from a hamlet in the vicinity of Kildare, extends through this county into Queen's County, King's County, Meath, West Meath, Longford, Tipperary, and Galway. In this hamlet is a celebrated hill, (anciently that of Temora,) in which is a cave that contains the remains of Oscar and other Ossianic chiefs. The hill is 300 feet in height, and from it there is an extensive prospect across the level of the moss. The Grand Canal passes through this bog, and affords a drainage to a considerable portion of it. How this immense tract of bog was produced is a subject that is involved in much philosophical conjecture, as at a considerable depth beneath the surface have been discovered whole forests of prostrate trees, apparently burnt off at the roots; and so antiseptic is the mass that covers them, that the finest oaks, firs, and yews, with all their branches, have been frequently dug up so perfect in condition as to be preferred to the same sort of trees felled by the woodmen. One great proof that the ground under the bog was once covered with rich fields and beautiful woods is, that in the vicinity of it are to be seen the finest specimens of monastic ruins; and no class of people knew how to select, appreciate, and enjoy the beauties and comforts of this life better than the cowled fraternity. The turf, when thoroughly heated, makes a good fire, and is an admirable substitute for coals. Many parts of Kildare are exceedingly fertile, producing large crops of corn and potatoes, and affording good pasturage for cattle. Its mineral productions are considerable. On the southern limits of the bog are copper-mines, which were opened thirty years ago; besides which, near Williamstown, is a deserted silver-mine.

WICKLOW.

Boundaries.—Dublin, Kildare, Carlow, Wexford, and St. George's Channel.
Towns.—1, Wicklow; 2, Arklow; 3, Rathdrum; 4, Kilcool; 5, Baltinglass; 6, Blessington; 7, Dunlavin; 8, Tinehaly; 9, Fort Chester; 10, Aghrim; 11, Macreddin; 12, Glendalough, or the Seven Churches; 13, Enniskerry; 14, Stratford-upon-Slaney; 15, Bray; 16, Ballymore Eustace.
Rivers.—a, the Leitrim; b, Avonmore; c, Avoca.
Capes.—A, Wicklow Head; B, Missen Head; C, Bray Head; D, Kippure Mountains.

MRS. ROWE.—WHAT are the boundaries, extent, and chief towns of Wicklow?

ANNA.—It is bounded on the north by Dublin, on the east by St. George's Channel, on the south by Wexford and Carlow, and on the west by Kildare. It measures 35 miles from north to south, and 30 from east to west. The most noted towns are Wicklow, Arklow, Rathdrum, Enniskerry, Stratford-upon-Slaney, Baltinglass, Bray, Blessington, Ballymore Eustace, and Glendalough.

MRS. ROWE.—Wicklow, the county town, is pleasantly situated at the mouth of the Leitrim, and notwithstanding the river is shallow, there are many fishing-vessels belonging to this port, and a considerable import and export trade is carried on here. It is also justly celebrated for its ale. On a rock at the mouth of the river are the remains of a singular fortification called the Black Castle, erected by William Fitzwilliam in the 14th century; and in a private garden may also be seen the vestiges of a Franciscan Monastery, founded in the reign of Henry II. It is said that James II. lodged in the barracks of this town after deserting his army at the battle of the Boyne. About a mile distant, on Wicklow Head, are three lighthouses, and at the foot of this promontory are some curious limestone caves. On the course called the Murrogh, which extends along the sea-shore for about six miles, races are annually held; and on the strand some very good pebbles of agate and chalcedony are sometimes found.

Arklow is a sea-port and market-town on the Avoca, over which it has a bridge of nineteen arches. Its harbour is so surrounded by sand-banks that it will admit only small vessels. The herring and oyster fishing employ 300 boats along this coast. The Castle, at the upper end of the town, was once the seat of the Earls of Ormond, and was of considerable importance. Near this are the barracks. This town also possesses the remains of a Dominican Friary, founded in the 13th century.

GEORGE.—On the 9th of June 1798, Arklow was attacked by the rebels, amounting to 20,000 men, 5000 of whom were armed with guns and the rest with pikes, besides having three serviceable pieces of artillery, whilst the regular troops stationed for the defence of this district amounted to only 2000. The commanding officer, Major-General Needham, after making a spirited but apparently useless resistance, came to the determination of forcing a retreat; when the resolution of Colonel Skirrett (then second in command,) saved the place; as he observed, " We can hope for victory only by maintaining our ranks; if we break them, all will be lost, and from the spirit I have seen displayed by the Durham regiment, I cannot bear the idea of giving ground." This magnanimous advice being acted upon was decisive, and the rebels, after a most furious assault, retired in despair. Their leader, Father Michael Murphy, was killed by a cannon shot, and the fall of this hero immediately damped the ardour of the insurgents, who from that moment began to lose ground.

MRS. ROWE.—Rathdrum is situated on the verge of the most beautiful part of the county, washed by the river Avon.

On the summit of the hill is the Flannel Hall, a square
building 200 feet in length, erected by Earl Fitzwilliam, in
which fairs are held every month, and every piece of cloth
deposited in it for sale must undergo the inspection of an
officer before it can be sold, by which means any attempt
to defraud is prevented, or punished by a heavy fine.   Not
far from hence are some lead-mines ; also the beautiful vale
where the great and lesser Avoca form the " Meeting of
the Waters," which Mr. Moore makes the subject of his
beautiful ballad commencing—

> " There is not in this wide world a valley so sweet
> As that vale in whose bosom the bright waters meet."

Near this place is Castle Howard, and the road to the mansion is cut round a rock.   The Avoca, after washing the
foot of the hill on which this noble mansion stands, (and
from which it commands extensive and varied views,) flows
between the mountains of Cronbane and Ballymurtagh,
both of which contain copper-mines.   The wild and romantic barony of Shillelagh (which, with the village, receives
its name from the ancient oak forest,) is in this vicinity, and
adds greatly to the picturesque scenery of the district.

Enniskerry is delightfully situated on the side of a steep
hill, at the foot of which runs a mountain torrent.   The air
of this place is esteemed for its salubrity.   In it is a school
erected by Lord Powerscourt, the noble patron of the village, near which his extensive and beautiful demesne is
watered by the river Glenislorean.   The grand Powerscourt waterfall, the Douce mountain, and the romantic
winding glen of the Dargle (it has been observed,) may, in
point of scenery, justly vie with any part of Italy.

Stratford-upon-Slaney is a well-built town, and is noted
for its manufactures of cotton and calico.   The great hill
above this town commands a view of ten counties.

Baltinglass is a market-town seated on the Slaney, in a
beautiful vale called Vallis Salutis, in which are the remains
of the Abbey of St. Mary, founded in 1151 ; also an ancient

Castle belonging to Lord Aldborough. The name of this town is derived from the Irish, and signifies Belus' or Baal's fires, in allusion to the worship of the sun which was observed here by the Druids, and in the vicinity of this place there are several Druidical altars. Baltinglass has extensive manufactures of woollens, linens, and diapers.

Bray is a sea-bathing town, separated from the county of Dublin by a river of the same name, noted for its trout. The immediate neighbourhood of this place is celebrated for its romantic scenery, and the angler may here amuse himself amidst wooded glens and awful precipices. On an eminence by the river side are the remains of an ancient Castle, near which a battle took place in 1690 between the forces of James II. and William III. The rocky promontory of Bray Head, which rises 807 feet above the level of the sea, is near this town : it is easy of ascent, and contains marble and other extensive quarries. The white pebbles found on the shore beneath this eminence, when cut and polished, are much prized. Along the coast are several Martello towers. About $3\frac{1}{2}$ miles from Bray is the Glen of the Downs, formed by two hills rising abruptly from 1200 to 1300 feet, which are entirely covered with wood. Between these there is just sufficient room for the road and a small torrent which runs parallel to it. This glen is adorned with many gentlemen's seats, and presents a view of some beautiful scenery. Not far from hence is one of the most picturesque dales in the county, called the Devil's Glen, where the Vartrey torrent forms a cascade 100 feet high, and the whole valley abounds with natural and artificial beauties.

Blessington, or Blisington, is a pleasant market-town, possessing a handsome church, which contains a monument in memory of Archbishop Boyle, who was a great benefactor to the town, at the end of which are the remains of the once magnificent seat of the Marquis of Downshire.

This mansion fell a sacrifice to the fury of the insurgents in 1798.

Ballymore Eustace forms a part of the county of Dublin, and has an ancient bridge across the Liffey.

GEORGE.—Near this is the grand waterfall of Pol-a-Pucha, which is formed by the river taking its course through a gap in a rugged rock. The grounds near it are beautifully laid out, and the effect is majestically striking. Near this are the curious ruins of a church, round tower and stone cross.

MRS. ROWE.—To the left of this, as you approach Baltinglass, is Sliebh Guth, or Church Mountain, on the top of which is a well, surrounded by rude stone-work, which is still frequented by pilgrims.

Glendalough, Glendaloch, or the Seven Churches, as it is commonly called, is situated in a valley amidst the mountain fastnesses of this county, being surrounded on every side except where it is entered by steep and lofty mountains. This ancient city enjoyed considerable celebrity in the early ages of Christianity, but now consists only of a few ruined edifices.

GEORGE.—Dr. Ledwick remarks upon this place, "That from the earliest ages it was a favourite seat of superstition. The gloomy vale, thick forest, and cloud-capped mountains were supposed by the wild savages who first fixed their abode here to have been the chosen seats of aerial spirits, and where they celebrated their nocturnal orgies : and from every rustling leaf and whispering gale they were so animated by fear, that invisible beings multiplied with the objects of the senses."

MRS. ROWE.—As superstition had thus filled Glendalough with evil spirits and devouring serpents, the Christian missionaries found it expedient to procure some Saint under whose protection the inhabitants would think themselves secure. Accordingly, being at a loss for a patron, the neighbouring mountain of Kevin was canonized, and the ideal Saint Kevin, in the person of the real Coemgene, soon dispelled all fear and performed numerous miracles. Coemgene was born in 498, and, upon taking the cowl, is said to have retired to these romantic wilds, where he founded its first abbey, wrote the Life of St. Patrick and other works, and died in 618 at the great age of 120 years. It shortly afterwards became a bishop's see, and continued so till 1214, when it was united to the Archbishopric of Dublin. A long resistance was however made to this union, till Friar White made a formal surrender of it, A.D. 1470. The ruins of the city are about the distance of a mile from the eastern entrance of the valley. The first object is the Ivy Church, so named from the vesture in which it is clad: this was a small chapel, which is now quite in ruins; a round tower formerly stood at one end of it, and about a quarter of a mile from it is the market-place, from whence a paved road, still in good preservation, led to Hollywood, on the borders of Kildare.

GEORGE.—Near to that is St. Kevin's rivulet, a small stream from Glendason river, said to possess miraculous powers on Sundays, Thursdays, and on the festival of any Saint, and in which a writer observes, " Superstition still directs weak and sickly children to be dipped," and certainly with the same efficacy that an early cold bath must produce on any other day of the week.

MRS. ROWE.—After crossing this river by a series of stepping-stones, you arrive at the area in which the Seven Churches, properly so called, are situated. This entrance is formed by a stone archway 16 feet wide. The most prominent object is the Cathedral, built by St. Kevin in the Saxon style of architecture, and beneath it are some curious sculptures. Near this are the ruins of the Priest's Cell and a stately tomb, and in the churchyard are the remains of some ancient crosses, one of which is an entire block 11 feet high; also a round tower in excellent preservation. Almost parallel

with the cathedral stands St. Kevin's Kitchen, the most perfect of the Seven Churches, and at the west end stood Our
Lady's Church, now in a ruinous state and overgrown with
ivy. On the other side of the stream which flows from the
upper lake in the valley, is the Rheafeart, or 'Sepulchre of
Kings,' which is celebrated as the burial-place of the princes
of the race of O'Toole. The church itself is a shapeless
ruin, and the cemetery is overgrown with brambles. Near
the Rheafeart is a conical heap of stones, to which pilgrims
resort to do penance. In a recess of Mount Lug Duff are
vestiges of Team-pell-na-Skellig church, or 'Priory of the
Rock,' or 'Temple of the Desert'; and in a rocky projection near it is St. Kevin's Bed, an almost inaccessible cave.
The abbey was dedicated to St. Peter and St. Paul, but is
now in so ruinous a state as to have nearly lost all architectural character. North of it is Trinity Church, with
part of a round tower and several smaller chapels and oratories, one of which contains the bones of St. Kevin. The
two lakes from which this valley derives its name (Glendalough, or Valley of the Two Lakes,) are situated to the
west of the cathedral, and are divided by a watery meadow.
The whole of this spot is well calculated to impress the
mind with the superstitious belief of the many legends that
are related respecting it.

ANNA.—Dr. Ledwick relates that St. Kevin, whilst ascending a neighbouring hill in a period of scarcity and famine, met a woman with a sack on her head, in which were
five loaves. The woman, being rather churlish, when the
Saint inquired what were the contents of her sack, told him
they were stones. "I pray they may be so," said the holy
inquirer, when instantly five stones tumbled out and rolled
towards Rheafeart church, were they were kept as sacred
relics for many years, but are now exhibited in the valley, weighing about twenty pounds each, and certainly
bearing a great resemblance to loaves, from whence this
idle story has arisen.

GEORGE.—South-west of this is the Vale of Glenmolaur: it is a wild district, bounded by steep mountains and almost inaccessible rocks. A river rises here and flows down the centre of the valley, and the road runs parallel with it along the entire length. This vale is of considerable celebrity in Irish history, as it was the retreat of Teagh O'Bryn in the time of Queen Elizabeth, and was the scene of a dreadful catastrophe to a party of English troops sent against him by Lord Grey, as, after a toilsome march, O'Bryn and his followers poured down upon the exhausted party and destroyed the whole of them: several officers of distinction were killed. In the middle of the vale are Drumguff barracks, capable of containing 300 men.

MRS. ROWE.—Which are the principal rivers of this county?

ANNA.—The Leitrim, Avonmore, and Avoca.

MRS. ROWE.—The Leitrim rises in the north-east, and for some distance pursues a southerly course, then, turning to the east, flows in that direction to the sea, which it enters at Wicklow.

The Avonmore rises a little westward of the last-mentioned stream, and flows southerly through Rathdrum to join the Avoca, which issues from the western border, and pursues an easterly course to the sea at Arklow.

Wicklow is very mountainous: Luguaquilla is the highest mountain, being 3070 feet above the level of the sea, and in the northern part of it there is an extraordinary fissure called the Scalp, which appears as if, by a wonderful convulsion of nature, the mountain had been rent asunder. Some have supposed it to have been cut by human effort, forgetting that neither Celtic nor northern tribes ever performed such works. The barren sides of the sloping hills, for there is a shelving precipice on either hand, present loose masses of stone, the largest fragments being the lowest. The width of this defile at the foot is just sufficient for the passage of the road. Although this county combines within itself all the rudeness of uncultivated nature, the romantic effect of wood and glen, the sublimity of mountain outline, and the charms of extended ocean, yet the interior is in many parts boggy. The sea-coast is rich in marine villas, and noblemen's and gentlemen's seats are numerous, as those fond of rural retreats are attracted hither by the vicinity of the capital and by the romantic beauties that abound almost everywhere, as well as by the uncommon mildness of the climate, which is peculiarly remarkable for the luxuriance of its foliage in evergreens. The larch is a favourite in all modern plantations, and the oak flourishes in the rocky glens.

ANNA.—This county is rich in mineral treasures, and considerable quantities of gold have been discovered.

MRS. ROWE.—The time when this precious metal was first found has never been clearly ascertained, as those who made the discovery endeavoured to conceal it, that the benefit might be reserved to themselves; but in 1796 a peasant youth who was angling in the mountain stream between this county and Wexford, perceived the glittering prize at the bottom of the stream, and judging it to be a treasure, dived for it and brought out a piece of gold, which he immediately carried and sold to a goldsmith, and from time to time finding more he entered into a traffic with him. His frequent visits to one spot were however soon perceived, and the important secret was speedily disclosed, which was no sooner known than the spade, plough, spinning-wheel and loom were laid aside, and all other occupations forsaken in search of treasures which they doubted not were to be found, and it has been asserted that 2666 ounces of gold were obtained by the peasantry in less than two months. The tumultuous throngs that assembled called forth the attention of Government, and it being necessary to subject the whole matter to some controul, a detachment of troops was sent to take possession of the prize in the name of the Crown, and to keep off all other visitants. A grant of one thousand pounds was offered to two gentlemen for the purpose of prosecuting their researches scientifically into the hidden treasures, but no mine or vein of the precious metal could be discovered upon the most diligent examination.

KILKENNY.

Boundaries.—Queen's County, Carlow, Wexford, Waterford, and Tipperary.
Towns.—1, Kilkenny; 2, Thomastown; 3, Gowran; 4, Callen; 5, Kells; 6, Urlingford; 7, Durrow; 8, Castle Comer; 9, Knocktopher; 10, Innistioge; 11, Parkstown; 12, Inchicore; 13, Kildalton; 14, Graignemanach.
Rivers.—a, the Nore; b, Barrow; c, King's River.

Mrs. Rowe.—WHAT are the boundaries, extent, and chief towns in Kilkenny?

Anna.—It is bounded on the north by Queen's County, on the east by Wexford and Carlow, on the south by Waterford, which with Tipperary bounds it also on the west. It measures from north to south about 50 miles, and from east to west 25. Its principal towns are Kilkenny, Thomastown, Callen, Castle Comer, Kells, Gowran, Graignemanach, Innistioge, Knocktopher, Urlingford.

Mrs. Rowe.—Kilkenny, the capital, is a bishop's see, situated on the river Nore, over which it has a handsome bridge of hewn stone. This city is built upon two hills, and was at first designated the Irish and English Towns. The former part is said to be the oldest town on the island, and is called by some of its inhabitants Bally Gaelloch, or the Town of the Lake. Some affirm that the name of Kilkenny was derived from St. Cannice or Kenny, while others assert that it arose from a transition from *Coil* or

Kyle-ken-ni, which mean the ' woody head or hill above the river,' upon which its Gothic cathedral was begun to be built by St. Cannice in 1202, and completed in 1252. It is esteemed one of the most delightful spots in Ireland, and possesses many architectural remains, as well as the public buildings appropriate to a city. Kilkenny coal is well known, and the vapour from it is by some thought dangerous. This city is also noted for its marble, with which the private buildings in all the chief streets are adorned ; the mills for sawing and polishing it are situated by the river side, near the main quarry, about a mile from the town. Its chalybeate and sulphureous spring is held in great esteem ; and it possesses manufactures of woollens and excellent blankets.

ANNA.—The episcopal see was originally at Aghavoe, in Upper Ossory (now the county of Meath), till the latter end of the 12th century, when it was removed to Kilkenny by Felix O'Dullam, Bishop of Ossory.

MRS. ROWE.—Thomastown derives its name from Thomas FitzAnthony, (one of the chiefs of Henry II.,) who founded the town and built the castle in it in 1180. It is seated on the river Nore, over which it has a handsome bridge, and its commercial importance is increasing from its river being navigable to New Ross and Waterford. Its principal remnant of antiquity is the Abbey, of which there is still a considerable portion, as one end of it has been kept in repair, and forms the parish church. Near it stands a venerable tower, which affords some fine specimens of ancient architecture ; and in the ruinous part of the abbey is a large sepulchral stone, which is said to cover the body of a giant. On the banks of the Nore, near this place, are the remains of Jerpoint Abbey, once a magnificent Cistercian establishment founded by O'Donoghue king of Ossory, of the same date as Thomastown. At a short distance from hence, forming all the way a most romantic walk, is the secluded dale and glen of Kilfaun where the rivulet, running through a lawn and flower-garden, and having on each side rocks ornamented with large evergreens, exhibits a most picturesque waterfall, with many other natural and artificial beauties.

Callen is a market-town, situated on the King's River, near the borders of Tipperary. This place was of considerable importance previous to the assault made upon it by Oliver Cromwell, when its three castles and old Gothic church were almost destroyed, and now present only the remains of their former greatness. The vicinity of this town is adorned with many gentlemen's seats, and is so fertile and rich as to be termed the Golden Vale. About one mile from it is a rath of very large dimensions.

Castle Comer is a market-town on the borders of Queen's County, and is noted for the coal-pits in its vicinity, which belong to the Ormond family, whose fine mansion near is surrounded by magnificent woods; and the Countess of Ormond grants premiums for industry and agricultural improvements to the small farmers and cotters of this neighbourhood. It is also a great butter-market. This town was a scene of action in the rebellion, and was partly destroyed by fire in 1798.

Kells is a small town on the King's River, and was formerly noted for its Priory founded by Geoffery FitzRobert in the reign of Richard I. Close to the bridge, at the entrance to the town, is a high mound of earth whereon may be traced the remains of strong walls.

Gowran stands on a pleasant stream: its church is in ruins, and in the cemetery are the bones of the officers of the castle garrison who were shot by order of Cromwell for their gallant defence of it.

Graignemanach stands in a sequestered vale on the romantic banks of the Barrow. Here are the ruins of an extensive Abbey founded in 1212, and particularly remarkable for having been the depositary of a " Doomsday Book," or Survey of the Island, begun under Henry II. and finished

by order of King John. This was a mitred abbey built in
the form of a cross, and its outline is still nearly entire.

Innistioge is a small town seated on the Nore, and noted
for its ancient Cross and the remains of a Monastery founded in 1210. Near it and overhanging the river is the picturesque seat of Woodstock with its extensive wood ; and
not far from hence is the romantic glen of Pulacuila, adorned with a beautiful waterfall.

Knocktopher was formerly of importance : it is pleasantly
situated on a stream which flows into the Nore, and possesses some remains of an Abbey founded in 1356. Near
it are the splendid mansion and demesne of Mount Juliet,
and the ruins of an old Castle.

Urlingford is noted for its race-course, on which races
are annually held. At this town are the ruins of an Augustine Convent founded in 1306.

Durrow, or Castle Durrow, is a handsome town seated
on the Erkin, and its vicinity is very picturesque. This
town formerly belonged to Queen's County, but the Earl of
Ormond procured an Act of Parliament to make it a part of
the county of Kilkenny.

Mothe is a small village about five miles north-west of
Kilkenny, and is noted for Dunmore Cave, the mouth of
which is on the slope of a gently rising hill near the church,
and is one of the greatest curiosities of the kind in the
island. This cave opens into a large oval pit about 40 or
50 yards wide, apparently formed by the sinking in of the
surface at the eastern end : to this there is a descent of 70
feet from the opposite quarter, but the other sides of the
pit are perpendicular ; the first cavern is spacious, but of
an irregular form, and to the left of it is a narrow passage
which leads by a slippery ascent to the interior cavern,
where a great variety of stalactitic concretions, added to the
rugged forms of the rocks, exhibit a most singular and
striking appearance. The upper end of this becomes much
narrower, but soon expands into a larger apartment ; and

beyond this there are some winding passages and other caves. It is said that one of the passages leads to the other side of the hill, where daylight may be seen through a small aperture. In one of the inner caverns the calcareous concretions are described as having assumed the form of an organ, in another those of a cross and altar. A stream of water passes through the cavern at a considerable depth below the entrance, and many skulls and other human bones have been found in it, some of which have become petrified or covered with calcareous spar. The bottom of this place is always damp and slippery, and it is rendered extremely rugged by the stalactites formed by the dripping water on its very irregular floorings.

Which are the principal rivers of this county?

GEORGE.—The Nore rises in Queen's County, and pursues a south-easterly course to join the Barrow at New Ross. The Barrow rises in the northern part of the same county, and flowing southward forms its eastern boundary; it then divides the counties of Carlow and Wexford from Kilkenny, and after receiving the Nore and Suir, falls into the sea through Waterford Haven.

The King's River rises on the confines of Tipperary, and after a short easterly course mixes its waters with the Nore.

MRS. ROWE.—This river derives its name from the circumstance of Nial, a king of the race of Hermon, A.D. 859, plunging into its waters to save the life of one of his attendants who had been carried down the stream by the force of the current, and in the attempt fell a victim to his humanity.

The surface of this county is generally level, though in some parts are to be seen furze-clad mountains interspersed with numerous antiquities. On the banks of its rivers the scenery is pleasingly diversified, and the soil productive; petrifactions or incrustations similar to those in Derbyshire, are to be found in many parts, but more especially on the banks of a stream which flows through the glen of Ballyragget, and the Irish agriculturists have discovered that these depositions, which form very rapidly, make an excellent manure. Kilkenny abounds with fine plantations and is, from the purity of its air, esteemed salubrious. It produces wool, marble and a species of coal, which, like charcoal, burns without smoke, and, according to the proverb, " Kilkenny boasts of fire without smoke, water without mud, air without fog, and streets paved with marble."

CARLOW.

Boundaries.—Kildare, Wicklow, Wexford, Queen's County, and Kilkenny.
Towns.—1, Carlow ; 2, Leighlin Bridge ; 3, Old Leighlin ; 4, Tullow ; 5, Hacklestown; 6, Rathville ; 7, Johnstown ; 8, Clonegall; 9, Bundaudy; 10, Shanskill; 11, Burris; 12, St. Mullins.
Rivers.—a, the Barrow ; b, Slaney.
Mountains.—A, the Blackstairs ; B, the Leinster.

Mrs. Rowe.—WHAT are the boundaries, extent, and chief towns of Carlow ?

Anna.—It is bounded on the north by Kildare and Wicklow, on the east and south-east by the latter county and Wexford, and on the west by Queen's County and Kilkenny. It measures 25 miles from north to south, and its extent is much the same from east to west. The towns most worthy of notice are Carlow, Leighlin Bridge, Old Leighlin, St. Mullins, Tullow, and Mount Leinster.

Mrs. Rowe.—Carlow, the capital, is a neat and flourishing town, well situated for inland commerce on the river

Barrow, and possesses a manufacture of coarse woollen. Its ancient Castle was built by King John, and was an important bulwark of the English pale.

GEORGE.—History records that in 1307 this fortress was taken by Donald MacArt, who styled himself King of Leinster, and that it remained in the possession of himself and his posterity till the reign of Queen Elizabeth, when it again became an English garrison.

MRS. ROWE.—This town surrendered to General Ireton in 1650, and was the scene of a sanguinary battle in 1798, when it was assaulted by the rebels before daybreak, but was successfully defended by a small party of the military and the loyal yeomanry. Here are also ruins of an extensive Abbey, said to have been founded before the English Conquest.

The vicinity of this town is remarkably pleasing, and the agriculture of the district is rapidly improving.

Leighlin Bridge is a market-town on the Barrow, and possesses the remains of an ancient Castle and some monastic ruins, which have also been castellated. The towers and battlements of the Black Castle, which extend along the river, have an imposing appearance. This was a strong hold of the powerful De Laceys, and in this vicinity are several castles that evince the warlike dispositions of the ancient lords.

Old Leighlin, once a city of considerable importance, now consists of only a few dwellings in a valley of the neighbouring mountains. Its celebrated church was founded in 632. It was erected into a bishop's see at an early date, and was incorporated with Ferns in 1600. A part of the cathedral is still kept in decent repair as the parish church. The monastery of Old Leighlin was founded by St Gobham, and acquired a character for sanctity in early times. Its ruin is deserving notice on account of its pinnacled spire and the rich tracery of its Gothic windows, erected, or at least reedified after a destructive fire, in the time of Henry II.

GEORGE.—Under some trees on the west side of the church is the once celebrated well of St. Laferien, which is still regarded with veneration by the lower classes of people, and near its brink is a rude ancient stone cross.

MRS. ROWE.—Some curious memorial stones erected by Bishop Harlewin in 1218, as boundaries of this ancient city, are worthy of notice. One of these is close by Leighlin Bridge, another near Wells, and a third on the mountains.

St. Mullins is a small village much noted for its antiquity, having been founded as early as the 7th century by a Saint of the same name who was bishop of Ferns, and built a church here, the ruins of which are surrounded by a cemetery. This noted Saint was a great patriot, causing the remission of a tax of oxen. He was also regarded as a prophet, and long inhabited the gloomy vale of Glendaloch. The ruins of this place, though not extensive, are very picturesque.

Tullow, once a walled town, is pleasantly situated on the river Slaney, over which there is a stone bridge, and immediately adjoining it is an Augustine Abbey in ruins. Its Castle, which was taken by Cromwell's army, is now converted into barracks. This place is noted for a brewery, and also for its butter- and corn-market.

Mount Leinster is celebrated for hares, foxes, and grouse, also for a well said to be unfathomable and much resorted to for medical purposes.—Which are the principal rivers of this county?

ANNA.—The Barrow and Slaney : the former runs from north to south along its western side, and the latter in the same direction skirts its eastern border.

MRS. ROWE.—Carlow is a small but interesting county. From the variety of its scenery in the south, from Mount Leinster to Blackstairs, it is awfully grand and majestic, and this mountainous range is impassable, except at Scullogh Gap, which resembles the passes in the mountains of India. In the western part of the county there is also another

mountainous range beautifully bordered with timber, even
to the summits of some of its loftiest hills ; and the banks
of the Barrow, in the immediate vicinity, are agreeably diversified by cultivation and the mansions of the opulent ;
and indeed some of the most delightful and picturesque
scenery in Ireland is to be met with in this county. It is
a curious fact that it is not inhabited by either a temporal
or spiritual peer, and yet, though without manufactures, it is
tenanted by more wealthy people than almost any other
part of the island. A considerable part of the county formerly belonged to Quakers. It produces limestone in
great abundance.—Can you mention any literary character
who was born here ?

Anna.—Edmund Burke, one of the most elegant writers
this age has produced : he was the author of many poetical
tracts, but his ' Essay on the Sublime and Beautiful' has
immortalized his name. He was also distinguished as an
orator.

WEXFORD.

Boundaries.—Wicklow, Carlow, Kilkenny, Waterford, and St. George's Channel.
Towns.—1, Wexford; 2, New Ross; 3, Taghmon; 4, St. Margaret's; 5, Bannow; 6, Fethard; 7, Enniscorthy; 8, Ferns; 9, Newtown Barry; 10, Gorey, or Newborough; 11, Glascarrick; 12, Wells; 13, Mochurry; 14, Dunbroady; 15, Clonmines; 16, St. Helen's; 17, Duncannon Fort; 18, Tintern; 19, Kyle.
Rivers.—a, the Barrow; b, Slaney; c, Bann.
Capes and Bays.—A, Raven Point; B, Wexford Haven; C, Greenore Bay; D, Carnsore Point; E, Bannow Bay; H, Hook Head.
Islands.—F, St. Patrick's Bridge; G, the Saltees.

MRS. ROWE.—WHAT are the boundaries, extent, and chief towns of Wexford?

GEORGE.—It is bounded on the north by Wicklow, on the east and south by St. George's Channel, and on the west by Waterford, Kilkenny, and Carlow. Its extreme length is about 42 miles, and breadth across the centre 28. Its chief towns are Wexford, New Ross, Fethard, Tintern, Enniscorthy, Ferns, Gorey, or Newborough, Kyle, Bannow, Clonmines, and Newtown Barry.

MRS. ROWE.—Wexford, the capital, is a handsome town situated on the banks of the Slaney, where the stream becomes contracted between two considerable rocks : across this river is a wooden bridge 2100 feet in length and 42 in breadth, which allows a passage for vessels in the centre. The harbour forms an inland bay, and this noble expanse of water is bounded by steep banks, all cultivated, and in some places covered with timber. Among the architectural beauties of this town are the ruins of the church and Abbey of Selksar, or the Priory of St. Peter and St. Paul, supposed to have been founded by the Danes; also

WEXFORD.

WATERFORD.

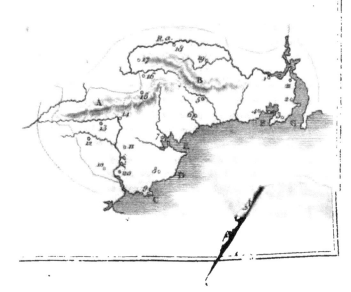

Tower, from which he very soon released him, and reinstated him in all his former possessions, Wexford excepted.

GEORGE.—FitzStephen was son to the celebrated Nest and Stephen, constable of Aberteivi, or Cardigan, and when he was in possession of the same high office, after the death of his father, he was treacherously delivered up by his own servants into the hands of Rhys prince of South Wales, who kept FitzStephen in close confinement for three years, and he was then only offered liberty on condition that he would assist Prince Rhys against Henry II. of England; but the noble youth refused, saying, "that as he claimed alliance with both the Welsh Prince and the English monarch, he would not subject his faith, credit, and fame to the slander, infamy, and reproach of himself and his posterity." He was soon afterwards released, through the earnest entreaties of his half-brothers, David the bishop and Maurice FitzGerald, when he chose rather to venture his life and seek his fortune in foreign countries, and undertook the cause of King MacMorogh.

MRS. ROWE.—Giraldus thus speaks, in commendation of this bold adventurer: "O noble man, the only pattern of virtue, and the example of true labour and industry, who, having tried the variableness of fortune, had tasted more of adversity than prosperity! O worthy man, who, both in Ireland and Wales, had traced the whole compass of Fortune's wheel, and had endured whatsoever good or evil fortune could give!"

GEORGE.—Wexford was the second town that Cromwell assaulted in Ireland, when he slaughtered Sir Edward Butler and the whole garrison.

MRS. ROWE.—In 1798 it was evacuated, and left in the possession of the rebels, who killed 97 of the inhabitants on the bridge, as they were retreating, and threw their bodies into the Slaney. Two miles north-west of this place, on a rock on the banks of this river, are the remains of the first military edifice erected by the Anglo-Normans on this island; and not far from hence, in the barony of Forth, live the descendants of an ancient colony, who were led over by the Welsh barons, in the time of Henry II., to assist King Dermod MacMorogh; these people retain their native language, possess great simplicity of manners, and are remarkably cleanly.

New Ross is a seaport and market-town on the Barrow, near its confluence with the Nore: there is a beautiful wooden bridge over this river, and vessels of 400 tons burden can come up to the quay, by means of which its importance, in a commercial point of view, is considerable. It is a staple port for wool, and great quantities of butter and beef are exported from hence. This town was once well fortified.

GEORGE.—In 1641 the Irish troops under Preston were defeated here by the Marquis of Ormond, and in 1798 the insurgents received a signal defeat upon attacking this town, when Lord Mountjoy was slain.

MRS. ROWE.—New Ross contains many architectural remains, amongst which are three of its entrance gates. Its church once formed the east end of a monastery of St. Saviour's, founded by Sir John Devereux, for Conventual Franciscans, the site of which had previously been occupied by a house of Crouched Friars, which was demolished by the people of Ross, and its inmates slaughtered, in retaliation for the murder of a citizen by one of the friars.

Fethard is a large town on the south-western coast of the county, and is noted for its Castle, the principal tower of which is an elegant specimen of ancient military architecture, from whence the enemy could be an_ _noyed in the old system of defence. It still retains the ren_ _ains of three of its entrance gates, and some of the high_ _en town walls. Here are also some Danish raths, and not _ far from hence is Duncannon Fort, which stands on a r_ _ock that overlooks

been its founder. Its Castle stands on an eminence, and is said to have been erected by King Dermod MacMorogh.

GEORGE.—It was to this place that he with difficulty retreated, through an enemy's country, after he landed at Glascarrick in August 1169; and here he passed the winter, as a private man, previous to the arrival of his allies, the English, in the following spring. He is said to have been honourably received and entertained by the clergy of the place.

MRS. ROWE.—The Bishop's Palace is a handsome building; and near the Cathedral is a holy well dedicated to St. Meoloch, its first bishop, who was consecrated in 598: his ancient tomb is to be seen in the edifice.

Gorey, or Newborough, is a market-town near the eastern coast, and possesses some extensive fisheries. The vicinity of this town was the scene of much devastation in the rebellion. At Clogh, a village about two miles from hence, is a chalybeate water, called "The Iron Well."

Kyle is a small village possessing the ruins of a monastery founded in 600. Near this place Major Lombard and one hundred militiamen were surrounded and slain in 1798.

Bannow is a small town situated on the east of the channel of Bannow Bay. Earl Strongbow is said to have effected his first landing here.

Clonmines is situated at the head of the same bay, and was formerly of note, as it possesses the ruins of an Abbey, and vestiges of seven churches.

Newtown Barry, or Bunclody, is situated between the junction of the rivers Slaney and Clody. The church was erected by Lord Farnham, and the churchyard is one or peculiar beauty.—Which are the principal rivers of Wexford?

ANNA.—The Barrow, which forms the western boundary of the county, and has been already described; the Slaney which rises in Wicklow, and, running southerly, falls into

the sea at Wexford; and the Bann, which finds its source
in the north-eastern part of this county, and pursues a
south-westerly course to join the Slaney.

Mrs. Rowe.—The Saltees are small islands and rocks,
situated off the southern coast, in Ballyteigh Bay; and
St. Patrick's Stepping-stones are rocks lying between these
islands and the coast. Begery, or Little Ireland, is an
island to the north of Wexford Harbour. St. Ivor is said
to have built a monastery here, and founded a school, over
which he presided so early as the year 420: he died
A.D. 500, and was interred on this island, and his relics
are still held in great veneration.

Wexford is deficient in mountain scenery, but possesses
many claims on our notice from its being the first active
scene of invasion by the Anglo-Norman adventurers, in
the reign of Henry II. It likewise merits investigation,
not only for the romantic views at every turn of the Slaney
(one of the most beautiful rivers of the island), but also
for the immense number of Gothic castellated ruins, the
relics of feudal barbarism and intestine hostility. Much
of Wexford is in a high state of cultivation, especially the
baronies of Bargie and Forth, which are, however, destitute
of all kinds of timber. It is believed that silver-mines
were once worked to advantage by the Ostmen in the
southern part of this county.

MUNSTER.

Mrs. Rowe.—HOW many counties are there in Munster!
Anna.—Six: viz. Waterford, Tipperary, Cork, Limerick, Clare, and Kerry.

WATERFORD.

Boundaries.—Tipperary, Kilkenny, Wexford, Cork, and the
Atlantic Ocean.
Towns.—1, Waterford; 2, Woodstown; 3, Rath; 4, Tramore;
5, Kilmacthomas; 6, Fox Castle; 7, Dungarvon; 8,
Hacket's Town; 9, Ardmore; 10, Strancally; 11, Clough;
12, Tallagh; 13, Lismore; 14, Cappoquin; 15, Ballyna-
mult; 16, Four-Mile-Water; 17, Killronan; 18, Glen;
19, Clonea; 20, Aglish; 21, Passage.
Rivers.—a, the Suir; b, the Blackwater.
Mountains.—A, the Kilworth; B, Munavolagh.
Capes and Bays.—C, Ardmore Head and Bay; D, Mine Head;
E, Dungarvon Bay; F, Tramore Bay; G, Waterford Harbour.

Mrs. Rowe.—What are the boundaries, extent, and
chief towns of Waterford?

George.—It is bounded on the north by the counties of
Tipperary and Kilkenny, on the east by Wexford, on the
south by the Atlantic Ocean, and on the west by the
county of Cork. It measures about 30 miles from north
to south, and about 50 from east to west. The places
of most note are Waterford, Lismore, Cappoquin, Dungarvon, Kilmacthomas, Aglish, Passage, Tallow or Tallagh, Strancally, and Tramore.

Mrs. Rowe.—Waterford, the capital of the county, is
an episcopal city, and large sea-port, situated on the south
bank of the river Suir, about four miles from its junction
with the Barrow. It has a noble quay, about one mile in
length, with a wooden bridge, 832 feet long and 42 feet
wide, having a drawbridge in the centre, which add much
to the beauty and convenience of the town. The harbour
is about eight miles long, and seven fathoms deep. Waterford carries on a very extensive trade, particularly with
Newfoundland, in the export of pork, bacon, butter, lard,

corn, and flour. It is also noted for its manufactures of
woollen cloth and glass, and has breweries, foundries,
and salt-works. The earliest remnant of antiquity to be
seen here is a circular tower, situated at the eastern angle
of the city walls, which is said to have been erected by a
Danish chieftain in 1003, and called, after him, Reginald's
Tower. It was converted into a dungeon by Earl Strongbow
in 1171, was the seat of a mint established by Edward IV.
in 1463, and was bombarded by Cromwell in 1643, and it
is said that at its summit one of the balls may still be seen:
it is now occupied by the police. This city formerly
possessed several monastic buildings, the principal of
which were the Priory of St. John, founded in 1185 by
King John, who resided here; St. Saviour Friary, founded
in 1226; and the Augustine Convent, built by Hugh lord
Purcel, of which the steeple remains. It still possesses a
Catholic Monastery. Its Cathedral was founded by the
Ostmen; but the present edifice is modern, has a fine
steeple, and the interior of it is handsomely fitted up. It
also possesses three parish churches. Waterford was
formerly strongly fortified, but fell before the arms of
Cromwell, and was also taken by William III. It confers the title of Marquis on the Beresford family: Clon-
egan Tower, erected by the late lord, in memory of his
son, is 72 feet high, and is deserving of notice. Steam-
vessels maintain a daily communication between this place
and Milford Haven, performing the passage in from eight
to twelve hours.

GEORGE.—Near this city is Dundonolfe Rock, where
Reymund, surnamed Le Gros, (a Welsh chieftain whom
Strongbow sent over before him with a small force,) landed,
in May 1170, and immediately threw up a slender fortress
of turf and wattles. But the citizens of Waterford no sooner
heard of their landing than they flew to arms, and, assisted
by Malachy O'Feolain, prince of the Decies, crossed the
Suir, and marched directly, with a force of 3000 men, to

attack the invaders. The gallant Reymund came forth to
meet them with his determined band; but the numbers
were too unequal, and after the first onset he was compelled to retreat towards his fort. The Danes and Irish,
thinking their victory complete, pursued them so closely
that they entered the gates fighting. Reymund, aware of
his desperate situation, boldly faced the enemy, and ran
his sword through the foremost who had gained admittance;
then, with a loud and animating voice, cried out to his
comrades, " Be of good comfort!" His troops rallied
around him, and made a desperate sally, which put the
enemy to flight: 500 were slain on the field of battle,
many others precipitated from the rocks into the sea,
and 70 of the principal citizens detained as prisoners of
war, whom the noble-hearted Reymund desired to treat
with mercy and pity; but his generous wishes were over-
powered by numbers, and the captives (like men condemned,) were brought to the rocks, and, their limbs being
first broken, were cast headlong into the sea.

ANNA.—On the 25th of August 1171, the city of
Waterford was attacked by Strongbow and his followers;
when the citizens who had escaped from the pursuit of
Reymund defended themselves manfully, and twice repulsed the English; but Reymund, (who is said to have
joined Strongbow the day after his landing,) espying a
small house of timber built upon posts, and connected with
the walls of the city, encouraged his soldiers to cut down
the posts; which having accomplished, the house fell,
and bringing down with it a large portion of the wall,
occasioned a breach, through which the English immediately entered the town, and, putting the inhabitants to
death without distinction, obtained a most bloody victory.
Amongst the prisoners were Reginald, prince of the Danes
at Waterford, and Malachy O'Feolain, prince of the Decies,
whose lives were spared, at the intercession of Dermod

MacMorogh, and they were confined by Earl Strongbow in Reginald's Tower.

MRS. ROWE.—Lismore is seated on the south side of the river Blackwater, over which it has a handsome bridge, erected at the sole expense of a noble individual. This was formerly an extensive city, though little now remains of its original splendour. It seems to derive its present appellation from a mount or ancient fortification standing a little to the east of the town, and now called the Round Hill, *lis*, signifying a fort, and *mor*, great. Its Castle was built by King John, upon the ruins of the Abbey of St. Carthagh, who also founded the Cathedral and University in 631. The see of Lismore was united to Waterford in 1363. The brave but unfortunate Sir Walter Raleigh was proprietor of the castle and manor. The castle was purchased by Sir Richard Boyle, who enlarged its fortifications : till lately it was in a dilapidated state, but the Duke of Devonshire has repaired it, and it is now a splendid modern mansion worthy of its ancient fame.

ANNA.—At the commencement of the rebellion in 1641, it was besieged by 5000 Irish troops, commanded by Sir Robert Beling, when it was bravely defended by the young Lord Broghil, third son of the Earl of Cork, who obliged the Irish to raise the siege ; but it was afterwards taken by Lord Castlehaven in 1645.

GEORGE.—Lismore is said to have formerly consisted chiefly of the habitations of the most learned monks, royal abbots, saints, and hermits, and the ruins of abbeys are still to be seen here ; but the ravages of the Danes, the conflagration of 1116, the assault by Earl Strongbow's son in 1147, another fire in 1207, and the attack of the Irish army in 1641, have occasioned the town to be repeatedly rebuilt, so that a clear detail of their foundations can scarcely now be given. Its vicinity is well wooded, and possesses some picturesque scenery.

Mrs. Rowe.—Below the town is a rich and very productive salmon-fishery, which is the greatest branch of trade here.

Cappoquin is a small neat town, which also stands on the Blackwater; and an extensive trade in corn is carried on between this place and Youghall, the river being navigable from hence for boats. Its Castle was built by the FitzGeralds, and is celebrated in history. It commands an extensive and enchanting prospect. The vicinity of the town is ornamented with several gentlemen's seats, with richly cultivated and well planted lands, amongst which is Salta Bridge, where resided the late Sir Richard Musgrave.

George.—When this gentleman was High Sheriff, he, on one occasion, could find no person who would flog a man sentenced to whipping for sedition, and therefore, as an imperative duty, he inflicted the punishment himself: for this he received the thanks of King George III.

Mrs. Rowe.—Dungarvon is an ancient and populous sea-port, situated on a bay of the same name.

The Nymph Bank, lying opposite to this coast, has always afforded facilities to the extensive fishery carried on by the inhabitants of the town, which is built on the beach, and which, from the mountain above it, appears as if it stood in the water. The corporation of this place had extensive privileges granted them by James I. The remains of its once extensive Castle are converted into barracks. Here also are the ruins of several monasteries, and across the river is a ruined Augustine Friary, founded in 1295: its steeple is 60 feet high, and springs from a curious vault, in which is the monument of Donald Magrath, who was buried here in 1400. The Gothic arch which supports the tower is also worthy of notice.

Kilmacthomas is a pleasing village on the Mahaghan river, which possesses good scenery and fishing. In the town are barracks, and the remains of an ancient Castle.

GEORGE.—About five miles west of this place, at the village of Whitechurch, may be seen a curious cave, called Con-a-glour, or Pigeon-hole: it is 150 feet long, with a subterraneous river, fantastical crystallizations, &c.

MRS. ROWE.—Aglish is a delightful village in the southern part of the county, noted for its very curious fortress, which is a quadrangular area, with four towers at the angles, connected by a curtain, in which are numerous loop-holes: the great gate was formerly fitted with a portcullis. The only apartments seem to have been in the angular towers, as the large inclosure does not appear to have been built on. This edifice is supposed to owe its erection to John lord of Ireland, in the reign of his brother Richard I. About a mile distant are to be seen the magnificent ruins of Aglish Abbey.

Passage stands on the Barrow, east of Waterford. Passengers embark for Milford Haven at its pier, which is constructed on the foundation of a fort, or block-house. Its church is built on the top of a mountain, and casts its broad shadow over this small town.

Tallow, or Tallagh, is a market- and post-town, on the Bride. Here are the ruins of Lisfinie, an old fortress of the Earls of Desmond; and near it is Castle Connough in ruins.

Strancally, on the Blackwater, possesses the remains of an ancient Castle with a curious cave, respecting which there are many traditionary tales: near it is the handsome seat of Headborough, with the venerable ruins of Molana Abbey.

Tramore is a pleasant sea-bathing village, on a bay of the same name: it possesses suitable buildings for the accommodation of strangers, and is much resorted to in the summer months.—Which are the principal rivers of this county?

ANNA.—The Blackwater and the Suir.

MRS. ROWE.—As the Blackwater may be more properly

styled a river of Cork, I shall describe it in the account of that county.

The Suir rises in Tipperary, and flows in a south-easterly course to Clonmel, where it becomes navigable; then, turning easterly, it forms the northern boundary of the county between Tipperary and Kilkenny; it then runs on to Waterford, where it forms a spacious harbour, and, after uniting with the Barrow below that city, it passes on to the sea, making a commodious estuary, or haven, deep enough for the largest vessels.

Waterford possesses some mountainous tracts on the borders of Cork and in the eastern part of the county, which are interspersed with rocks and frightful precipices; and amongst these are some loughs, abounding in trout and char. The other parts of the county may be generally considered fertile and rich, yielding good corn and pasturage, and affording much picturesque scenery, and on its coasts are very productive fisheries. Of its mineral stores, granite is the principal. A stratum of clay equal to that of Stourbridge for glasshouse pots is also found here.—Can you name any great character who was a native of this county?

GEORGE.—Robert Boyle, a celebrated natural philosopher, whose numerous works on theology and philosophy are highly esteemed. He was born in Lismore Castle, and it has been justly remarked of this great man that he revived the memory of its ancient university.

o 5

TIPPERARY.

Boundaries.—King's County, Queen's County, Kilkenny, Waterford, Cork, Limerick, and Clare.

Towns.—1, Cashel; 2, Tipperary; 3, Clonulty; 4, Burrosaleigh; 5, Tullo; 6, Silvermines; 7, Clothonan; 8, Nenagh; 9, Annagh; 10, Clonlish; 11, Lorhoe; 12, Longford Pass; 13, Thurles; 14, Holy Cross; 15, Trasny; 16, Killenaule; 17, Bally Patrick; 18, Carrick-on-Suir; 19, Fethard; 20, Blackcastle; 21, Ballycarrin; 22, Clonmell; 23, Cahir; 24, Clogheen; 25, Ballyporen; 26, Golden Bridge; 27, Roscrea; 28, Toomavara; 29, Castle Connell; 30, Ardfinnan; 31, Templemore; 32, Emly.

River.—a, the Suir.

Mountains.—A, the Reeper; B, Devil's Bit; C, Galty.

Lough.—D, Lough Derg.

Mrs. Rowe.—WHAT are the boundaries, extent, and places most worthy of note in Tipperary?

George.—It has King's County on the north and north-east, Queen's County and Kilkenny on the east, Waterford on the south, Cork, Limerick, and Clare on the west, and Galway on the north-west. It measures from north to south about 60 miles, and from east to west, in its widest part, about 40. The principal towns are Clonmell, Cashel, Holy Cross, Tipperary, Carrick-on-Suir, Golden Bridge, Roscrea, Toomavara, Silvermines, Castle Connell, Ardfinnan, Clogheen, Templemore, Burrosaleigh, Emly, Killenaule, Fethard, Cahir, Nenagh, and Thurles.

Mrs. Rowe.—Clonmell, the county-town, is a well-built place on the north bank of the river Suir, over which it has three bridges, and by means of which its trade with Waterford, in provisions and corn, is very great. It also possesses manufactures of woollens and cottons, introduced into it by a society of Quakers. In 1269 the Dominican Friary was founded, and at the same time Otho de Gran-

CPSIA information can be obtained at www.ICGtesting.com
Printed in the USA
BVOW06s0642130716

455315BV00022B/200/P